AN INTRODUCTION
TO PHILOSOPHY

An Introduction

To Philosophy

GEORGE NAKHNIKIAN

WAYNE STATE UNIVERSITY

Alfred·A·Knopf  *New York*

THIS IS A BORZOI BOOK,
PUBLISHED BY ALFRED A. KNOPF, INC.

© Copyright, 1967, by George Nakhnikian

All rights reserved under International and Pan-American Copyright Conventions. Distributed by Random House, Inc. Published simultaneously in Toronto, Canada, by Random House of Canada Limited.

FIRST PRINTING

Library of Congress Catalog Card Number: 67–10714

Manufactured in the United States of America

*To Jean
and our daughters*

PREFACE

THIS BOOK is designed for introductory courses in philosophy. Parts II and III contain material that would also be of interest in courses or seminars on Descartes. I believe that the book is also a useful guide for those who may want to study philosophy at home.

The problems discussed are in ethics, metaphysics, philosophy of mind, philosophy of religion, theory of knowledge, theory of meaning, and theory of definition—particularly as this last relates to the nature of philosophical analysis. These problems are discussed within the context of a critical examination of the early books of Plato's *Republic,* the whole of Descartes' *Meditations,* and three essays by William James. The book is intended to be read along with these primary sources. Part I should be read concurrently with pp. 1–59, 119–143, and 211–220 in F. M. Cornford's edition of Plato's *Republic,* available in paperback (Oxford University Press). Parts II and III should be read concurrently with Descartes' *Meditations on First Philosophy.* It is included in Vol. I of *Philosophical Works of Descartes,* E. S. Haldane and G. R. T. Ross, trans. (Cambridge University Press). Although all quotations in the text are from that edition, the reader may use one of a number of other available translations. Unlike what I have to say about Plato, what I have to say about Descartes is not tied to any particular English translation. Part IV should be read concurrently with James' "What Pragmatism Means," "Pragmatism's Conception of Truth," and "The Will to Believe": these essays are reprinted in William James' *Essays in Pragmatism,* A. Castell, ed., available in paperback (Hafner). In lieu of "What Pragmatism Means" or in addition to it, the student may read James' "Philosophical Conceptions and Practical Results," reprinted, with minor omissions, in *Readings in Twentieth-Century Philosophy*, W. P. Alston and G. Nakhnikian, eds. (The Free Press of Glencoe). This essay is an earlier statement of James' views in "What Pragmatism Means."

I have tried to explain and to interpret as clearly, precisely and accurately as I can what it is that Plato, Descartes, and James are saying in these works. I have tried to formulate their arguments in detail, in order to examine them closely so as to see if they succeed in proving their conclusions true. I have, in short, tried to show the reader how to read a philosophical text philosophically.

By going through the sort of detailed philosophical scrutiny of philosophical problems that he will find in this book, the reader is certain to develop a knack for discerning philosophical problems, and to begin to appreciate their enormous difficulty and complexity as well as their resistance to neat and final solutions. He will also acquire some facility in philosophical reasoning and gain some understanding of the opposition between rationalism and empiricism. Plato and Descartes are two of the best representatives of rationalism. And, although James is neither a philosopher of the stature of Plato or Descartes nor a strong representative of empiricism, he is disarmingly forthright and provocative, even when he is propounding outrageous theses. Part IV on James and the section on logical positivism's verifiability criterion (Part III, Section 2) are, among other things, intended to be an introduction to empiricism. All in all, the attentive reader of this book and of the primary sources that have inspired it should have obtained a good start in philosophy.

I am indebted to the many students in my introductory course during my sixteen-odd years of teaching. From my departmental colleagues I have learned more than I can hope to acknowledge. For some of the ideas in this book I am particularly indebted to my colleagues, Hector-Neri Castaneda, Edmund L. Gettier, Robert C. Sleigh, Jr., to William Rowe of Purdue University and to Helen Cartwright.

W. P. Alston, A. W. Burks, R. M. Chisholm, Raphael Demos, Martin Lean, and A. D. Woozley supplied extremely helpful comments on the manuscript in various stages. They are responsible for many of the improvements and for none of the faults in the final product.

I would like to express my appreciation to V. C. Chappell, the consulting editor, David Dushkin, the editor, and Sylvia Moss, the assistant editor, for their many helpful suggestions.

I thank Mrs. Dorothy Coleman and Miss Marilyn Weiss for hours of patient typing.

To Jean and our three daughters I owe the happiness and peace of soul that I need to work. I dedicate this book to them.

June 1966   G. N.

CONTENTS

PART I

Plato's Definition of a Good Man

PRELIMINARY EXPLANATIONS ON THE NATURE OF DEFINITIONS AND ETHICAL QUESTIONS

The Republic THAT WE are reading is an English translation of the original in classical Greek. Words, phrases, and sentences that are philosophically important may have been inaccurately or misleadingly translated. A philosopher at home in classical Greek would very likely find in the original a Plato who is different from the one who appears in our translation. The other Plato may even be more subtle and more profound. But we are in no position to make such comparisons. We shall content ourselves with examining the ideas of our Plato, with a view to determining what they mean and whether or not they are true. Whenever I speak of Plato in this Part, one must remember that I am talking about the Plato we find in F. M. Cornford's translation of *The Republic*.

In that work, Plato discusses the nature of human goodness with three people: Cephalus, Polemarchus, and Thrasymachus. The *dramatis personae* are actually these three and Socrates. To simplify matters, however, we shall assume that Socrates is speaking for Plato.

In order to make it easier for the reader to understand the tactics and strategy involved in Plato's arguments with Cephalus, Polemarchus, and Thrasymachus, it will be useful for us to begin with certain preliminary explanations. These preliminaries will take up the rest of Section 1. They will be long, and they will involve many fine details. I would ask the reader to study these pages patiently. He will come to see their relevance to the examination of Plato after he has completed studying the whole of this Part.

In *The Republic* Plato is concerned with an important question: What is a good man? Because Plato believes that as a matter of fact the human infant becomes a person only as a member of society, his first question necessarily leads to another: What is a good society? Plato thinks of the good society as the good man writ large. He also thinks of it as being the only society that can be counted on to produce good men. In the early books of *The Republic*, which is what we shall study in detail, the main question is: What is justice?, i.e., What is a just man? The answer to this is part of Plato's answer to the question: What is a good man? For Plato's view is that a good man is a man who is just, wise, temperate, and courageous, just as a good society is a just, wise, temperate, and courageous society.

Plato would grant that a good man is one who loves and cherishes his wife and children, and that a good society is one in which no one need go hungry or homeless; he would also agree that a just man will not cheat his customers. Yet these propositions are inadequate to answer his questions. We must therefore try to understand first what it is that the questions: "What is a good man?" and "What is a just man?" are asking respectively about their subjects. Second, we must try to understand what function the answers are expected to serve.

Let us begin by concentrating on the question: "What is a good man?" Whatever we say about it as a philosophical question applies as well to the other questions, "What is a just man?" and "What is a just society?"

What is the question "What is a good man?" asking? It is asking for a complete description of the essentials of being a good man. It is asking for a definition in which the defining expression states the meaning of 'good man'[1] and hence specifies a set of logically necessary and sufficient conditions[2] for being a good man. Consider the following definitions:

---

[1] Throughout this book I shall use single quotes exclusively to indicate that I am talking about the word or linguistic expression that occurs within the single quotes. The linguistic expression may be a syllable, a word, a phrase, or a sentence. Cats, for example, are mammals, but not monosyllabic. The word 'cat' is monosyllabic, but not a mammal. I shall use double quotes to indicate that I am quoting somebody or to mark off colloquialisms, e.g., "sets us up," "get away with," or to mention a proposition, e.g., "All squares have four sides," or to register mental reservations, e.g., the "miracle" Jones reported was witnessed by no one else.

[2] The logically necessary and sufficient conditions for being, say a mammal, are conditions such that whatever satisfies them cannot fail to be a mammal, and whatever lacks them cannot be a mammal.

(i) An even number is, by definition, a number divisible by 2 without remainder.

(ii) A bachelor is, by definition, an adult human male who has never been married.

(iii) A brother is, by definition, a male sibling.

(iv) 'x is a sibling of y' means that the father and mother of x are also the father and mother of y.

We find such definitions, or their equivalents, in dictionaries of the English language, and their counterparts exist in the dictionaries of many other languages. The main function of these dictionaries is to record what meanings a word has. They are attempts to report, as accurately as possible, how words are used by the community of literate users of the language. The definitions are not inventions or stipulations. That they are not is consistent with the fact that lexicographers sometimes make decisions—for example, when they decide that a hitherto unacceptable expression has acquired a sufficiently wide currency to be treated as standard.

But if we go to the dictionary for a definition of such words as 'table', 'chair', 'cup', 'vehicle', 'game', and thousands more, we will notice an important difference between their definitions and some from among (i)–(iv) above. Take, for example, (i). This defines an even number in terms of its necessary and sufficient conditions which are stated precisely and clearly. There is no dictionary definition of 'table', for example, in terms of necessary and sufficient conditions that are stated precisely. In our ordinary conversations we have no trouble communicating with each other about tables, chairs, cups, etc., even though none of us is prepared to produce a clear and precise definition of the words involved in terms of logically necessary and sufficient conditions. Plato *assumes* that if we want to be clear about anything, we must first find its definition, and that even if the definition is not already written down for us in a dictionary, we can always arrive at a clear and precise statement of it, if we work hard and long enough.

The term 'good man' is not clearly and precisely defined for us in any standard dictionary. Plato wants to find, by philosophical reflection, what the essence of a good man is. He is looking for a definition in which *the definiens* (the defining term) states the meaning of 'good man' and hence specifies a set of logically necessary and sufficient conditions for being a good man, which is *the definiendum* (the term to be defined). This is what the answer to Plato's question "What is a good man?" is supposed to provide.

Real and Arbitrary Definitions

BUT HOW are we to tell the difference between a correct and an incorrect definition of a good man? In the case of arbitrary definitions, this question would not arise. In an arbitrary definition, an expression is assigned a meaning that it did not have before, or it is made to name a thing or a collection of things that it did not name before. An arbitrary definition is really a verbal stipulation, e.g., "Let us mean by 'electron' a negatively charged small particle." This is like christening or giving a name or attaching a label to something. We cannot raise serious questions about the correctness of labeling as 'electrons' the small particles in question. There is nothing here to be either correct or incorrect about.

Another type of case is exemplified in Newton's invention of the concept of vector. There is in it an element of verbal stipulation. Part of what Newton did was to say in effect: "Let us mean by a 'vector' a quantity that requires for its complete specification a magnitude, a direction and a sense, and let us represent this quantity by an arrow whose length indicates the magnitude of the quantity, whose orientation represents the direction, and whose arrowhead represents the sense of the quantity." But there is more to what Newton did than this. In the case of the electron, the existence of certain particles had already been discovered or suspected, and the verbal stipulation simply labeled them. Newton, on the other hand, *invented* a concept. He did not merely provide a name for a class of things that had been found or suspected to exist. He *conceived* of representing forces in statics in terms of vectors, and it was this *conception* that made it possible to treat the branch of mechanics known as statics with complete theoretical elegance. Now any finite number of forces could be considered together and their resultant calculated with precision. This is an example of conceptual innovation, comparable to inventing the calculus. Without such conceptual innovations, science cannot make advances. To leave no doubt as to the difference between merely labeling things and inventing useful concepts, remember that the *phenomena* that Newton proposed to represent in terms of vectors were already well known. A spring balance with a weight hanging on it exhibits quantities that are capable of being represented in terms of vectors. Newton did not merely propose a name for the phenomena. He proposed a way of representing them that introduced mathematical order into an important branch of physics.

In the case of the vector, also, it would make no sense to ask whether or not the definition Newton introduced was correct. The only appropriate characterization of it is that it was an extremely *useful* concept, relative to the purposes of the physicists. The question of the correctness of definitions arises only when the definitions in question are *real* as against *arbitrary* (stipulative).

Plato and other philosophers who have been influenced by him (e.g., G. E. Moore) seem to think that real definitions have nothing to do with words, that only stipulative definitions have to do with words. Their view may be fairly reported as follows: A real definition identifies a property, P, as being either a conjunction or a disjunction of properties $P_1 \ldots P_n$, where n is greater than 1 and where each one of $P_1 \ldots P_n$ is distinct from the others and from P. For example, the property of being a father is identical with the conjunction of the properties of being a male *and* a parent. The property of being a grandfather is identical with the disjunction of the properties of being *either* a mother's father *or* a father's father. The property of being red is clearly different from the property of being blue. Further, red and blue are not only different, they are incompatible: it is impossible for the same thing to be uniformly red and blue all over at the same time.

In the overwhelming majority of cases, we have no difficulty seeing that P_1 and P_2 are the same property, or else that they are different properties. But this practical facility does not satisfy theoretical requirements. We do not fully understand the Platonic notion of (i) a *real* definition, and (ii) a *correct* real definition, unless we have a criterion of the identity of properties. Under what conditions can P_1 and P_2 be said to be identical? No one has yet been able to provide a satisfactory answer, and the prospects of finding one are, I think, dim. I shall therefore, introduce another view of real definition in the hope that it will be more immediately useful than Plato's own theory of real definition for an understanding of Plato's strategy and tactics against Cephalus, Polemarchus, and Thrasymachus.

While a real definition is about words, it is neither a stipulation nor a conceptual innovation. Stipulations and conceptual innovations can be either useful or pointless, but they cannot be true or false, correct or incorrect. Real definitions, by contrast, can be true or false, correct or incorrect. Thus it is true that, as used in the sentence, 'My father can lick your father', the word 'father' in both its occurrences means *male parent*. When you ask: "What does the word 'father' in that sentence mean?" and I answer: "In both its occurrences it means *male parent*," I am not proposing a convention or making a stipulation or announcing a resolution. I am simply stating a fact: one of the ways in which the word 'father' is used is such that, in that use, the word 'father' means *male parent*.

Real definitions are explications of meaning. I shall explain this further by way of examples, but before we go into details, it may be useful to furnish a preliminary idea of what it means to say this. Take a word such as 'father'. It is a word that has different meanings in different contexts. In the Lord's Prayer, for example, the word does not mean *male parent*. The believer is addressing God, the Father, when he begins his prayer with 'Our Father'. In the sentence 'The wish is father to the thought', the word 'father' does not mean *male parent;* the *whole* sentence means that one believes because one wishes to. It would be very difficult to say what the word 'father' means by itself in that sentence. Perhaps it means *is the determinant of*. But if we want to explain meanings in this type of case, the safest procedure is to take the *whole* sentence as the unit to be translated. Likewise, in the sentence 'The child is father to the man', the *whole* sentence means that the lines of our development as adults are laid down in our childhood. Again, the word 'father' does not mean *male parent*.

Now in all these instances we have the same word used in different ways. Yet every one of these uses is familiar and standard, and none of them is technical. That is, none of these uses occurs in some technical subject, such as physics or mathematics or psychoanalytic theory or philosophy. Every one of those sentences has a standard use in non-technical, everyday English. As speakers of plain English, we are expected to understand them.

In the sentence, 'My father can lick yours', the word 'father' is clearly used to mean *male parent*. If someone did not know that fact, we would have to convey it to him; in so doing, we would be explaining to him what the word 'father' meant in that sentence. This explanation is an example of explicating the meaning of a word for one of its standard uses.

However, not all explications of meaning are as easy as this one. The difficult ones are usually the ones of most interest to philosophy. An example of an explication that is more than a straight report of what a word means in plain English as used in a certain standard way, is Peano's[3] definition of arithmetical addition. I shall later develop this example in some detail. (It happens to be an explication of the meaning of an expression for one of its standard *technical* uses.) The interesting distinction between this explication and the explication of 'father' as meaning *male parent*, is not that one is the explication of a *technical* term, while the other is the explication of a *non-technical* term. It is this: the explication of 'father' is a simple report of a linguistic fact that is familiar to every competent speaker of the English language. Not so in the case of 'plus' or '+'. Peano did not simply report a familiar linguistic fact. His explication, as we shall see, is an explanation of the nature of addition, an explanation which makes clear *for the first time* a meaning of 'plus' or '+'; or, to put it in different terms, it is an explanation that makes clear *for the first time* what the nature of arithmetical addition is.

The distinction between *real* and *arbitrary* definitions is based upon one principle. There is another distinction, based upon a different principle, according to which a *real* definition may be explicit, recursive, or contextual—and so too may an arbitrary definition. Peano's definition of 'plus' or '+' is a real recursive definition. What Plato is looking for is a real explicit definition of 'good man'.

I shall now distinguish explicit, recursive, and contextual definitions by way of examples of real explicit, real recursive, and real contextual definitions. My aim will be to shed some light thereby on the nature of the philosophic enterprise, insofar as that involves providing analyses or explications. Plato's question

[3] Giuseppe Peano, the Italian mathematician (1858–1932).

"What is a good man?" is, after all, a request for an analysis or explication of what it is to be a good man. I have already said that some explications are easy—e.g., the explanation of what it is to be a father; some explications, by contrast, are difficult—e.g., the explanation of the nature of addition. It is rather obvious that Plato thinks that the explication of what it is to be a good man is one of the hard kind. This is not because 'good man' is a technical term; it is, like the word 'father', a term of everyday non-technical discourse. But it is unlike 'father' in one important respect. Competent speakers of English would have no hesitation in seeing at once—and probably without exception—that, as used in a certain sentence on a given occasion, the word 'father' meant *male parent*. But there is no comparable assurance as to what 'good man' means as it is used in the sentence 'My father was a good man' on the occasion of my uttering this sentence to tell my children that my father was a good man. What does 'good man' mean in such a context? That is Plato's question, and it calls for philosophical analysis or explication.

Explicit Definitions

"FATHER = Df. male parent" is an example of a real explicit definition. What Plato wants to find is a real explicit definition of the words 'justice', 'courage', 'temperance', and 'wisdom'. They denote respectively the four cardinal virtues that, according to Plato's doctrine in *The Republic*, together make up the essence of a good man. We could alternately describe Plato's enterprise by saying that he wants to find a real explicit definition of 'just (man)', 'courageous (man)', 'temperate (man)', and 'wise (man)', and to define a good man as one who is just, temperate, courageous, and wise.

By 'a real explicit definition of a term', we mean a definition that satisfies the following conditions:

(1) it is of the form: *definiendum* = Df. *definiens;*
(2) the *definiendum* and the *definiens* are different expressions;
(3) the *definiendum* is a term having a certain standard use;
(4) The *definiens* undertakes to give the meaning of the *definiendum* for that standard use by listing a number of condi-

tions that, either conjunctively or disjunctively, constitute logically necessary and sufficient conditions of being the sort of thing to which the *definiendum,* in that standard use, applies.

There are, however, logically necessary and sufficient conditions that are not, strictly speaking, part of the meaning of a term. An equilateral Euclidean triangle, for example, is by definition a Euclidean triangle that has three equal sides. It is true that being a triangle that has three equal angles is also a logically necessary and sufficient condition for being a Euclidean equilateral triangle, yet being a triangle that has three equal angles is not part of the meaning of 'equilateral Euclidean triangle'. On the other hand, whatever is specified in the meaning is thereby logically necessary and sufficient.

An example of conditions being *conjunctively* definitive is to be seen in the *definiens* of 'father'. To be a father is to be male *and* parent. An example of conditions being *disjunctively* definitive is to be seen in the *definiens* of 'grandparent'. Grandparent = Df. mother's mother *or* mother's father *or* father's mother *or* father's father. Both of these are examples of the type of definition that Plato's program of defining the goodness of a man assumes to be possible. They are explicit definitions that are also real. Hence, the assumption is correct that there are real explicit definitions of some terms. It remains to be seen what are the ways of finding out the real definition of a given expression. It also remains to be seen whether the words 'just', 'courageous', 'wise', and 'temperate' can each be defined, and, if so, whether their conjunction constitutes a real explicit *definiens* of 'good man.'

But first let us attempt to gain better understanding of explicit definitions by contrasting them with two other important kinds of definition—recursive and contextual.

Recursive Definitions

FOR PURPOSES of comparison, we may think of an explicit definition as a one-step rule of elimination, and a recursive definition as a two-step rule of elimination. The explicit definition, "father =

Df. male parent," licenses the elimination of the word 'father' from any suitable context. Thus, I can say either that my father is alive or that my male parent is alive. By virtue of the explicit definition, these would be two different ways of saying the same thing.

The easiest way to explain why a recursive definition may be thought of as a two-step rule of elimination is by way of an example: Peano's definition of the arithmetical operation of adding numbers. This is a clear and simple example of a recursive definition. But that is not the only reason why I have chosen it. Peano's definition is also a clear and philosophically uncontroversial example of the difficult kind of explication or analysis. It is a real and correct definition of addition, and it makes clear *for the first time* what the nature of arithmetical addition is.

Addition is a familiar operation in arithmetic. We all know how to tell a right from a wrong answer in addition. But those of us who have not thought about the matter would not be expected to produce a definition of '+'. Peano's definition purports to be an explanation of the essential nature of a familiar arithmetical operation. It is a recursive definition that is also real.

Let 'x', 'y', 'z', 'x'', 'y'', 'z'', 'x''', 'y''', 'z''', etc., take as values non-negative whole numbers including 0, and let 'S(x)' be an abbreviation for 'the successor of x'. Peano's definition of '+' consists of two steps:

(a) $x + 0 = x$
(b) $x + S(y) = S(x + y)$

If we arrange the non-negative whole numbers, starting with 0, in a succession, we get the sequence $0, 1, 2, 3, 4$, etc., to infinity. In this sequence every number has exactly one successor. This fact about the sequence ensures that, between them, (a) and (b) will enable us to eliminate the '+' sign from any formula, 'x + y', where the place of 'y' is occupied by a numeral designating a non-negative whole number, including 0. Thus, Peano's two steps will enable us to produce a formula equivalent to 'x + 3' in which there will be no occurrence of '+'. Let us see how this is done. As 'x + 3' stands, neither (a) nor (b) applies to it. (a) would apply only if the place of '3' were occupied by '0'. But (b) will apply if we first write 'x + 3' in an equivalent form: $x + S(2)$, (read: x + the successor of 2). By (b), $x + S(2) = S(x + 2)$. But $S(x + 2) =$

$S(x + S(1))$. By (b), $S(x + S(1)) = S(S(x + 1))$. But $S(S(x + 1)) = S(S(x + S(0)))$. By (b), $S(S(x + S(0))) = S(S(S(x + 0)))$. Now we are ready to apply (a), which tells us that for 'x + o' we may substitute 'x'. Hence, $S(S(S(x + 0))) = S(S(S(x)))$. According to Peano's definition of '+', then, $x + 3 = S(S(S(x)))$. For example, let $x = 1$. Then, $x + 3 = 1 + 3 = S(S(S(1))) = 4$, which is true. By repeated applications of step (b) to instances to which it applies, and by a single application of (a) to the single instance to which it applies, we have succeeded in producing a formula equivalent to 'x + 3' but not containing the sign '+'.

This example shows three things: first, that Peano's definition is a correct real definition, inasmuch as it yields correct results; second, that Peano's definition is not viciously circular, appearances to the contrary notwithstanding. It is circular inasmuch as the two steps of the *definiens* contain the very sign that is being defined. But a comparison with a viciously circular definition will show that the definition is not viciously circular. A viciously circular definition would be the following:

Curved line = Df. line that is curved.

The *definiens* in this case provides no means whatever of eliminating the *definiendum* from any context at all. But, as we have already seen, Peano's definition does enable us to eliminate '+' from an endless number of formulas. The third point is that Peano's definition is a rule of substitution, and a correct one. It differs from the definition of 'father' or of 'grandfather', however, in an important respect. Peano's definition is a rule of substitution in two parts, each part applying to a different type of case. In fact, step (a) of Peano's *definiens* amounts to saying that if $y = 0$, then $x + y = x$; and step (b) amounts to saying that if $y \neq 0$, then $x + y = S(x + z)$, where $y = S(z)$. This is correct because every non-negative whole number has exactly one successor. Hence, if $y \neq 0$, $x + y = x + S(z)$. But step (b) in Peano's *definiens* states that $x + S(z) = S(x + z)$. Hence, $x + y = S(x + z)$, where $y = S(z)$. The definition of 'father', on the other hand, is a single rule. It does not provide a different rule of substitution for different conditions. It licenses substituting 'male parent' for 'father' in any context.[4] In short, recursive definitions and explicit definitions are alike in that both are rules of substitution, but

[4] For a brief word of caution, see footnote on p. 182.

they differ in that explicit definitions are single-step rules, while recursive definitions are case-by-case rules, in the sense just explained.

Contextual Definitions

THE SECOND type of definition to be compared to an explicit definition is a contextual one. Some philosophers, following Bertrand Russell, believe that contextual definitions are particularly important for philosophy. By 'a contextual definition' we mean a definition that tells us how to translate sentences that contain some specific word or phrase into synonymous sentences that do not contain that word or phrase or any of its synonyms. By 'a real contextual definition' we mean a definition that purports to tell us how to translate sentences containing a word or phrase that has a certain standard use into synonymous sentences that do not contain that word or phrase or any of its synonyms. In both the definition of 'a contextual definition' and that of 'a real contextual definition', the word 'sentence' is used in a technical sense. Everyone would grant that 'Jones is tall' is a sentence. But when confronted with 'x is tall', people either would say that it was not a sentence or they might not know what to say. Now the word 'sentence', as it occurs in the above definitions of 'contextual definition' and of 'real contextual definition', is being used in such a way that both 'Jones is tall' and 'x is tall' are sentences, the former being a "closed" sentence—one that has no "free" variables —the latter being an "open" sentence. Accordingly,

x is a father = Df. x is a male parent,

is a contextual definition. Its *definiens* and *definiendum* are sentences, in this case open sentences. On the other hand,

father = Df. male parent

is an explicit definition. Neither its *definiens* nor its *definiendum* is a sentence, open or closed. But if this was all that there was to the difference between explicit and contextual definitions, the distinction would be hardly worth making. For every explicit definition has a contextual counterpart; from the logical point of view, therefore, the difference between the explicit definition of 'father' and its contextual counterpart would be merely a matter of diction.

What makes the distinction logically and philosophically interesting is the belief of certain philosophers that some words or phrases cannot be defined explicitly, but that sentences in which they occur can be translated into synonymous sentences that do not contain those words or phrases or any of their synonyms. This is precisely the assertion that Russell makes about definite descriptions, and his analysis of definite descriptions is itself an example of a real contextual definition.

Not all philosophers think that this is a correct analysis. My present purpose is not to attack or to defend Russell. Right or wrong, his analysis is an example of what I mean by 'a real contextual definition'. Russell would draw our attention to two distinct uses of the phrase 'the so and so.' In the sentence, 'The whale is an aquatic animal', the phrase 'the whale' is not a definite description. The whole sentence is synonymous with 'All whales are aquatic animals.' Here 'the so and so' is used to make a universal generalization. There is another use of 'the so and so' as, for example, in 'The present King of France is bald'. In this sentence, 'the present King of France' is a definite description. It is of this use of such expressions that Russell's theory of definite descriptions is an analysis. In particular, Russell's analysis of definite descriptions may be regarded as a real definition of the word 'the' in one of its uses—namely, that which it has in expressions such as 'the present King of France'. Russell's view is that there is no explicit or recursive definition of definite descriptions. The meaning of such expressions can be explained only within a larger context, namely, in that of sentences. "... we do not define 'the x which satisfies $\phi \hat{x}$', but we define any proposition in which this phrase occurs."[5] Thus, 'The present King of France is bald' is synonymous with 'At least one man is now King of France and at most one man is now King of France and he is bald'. In other words, Russell is contending that the proposition, "The present King of France is bald" is identical with the proposition, "At least one man is now King of France and at most one man is now King of France and he is bald." As Russell puts it, that at least one man

[5] A. N. Whitehead and B. Russell, *Principia Mathematica to * 56*, paperback edition (Cambridge, Eng.: Cambridge University Press, 1962), p. 173.

is now King of France and that at most one man is now King of France "must be part of what is affirmed by any proposition about [the present King of France]."[6] Thus, the logically and philosophically interesting feature of contextual definitions is that by means of them we can explain what certain words or phrases contribute to the meaning of a sentence even though we cannot define the words or phrases themselves in isolation—i.e., explicitly.

It is quite clear in *The Republic* that Plato is looking for an explicit definition of what it is to be a good man. Furthermore, it is clear that he is trying to discover a *real* definition of 'good man'. None of the arguments with Cephalus, Polemarchus, and Thrasymachus would make sense if we thought otherwise.

Discovering a Real Definition

WHAT ARE we to understand by 'discovering' a real definition? Let me first indicate in what sense it is *impossible* to discover a real definition. If we have an arbitrarily selected class of entities and we stipulate that a certain word W is to apply to each one of those entities, and the word W has—for all we know—no other meaning, then it is impossible to discover a real definition of W by observing what property or properties are common and peculiar to the members of the arbitrarily selected class. First, I shall use an example from arithmetic, and then an example from the physical world to make my point.

I select, arbitrarily, a class whose members are every other positive integer, and every other negative integer, beginning with zero. This class includes . . . −8, −6, −4, −2, +2, +4, +6, +8. . . . I decide to use the expression 'even integer' to refer to any member of this class. I have, if you will, stipulated a definition of 'even integer'. Let us suppose that I next observe that there is a property that is common and peculiar to every even integer,— namely, being divisible by 2 without remainder. Now arithmetical operations can be construed in such a way that being divisible by 2 without remainder is a principle of selecting numbers that is distinct from the arbitrary principle with which I began. Hence, my observing that even integers and only even integers are

[6] *Ibid.*, p. 68.

divisible by 2 without remainder is a discovery. Moreover, it is *necessarily* true that all and only those numbers that are (by my stipulation) even integers, are divisible by 2 without remainder. In other words, being an even integer is a logically necessary and sufficient condition for being divisible by 2 without remainder.

But have we discovered a real definition of 'even integer'? No, because a set of logically necessary and sufficient conditions for being an even integer is not necessarily the meaning of 'even integer'. It is logically necessary and sufficient for a triangle to be equilateral that it be equiangular. But 'equilateral triangle' does not mean *triangle having equal angles*. It means *triangle having equal sides*. The example shows that, starting with a stipulative definition of 'even integer' we can discover a number of conditions that are logically necessary and sufficient for being an even integer. But these necessary and sufficient conditions do not yet make up the real definition of 'even integer' simply be-cause, although in an explicit definition the *definiens* of a term purports to specify logically necessary and sufficient conditions for being the sort of thing to which the *definiendum* correctly applies, not every set of logically necessary and sufficient condi-tions is identical with the meaning of the *definiendum*.

As a matter of fact, the expression 'even integer', as used in arithmetical contexts (not, for example, in a code language), does mean *number divisible by 2 without remainder*. But we can re-port that fact only because there is an antecedently established convention to the effect that 'even integer' is to mean integer divisible by 2 without remainder. This would not be a good stipulation, if being divisible by 2 without remainder were not common and peculiar to every number denoted by the term 'even integer'. But, in principle, there can be more than one set of logically necessary and sufficient conditions for being a certain sort of thing. And from among them we have to make a choice, usually guided by our needs and interests and purposes, as to which set will be *definitive* of being that sort of thing. That choice is a stipulation as to what a certain expression is to *mean*, or as to what is to be treated as being *constitutive* of being a certain kind of thing.

I shall next use an example from the physical world to illus-trate the same general point—namely, that if we have an arbi-trarily selected class of entities and we stipulate that the word, W, is to be used to apply to any one of them, then it is impossible to discover a real definition of W by observing what property or properties are common and peculiar to the members of the arbitrarily selected class. Imagine someone who for the first time observes that certain animals that live in the Nile resemble each other anatomically in ways in which they resemble no other animals known to him. He captures one of them, and has it put on exhibit in the zoo. Assume that the expression, 'the animal that is on exhibit in the zoo', uniquely refers to it. Imagine further that he decides to use the word 'crocodile' to refer to any animal that resembles anatomically the animal in the zoo. He has thereby stipulated that he will mean by 'crocodile' any animal that resembles anatomically the animal in the zoo.

Imagine further that his stipulation is generally adopted. (This sort of thing happens frequently: Newton's stipulative definition of 'vector' was adopted by physicists, and the word thereby acquired a standard use. When a physicist talked about vectors, other physicists understood him to be talking about a quantity that requires for its complete specification . . . , etc.) We are to imagine that, in like fashion, the word 'crocodile' acquires a standard use. People use it to mean an animal that resembles anatomically the animal on exhibit in the zoo. At first, people apply the word 'crocodile' to crocodiles and alligators indiscriminately. After all, crocodiles do resemble alligators anatomically more closely than crocodiles and alligators resemble anatomically any other animals we know of. But one crocodile resembles anatomically another crocodile more closely than any crocodile resembles an alligator. Hence, it will be possible to observe that, within the class of crocodiles, a finer discrimination can be made; we then make it. Now we apply the word to the crocodiles and withhold it from the alligators, even though we have no theory as to what makes for the difference between the animals we call 'crocodiles' and the others that look so much like them, and yet are different. With this standard use of the word 'crocodile' at hand, it is possible to discover facts about crocodiles that are unique and peculiar to them. One may find out that crocodiles and only crocodiles are large, thick-skinned, long-bodied aquatic reptiles that have a broad head tapering to the snout, their natural habitat being in or near tropical or subtropical waters.

What we have discovered, however, is a *matter-of-fact* correlation. This is a crucial *disanalogy* between this case and the mathematical case. This matter-of-fact correlation is not enough to give us *logically* necessary and sufficient conditions. (a) It is necessarily true that crocodiles and only crocodiles resemble in certain definite respects anatomically the animal in the zoo. The necessity of this is fixed by an initial stipulation and a subsequent finer discrimination. (b) But it is only contingently true (it happens to be true, but it might have been false) that animals and only animals that resemble in certain definite respects anatomically the animal in the zoo are long-bodied, thick-skinned, and all the rest. From (a) and (b) it does *not* follow that *necessarily* crocodiles and only crocodiles are long-bodied, thick-skinned and all the rest. But in order for it to be a *real definition* that a crocodile is a long-bodied, etc. animal, the proposition that crocodiles and only crocodiles are long-bodied, etc., must be *necessarily* true. We have, in other words, *discovered a correlation:* something is a crocodile if, and only if, it is long-bodied, thick-skinned, etc. But we have not so far *discovered a definition*. To get a definition out of this situation, we must make a *decision* or a *stipulation*. We must decide which among the properties that are common and peculiar to crocodiles are to be treated as *essential* to being a crocodile.

The example of the crocodiles illustrates a general point. If we have an arbitrarily selected class of physical objects, and we stipulate that the word, W, is to be used to apply to any one of those physical objects, and the word, W, has, for all that we know, no other meaning, then it is impossible to discover that W has another meaning, which is its real *definiens*, by observing what property or properties are common and peculiar to the class of physical objects denoted by W. Let $P_1 \ldots P_n$ be properties that are observed to be common and peculiar to the members of an arbitrarily selected class of physical objects. The fact is that these properties are not *observed* to be *necessarily* common and peculiar to those objects. Moreover, as illustrated in our arithmetical example, even if they were "seen," by a rational intuition, to be necessarily common and peculiar, in principle there may be more than one set of necessary and sufficient conditions. There is no rational intuition by which we can "see" which set of necessary and sufficient conditions is *definitive*. It is logically necessary and sufficient for a triangle to be equilateral that all of its sides be of the same length. But it is also logically necessary and sufficient for a triangle to be equilateral that it be equiangular. We do in fact identify the meaning of 'equilateral triangle' with "triangle whose sides are of the same length"; but this cannot be because the only set of logically necessary and sufficient conditions of being equilateral is being equal-sided.

I have described the conditions under which one cannot discover a real definition. I shall now describe two conditions under which one can. The first condition is an obvious one. If a word is defined in an authoritative dictionary, one can find out what it means by consulting the dictionary or by asking an adult, well-educated speaker of the language. Any adult who speaks English well can tell you that in such a sentence as 'My father is taller than yours' the word 'father' means *male parent*. Not every well-educated adult can tell you what 'tweeter' means, but a hi-fi engineer can, and an authoritative dictionary of hi-fi terms will also tell you what the word means.

However, the dictionary definition of many a familiar word may be unsatisfactory for one of a number of different reasons. The dictionary tells you that a good man is a man of praiseworthy character; but if you then look up 'praiseworthy', you are told that it means *good*. This is going around in circles. No thinking man, let alone a professional philosopher, can be satisfied with such a "definition." Another reason why some dictionary definitions are unsatisfactory is that they are often so vague as to be almost without meaning. Vagueness is in itself no vice. Many useful definitions are vague. 'Bachelor', for example, is defined as "adult human male who has never married." Although this is vague (what exactly is an adult?), it is useful for making distinctions and classifications. It is when a definition is vague beyond a certain degree that it becomes almost pointless. For example, *Webster's New Collegiate Dictionary* defines the arithmetical operation of addition as follows: "the operation of combining numbers so as to obtain an equivalent simple quantity." This is evidently intended to be an explicit definition. But it is too imprecise to be of any use in explaining what addition is. What is "combining numbers"? How does this distinguish multiplication from addition?

As compared with Peano's definition, the standard laymen's

dictionary definitions of '+' are very poor. Presumably both Peano and the lexicographer are trying to articulate the meaning of '+' that is implicit in our basic arithmetical intuitions and practices. Why is it, then, that Peano's definition is so much better? Perhaps it is because the lexicographer is chiefly interested in articulating the layman's notion of what addition is. Perhaps that notion comes to something like this: "addition is the process denoted by the sign + of combining two or more numbers so as to obtain their sum" (*Webster's Third New International Dictionary*). At any rate, this is the sort of definition a supposedly carefully prepared dictionary contains. But no such definition will satisfy anyone who wants to know precisely what addition is. That is what Peano is chiefly interested in. He wants to understand the nature of the operation precisely, and it is obvious that what we are taking to be the layman's notion contributes very little toward that. Or perhaps the run-of-the-mill lexicographer is simply not equipped to articulate the implicit meanings of certain technical terms. That may be another reason why such terms are so badly defined in standard laymen's dictionaries. Of course, there is nothing to prevent an editorial board from commissioning a Peano to articulate for a laymen's dictionary the meanings of technical terms in arithmetic. Peano, the mathematician, can also be a lexicographer. A lexicographer who is ignorant of the foundations of arithmetic is less likely to succeed in articulating the meaning of '+' than a Peano. A good lexicographer's definition of a term may be as good as that of a theoretically sophisticated expert in the field in which the term that is being defined has its typical use. But in order to produce a *good* definition, one that correctly articulates the essential core of our relevant intuitions and practices, one would have to have a theorist's interests and capacities.

The same thing holds true for philosophy. The difference between a good philosopher's definition of a term that is almost a technical term in philosophy, or that is particularly important for philosophy, and a philosophically naive lexicographer's definition of the same term is not hard to explain. The philosopher-expert is aware of more subtleties and nuances, more examples and counter-examples, than is the non-philosopher. The philosopher understands the philosophical problems; he is familiar with the conceptual confusions that the sought-for definition is intended to solve and clarify. The layman certainly has some idea of what, for example, an incorrigible belief is. But the philosopher's definition of incorrigibility[7] is bound to be more subtle because he is interested in articulating the meaning that will be most helpful in dealing with certain conceptual problems with which the layman is not concerned. The philosopher's term is a technical one, as we shall see in Part II. Nevertheless, he is not stipulating a meaning. He is rather articulating a meaning that is at one and the same time designed to be a tool in a certain area of philosophical investigation, and also to state clearly one meaning that is implicit in our intuitions and practices. Perhaps another reason why laymen's dictionaries do not contain definitions of such precision and subtlety is that these are in fact much too refined for the purposes that laymen's dictionaries are intended to serve. There are exceptions, of course. *Webster's Third New International Dictionary* has an exact definition of 'vector'. Presumably, the editors made it a point to include exact definitions of a considerable number of scientific terms. This may reflect their conviction that the layman nowadays needs to know the exact meaning of at least some scientific terms.

Peano's Definition as an Example of Discovering a Real Definition

The standard lexicographer's definition of '+' fails, while Peano's definition succeeds in telling us what '+' means, in the sense that Peano's definition articulates our basic arithmetical intuitions and accords exactly with our arithmetical reckonings. Peano articulates successfully what the rest of us are inarticulately committed to by our intuitions and practices. This is analogous to a mathematician who discovers a proof that the rest of us are not clever enough to discover; once it is discovered, however, we can check it and see that it proves its point. Peano's definition of '+' is thus an example of a real definition. It explicates a meaning of '+' in that it formulates in precise and understandable terms a meaning of '+' that is implicit in our arithmetical intuitions and practices. Lexicographers do try to provide real definitions, and their defini-

7 See Part II, esp. Section 1.

tions, if good, are genuine explications of meaning. The most important difference between Peano's and the ordinary lexicographer's definition of '+' is that Peano's *succeeds* in explicating a meaning of '+' adequately and precisely, where the mathematically ignorant lexicographer fails. An original explication of meaning, if successful, is a discovery. It is not a stipulation.

There is no way of delimiting precisely the conditions under which a definition could be said to be formulating in understandable terms a meaning that is implicit in our intuitions and practices. The latter terms are admittedly vague. But my characterization of explication is, I hope, not useless. For, although we cannot pretend that it is precise we can, in given cases, explain how a certain definition may be an instance of a correct explication.

Let us look at Peano's definition of '+' once more. Almost everybody knows how to add. The sign '+' has a standard use in arithmetic, in which it symbolizes the operation of adding numbers. We want to understand the nature of this operation. Peano's way of achieving this understanding is to begin by understanding addition as it involves the natural numbers, 0, 1, 2, 3, 4, . . . etc. Once we understand addition as it involves the natural numbers, we can define addition for other sorts of numbers. Now before Peano the sign '+' had a use, but it did not have an adequately articulated meaning in the way that such words as 'father' and 'brother' have. The standard dictionaries define these latter words in a perfectly adequate way; but their definitions of '+' are hopelessly vague. Well, then, let us look at a true addition equation that involves natural numbers; perhaps that equation will give us some idea about the nature of addition. Let us look at $1 + 1 = 2$. The operation $1 + 1$ uniquely determines a natural number, the number 2. That is one thing the equation tells us. Another thing it tells us is that the uniquely determined number is identical with $1 + 1$. What sort of operation then is the addition of natural numbers? It is not unreasonable to think that one way of explaining precisely the nature of this operation would be to set down a rule or set of rules that will tell us precisely how to express that uniquely determined number in terms every one of which is clear and precise and is different in meaning from '+'. That is exactly what Peano's recursive definition does for addition involving natural numbers. If you think about Peano's definition, you will see that where m and n are natural numbers, the operation, m + n, uniquely determines the nth successor of m. If n = o, the nth successor of m is m itself. This is the first step of Peano's recursive definition, m + o = m. This accords very nicely with the sense we all have that to add o to a number is to add nothing to it. If n $\neq$ o, then it is easy to see what the nth successor of m is, in any given case in which the value of n is a given natural number. Thus, 1 + 1 determines the first successor of 1, namely 2. 1 + 2 determines the second successor of 1, namely, the successor of the successor of 1, namely, 3. This, too, accords very nicely with our sense that, when we add a number other than o to a given number, we are adding something to it. That comes to saying that the number identified is a number different from the number to which a number has been added. m + o "takes you nowhere"; m + n, where n $\neq$ o, does take you beyond m, to something different. We may note in passing that because addition is commutative, i.e., because m + n = n + m, it makes no difference whether we say that m + n determines the nth successor of m or that it determines the mth successor of n.

The root idea is that the operation of adding natural numbers is an operation that uniquely identifies a certain natural number in terms of the successor relation. Peano's definition tells us exactly how that number is identified for each case of m + n, where n is a specific natural number. As we saw in an earlier example, x + 3 identifies the successor of the successor of the successor of x, i.e., the third successor of x. Peano's choice of the successor relation to explain the nature of addition is a good one. The relation is clearly enough understood and it is certainly different from the operation denoted by '+'. The fact that Peano's definition *explains the nature* of addition is the reason for saying that it is a discovery, not a stipulation. It brings out in the open a fact that was there for any of us to see all the time. The fact is that to add natural numbers is uniquely to determine a natural number. The problem is to explain clearly the manner of that unique determination, and Peano's recursive definition does just that. When the rest of us think about it, we see that Peano's definition is a perfectly good account of the nature of addition.

This is not to say that there may not be others just as good. Peano's work in the foundations of arithmetic was done without assuming set theory. However, if set theory is assumed, addition can be defined explicitly. The recursive and explicit definitions may both be explicative. It may be a good thing to have both. Each may be useful in one specific context of inquiry. But even if there were no practical significance in the fact that both definitions are possible, it is theoretically interesting to know that a given term can be defined equally well either explicitly or recursively.

Problems About Ethical Concepts

IF CONSULTING dictionaries and producing explications of meaning are the only ways to discover real definitions, then we should be able to discover the meaning of 'good man' either by consulting an authoritative dictionary or else by explicating the meaning of 'good man'. A little effort should be sufficient to convince anyone, however, that the dictionary does not contain an illuminating answer. As I have already noted, the dictionary will say, for example, that a good man is a man of praiseworthy character; if we look up 'praiseworthy', we will then be told that it means 'good'; and so we will be going around in circles. Or else we will be told that 'good' is "the most general adjective of commendation in the English language" (*Oxford English Dictionary*). This means that a good man is a man to whom the adjective 'good' applies—which, again, is not very illuminating. We are thus left with the alternative: the only way to discover the meaning of 'good man' is to discover its explicative definition.

The search for real definitions is a characteristic philosophical activity. It is precisely the activity that Plato is engaged in, with respect to the question: "What is a good man?" His dissatisfaction with a number of answers offered makes it quite plain that he does not expect to find a ready-made real definition. He sets out instead to formulate a definition that, he hopes, will be recognized as explicating what a good man is. (In the vast majority of cases, a dictionary definition will not satisfy a philosopher's needs. Typically, a philosopher discovers a real definition not by consulting a standard dictionary, or any other such accomplished work, but by being the first to articulate a relevant implicit meaning.)

Plato, it must be remembered, is looking for a *correct* real definition of human goodness. But what is the standard of correctness here? What sorts of facts about a man could help us to determine the correct meaning of the expression 'good man'? Surely not a man's physical attributes. The size of a man's muscles or the color of his skin are not *constitutive* of his being a good or a bad man. There is no contradiction in thinking that a black-skinned man is a good man, nor is there any contradiction in thinking that he is a bad man. While there are such things as the dispositions, feelings, attitudes, principles, habits of a good man, there is no such thing as the color of a good man. Every good man has some color or other, but no one color is the color of a good man. The same is true of any other typically human physical attribute.

Perhaps we should look at human dispositions, feelings, attitudes, principles, and habits in order to discover the real definition of a good man. But studying dispositions and the rest as brute occurrences will not help us to discover the real definition of a good man. We need to know which dispositions and habits make for goodness in a man. In other words, we seem to be driven to suppose that the material from which we may be able to elicit an explication of 'a good man' consists of the true judgments we make about what is or is not right, proper, fitting, and good for a man to do and to be. Accordingly, let us agree that a correct real definition of a good man must conform to the true judgments we actually make as to what is and what is not good for a man to do or to be, or, in other words, about what a man ought to do and what sort of person he ought to be. This is a necessary condition for any definition being a correct real definition of 'good man'. It is not, however, a sufficient condition.

This sort of standard involves two major complications. The first has to do with the requirement that the definition must conform to, be consistent with, our *true* judgments. The second concerns the requirement that it must be true to *our* judgments. How are we to tell which of our judgments of evaluation are true? And who are the "we" whose true judgments are to be the acid test? Are "we" the majority of mankind? All of mankind? Any reflective person? Only those who agree with us? Any group of people who agree among themselves, whether or not they agree with us?

The first major complication is really in three parts. First, what sort of thing is a judgment about what a man ought to do and the sort of man he ought to be? Second, how do we determine what are a man's actual judgments about such matters? This issue we must face as a preliminary to the third: how do we tell a man's true value judgments about human beings from his false ones?

Ought-Judgments

LET US CALL a judgment about what a man ought to do and what sort of man he ought to be an *ought-judgment*. And let us characterize such judgments as follows: Ought-judgments are statements that (a) we can correctly assert by using sentences that contain words like 'ought', 'right', 'wrong', 'obligatory', 'forbidden', 'may', 'permitted', 'must', 'has to', and (b) are judgments about the actions and character of human beings; they guide choices, and enter into deliberations about what to do or what not to do. Accordingly, "It ought to rain tomorrow" is not an ought-judgment, in our sense, while "Inasmuch as you promised to pay Smith five dollars, you ought to make every effort to pay him" is an ought-judgment. "I wouldn't do that if I were you" does not contain 'ought', 'right', etc., although in certain contexts it would be an ought-judgment: it could be expressed equally correctly by using the sentence, 'You ought not to do that'.

Determining what a man's ought-judgments are is a complex matter. There are certain facts about a man that we can determine by observing his appearance and behavior. We can tell in that way what color his hair and eyes are; we can also tell that one man steals while another is scrupulously honest, or that one man is careless about keeping his promises, while another takes his promises with the utmost seriousness. But by simply observing a man's appearance and behavior, we cannot tell what ought-judgments he makes. For a man who is habitually careless about keeping promises may yet firmly believe that one ought not to be careless about one's promises. He may, without giving any external signs of it, have feelings of guilt or self-deprecation each time he acts carelessly about keeping a promise. In such a case we cannot tell, merely by observation, what he believes about the obligatoriness of keeping one's promises. It is also possible that a man may not have thought at all about the worth of an action; it may be that, when he does think about it, he will find himself appraising it in a certain way. If we call this sort of appraisal a *latent ought-judgment*, then there may be many ought-judgments that a man would make, but what they are we could not now tell merely by observing his appearance and behavior. I am not implying that a man's actual ought-judgments are sometimes an unfathomable mystery. I am merely warning against the mistake of supposing that the process of discerning what a man's ought-judgments are is a relatively simple matter.

Third, how do we tell true from false ought-judgments? There is no easy answer to this question. Some philosophers tell us that ought-judgments are not genuine judgments: they are neither true nor false. Others say that they are, indeed, true or false, but that the criteria of truth for ought-judgments are different from those for scientific judgments. According to these philosophers, an ought-judgment is true for someone if, and only if, he continually reaffirms it, whenever he re-examines the judgment in the course of deliberating about a practical problem. On this view, an ought-judgment is true, as far as Jones is concerned, if, and only if, Jones finds himself sincerely reaffirming it upon every occasion of his reconsidering the judgment within the context of further experience. Philosophers who hold this view acknowledge that the truth of ought-judgments is relative to the individual. Jones may conscientiously reaffirm an ought-judgment, while Smith may conscientiously reaffirm its contradictory. Both would be judging truly. The philosophers who hold this view are led to it because they believe that there is no ought-judgment that can be proved true or false, that there is no ought-judgment, no matter how outlandish, that a person cannot consistently believe.

Plato disagrees both with those who propose that ought-judgments are neither true nor false, and with those who relativize their truth to the conscientious reaffirmations of an individual. Plato assumes that ought-judgments are true or false in a straightforward way. On Plato's view, two contradictory ought-judgments cannot both be true. Unfortunately, Plato does not provide a clear method of determining the truth-value of ought-judgments. He asserts repeatedly that their truth-value is discovered by reason.

And up to a point he is right. There are ought-judgments that are indubitably true or conclusively justified, and hence can be discovered by reason. It is, therefore, a mistake to believe that no ought-judgment can be proved true or false. Suppose, for instance, that I had promised my mother to meet her downtown at 6:00 P.M., on a certain day. Just a few minutes before it is time for me to start, I learn that if I get there on time a gang will kill me. I don't want to be killed, and my mother doesn't want me to be killed. Under the circumstances, it is clear that I ought to break my promise to my mother: I ought not to go to the meeting place on time. The reasons against my going far outweigh the sole reason why I ought to go: namely, that I promised. This is one example of concluding what one ought to do by rational deliberation. It will not do to say that the conclusion is by no means fully justified, on the grounds that perhaps all promises ought to be kept, no matter what. While Kant, for example, thought that all promises ought to be kept, no matter what, I believe that principle to be demonstrably false. Suppose it were indeed true. Now consider the following propositions:

(a) I promise to give you a bottle of whiskey.
(b) I promise your wife not to give you a bottle of whiskey.

From (a) and the principle, it follows that (c) I ought to give you a bottle of whiskey. From (b) and the principle, it follows that (d) I ought not to give you a bottle of whiskey. But "I ought not to give you a bottle of whiskey" entails (e) "It is false that I ought to give you a bottle of whiskey." (c) and (e) are contradictories. We have, then, deduced a contradiction from the principle, used in conjunction with (a) and (b). Hence, it must be that at least one of the three—the principle, or (a), or (b)—is false. There appears to be no reason to suppose that (a) and (b) cannot both be true. Hence, it must be that the principle, "All promises ought to be kept," is false.

This argument does not depend upon anything but logic—provided that the assumption is correct that (a) and (b) can both be true. Until someone shows that assumption to be false, the whole argument remains as an example of a logical refutation of an ought-judgment. The view that, when it comes to questions of what is good and what is right, one man's opinion is as good as another's, for there is nothing but opinion about such things, is, I think, false. At the same time, there are ought-judgments whose truth-value is difficult, perhaps even impossible to determine.

Up to a point, then, Plato is right when he says that the truth-value of ought-judgments can be discovered by rational deliberation. It may even be the case that, if we could know everything that would happen as a result of our intentional acts, and if we knew everything about the facts as they are before we acted, then there would be no doubts about the truth-value of any ought-judgment. But, unfortunately, our information is incomplete, and hence in practice not every ought-judgment is as indubitable as the one in our example.

Besides, there may be ultimately irreconcilable differences among different persons' ought-judgments. Imagine a person X who is so powerful that he can torture people at will without being detected or punished. If X positively enjoys torturing people from time to time, if he feels no remorse or guilt when he does torture anyone—in fact, his life becomes "weary, stale, flat, and unprofitable," if he never tortures anyone—then he may decide that, all things considered, he ought to torture people from time to time. You and I, however, who abhor the idea of anyone torturing anyone, would judge that, all things considered, X ought not to torture anyone. This may be an irreconcilable ultimate disagreement between us and Mr. X; it may be a disagreement, that is, that cannot be resolved by further rational deliberation. In the event that we were confronted with such an impasse, it might be very hard for us to tell which of the two incompatible ought-judgments was true. If we went along with Plato's assumption that one of the two judgments—"Mr. X ought from time to time to torture people" and "Mr. X ought at no time to torture people"—must be false, and if we had no way of proving which of them was true and which false, we could not very well settle questions about which definition of 'good man' is correct. For surely it is important to know whether or not torturing people for self-gratification is what a good man would do.

Because of these uncertainties, we should be wiser if we did not expect with certainty to find an explicative real definition of 'good man' supported by our true ought-judgments. More modest expectations, however, are quite in order. For example, we could use the standard of correctness even in its present form to determine whether or not an individual or a group was being consistent in proposing a certain definition of 'good man', while making certain ought-judgments. We could, thus, eliminate inconsistent theories (definitions), even if we couldn't with certainty prove that any proposed theory (definition) was both consistent and correct. These, in fact, are among the tactics that Plato uses against Cephalus, Polemarchus, and Thrasymachus, as we shall shortly see.

Our second major complication has to do with the "we" whose ought-judgments are to serve as a check in the definition of 'good man'. On any occasion when we apply the standard for a correct explicative real definition of 'good man', we have to make up our minds as to who are the "we" whose actual and true ought-judgments are to be accommodated by the correct definition. The first fact to note is that, no matter how we decide to restrict the range of "we," there will still be an element of guesswork as to what are the actual ought-judgments that are to serve as our point of reference. The one possible exception is to restrict the "we" only to those who agree with us. But even if the presumption were unquestionable that we know our own ought-judgments, this way of restricting the "we" could give us a standard only for what would be a correct definition of 'good man' *for me and for those who agree with my ought-judgments*. This, as we shall see shortly, is a useful standard in a specific context of philosophical inquiry, but it falls short of being a standard for a correct definition of 'good man' *per se*. Taking the "we" as any group of people who agree among themselves proves to be similarly restrictive. It cannot provide a standard of correctness for defining 'good man'; it can provide one only relatively to the ought-judgments *of some group or other*.

The remaining alternatives include the possibilities that the "we" refers to all of mankind, to the majority of mankind, to any reflective person. These seem to be more promising, but they are ultimately indecisive. This is because the conclusion seems to be inescapable that it is not logically necessary that all of mankind, or the majority of mankind, or all reflective persons agree in all their ought-judgments—even after all the facts that are relevant to ought-judgments are known to everyone concerned. In other words, the proposition "All people (or the majority of mankind, or all reflective persons) who agree as to what the ought-relevant facts are will agree in their ought-judgments" is contingent and it may be false. If I find that X enjoys torturing babies, I may think that he doesn't really know what being tortured is like, and that if I can only get him to know what experiencing torture is, he would stop torturing babies, because he would then see the monstrous quality of his act. It is quite possible, however, that even if I am right in thinking that X doesn't really know what being tortured is like, I am wrong in thinking that he will see the error of his ways if I get him to know the feel of being tortured. To my horror, he may want more than ever to torture babies precisely because he hadn't really known until now what he was doing to the babies. Now that he does know, the more they suffer, the better he likes it! I may call X a monster; I may think he ought to be killed or imprisoned. But the one thing I cannot do is to argue him into believing that, all things considered, he ought not to torture babies. Nor can I prove that he is any less reflective than I am. (Here I am anticipating my disagreement with Plato. In the parable of Gyges, Plato undertakes to prove that, even when one is immune from detection and punishment, one ought not to misbehave. Plato thinks, I believe mistakenly, that this thesis is demonstrable to any reflective person.)

I have just spoken about all the facts that are relevant to ought-judgments being known to everyone concerned. But here, too, there are complications. The truth is that a fact that is ought-relevant both for you and for me may not be ought-relevant in the same way. Both for me and the sadist, the fact that torturing children will cause them horrible suffering is ought-relevant. On it I base my judgment that I ought not to torture children, while what the sadist concludes from the very same fact is that he ought to torture children. The sadist treats his own enjoyments as taking precedence over the suffering of his victims. Knowledge of the victim's sufferings is relevant, as far as the sadist is concerned, but only in that it ensures and augments his own enjoyments. Moreover, not all men, not even all reflective men, will agree on what are the ought-relevant facts. There are people who base some of their ought-judgments on their belief that God commands certain things. For them God's commands are ought-relevant. The unbeliever dismisses such appeals to God's commands as being irrelevant, because he believes that there are no such commands, because for him there is no God. Here is an example of how a disagreement about the ought-relevance of a given proposition is actually rooted in a metaphysical disagreement about God's existence. There are many other such examples.

The foregoing remarks serve as reminders that there is no single standard for judging the correctness of a given definition of "good man." Sometimes we may appeal to what everyone we know would say about some matter of what ought to be. Sometimes we may appeal to what a reasonable or reflective man would say. We should be as clear as we can about which version of the standard we are employing in a given context. If we did this, we would be spared some avoidable confusions, and we would be forewarned against expecting what, given the nature of the subject, may not be forthcoming—namely, a demonstrably satisfactory explicative real definition of 'good man'.

What I have just been saying is that we should not be too optimistic about finding a definition of 'good man' that is consistent with everyone's true ought-judgments or with the true ought-judgments of all reflective people. I should like at this point to avoid a possible misunderstanding. I would not want the reader to confuse my position with that of those cultural relativists who argue from cultural relativism to ethical relativism.

Cultural and Ethical Relativism

CULTURAL relativism is a controversial empirical hypothesis. It asserts that among different societies there are *basic* disagreements about values (including ought-judgments). A basic disagreement about values involves agreement about all the facts in a given situation, yet a disagreement about what is good or appropriate or right in that situation. For this to be an empirical hypothesis, however, the basis for there being two different societies cannot be that there are basic disagreements between them about values. Otherwise, the statement of cultural relativism would not be an empirical claim but a tautology: "There are basic disagreements among societies among which there are basic disagreements." The criteria for these being two different societies will instead include such factors as different tribal or national boundaries, languages, customs, practices.

Not all writers on the subject agree that cultural relativism is true. There is disagreement, for example, as to whether or not there are clear cases of basic disagreement about values among individuals. I myself am inclined to believe that among individuals there are basic disagreements. The example of the sadist seems to present a clear case of basic disagreement about values between an individual like myself and an individual sadist. It is less certain in my mind that there are basic disagreements among different societies.

Even if cultural relativism is proved to be true, however, the move from cultural relativism to ethical relativism is invalid. By 'ethical relativism' I mean the view that, given a basic value disagreement between two different cultural groups, it is impossible to prove that one of the two incompatible judgments is true and the other false. The thesis I have proposed should be sharply distinguished from this. My thesis is that the proposition, "All those who agree as to what the ought-relevant facts are will agree in their ought-judgments," is contingent and almost certainly false.

The argument from cultural relativism to ethical relativism is roughly but substantially this: there are in fact enormous disparities in the basic goals pursued by different societies. This rules out the possibility of inter-societal arguments to prove that a certain ought-judgment made by the members of one society is true, while an ought-judgment that is incompatible with it and made by the members of a different society is false.

That there is something inconclusive about this inference can be seen if we observe that an exactly parallel argument will yield the conclusion that there can be no inter-societal validation of scientific judgments. Here is the argument: "It is a fact that there are enormous disparities in the basic factual beliefs of different societies. (Let a basic factual belief be a belief about what is the case—a belief that is taken for granted and which functions as an axiom relative to many other beliefs about what is the case. For example, that cows get sick because there are evil spirits at work is a basic factual belief in certain societies; Martin Luther's contemporaries, and Luther himself, believed this.) This rules out the possibility of inter-societal agreement on basic factual beliefs. And this, in turn, rules out the possibility of inter-societal arguments to prove that this factual judgment is false and that one is true." Although the initial premise of this argument is known to be true, we are generally disinclined to accept the conclusion, because we believe that, even if initially there is a wide diversity of opinion about scientific subject matter, anyone whose faculties are unimpaired can be taught how to reason and experiment and observe, according to the canons and practices that are characteristic of the natural sciences. And we take it for granted that, notwithstanding the fact that X and Y are members of different societies, if they both proceed scientifically, they will, in the long run, arrive at the same conclusions about scientific subject matter. The argument from cultural relativism to ethical relativism offers no reason at all why we cannot make the same assumption about values that we make about scientific subject matter. For all we know, X and Y might very well come to accept the same basic ought-judgments—if they were both fully enlightened, in a responsible frame of mind, and shared the same scientific and metaphysical beliefs.

What I am saying is that we are inclined to believe that X, who is a European scientist, and Y, who is a Bushman, may come into contact with each other under circumstances that make it possible for X to train Y to be a scientist. In other words, two people, *each from a very different type of society initially,* can conceivably so interact that at the end they share the same factual beliefs, as the result solely or chiefly of rational and uncoercive communication. If this is imaginable concerning scientific subject matter, why is it not imaginable as far as basic values are concerned? The argument from cultural relativism to ethical relativism does not present the slightest ground for believing that there is a difference here.

＊　＊　＊　＊　＊

THE PRECEDING explanations are intended to prepare the reader to understand what Plato is trying to do in the early books of *The Republic.* They are also intended to indicate the complications that are involved in some of Plato's methodological presuppositions—in particular, the difficulties in the presupposition that the nature of human goodness is susceptible of an explicative real explicit definition. It may be that being a good man is not definable explicitly. Plato may be wrong (indeed, I believe he is wrong) in assuming that there is a real explicit definition of 'good man'. But even so, he is surely right in believing that the expression 'good man' is meaningful, and that we may become clearer about what it means if we reflect philosophically.

Plato begins the philosophical reflection on what it is to be a good man by first criticizing five definitions. He rejects all of them. Although most, if not all, of these definitions are pretty obviously inadequate, one can still learn a good deal about philosophical thinking by examining Plato's own remarks about them.

Section 2

THE ARGUMENT WITH CEPHALUS

THE DEFINITION of 'just man' that Plato first criticizes is Cephalus'.

Df. I: A just man = Df. a man who tells the truth and keeps his promises.

The essence of Plato's objection to this definition is to be found in one rhetorical question, which Socrates puts to Cephalus: "Are not these acts [telling the truth and keeping promises] sometimes right and sometimes wrong?" Plato believes that the answer is obviously "Yes." If we had accepted Cephalus' definition, then we should be committed to believing that "If a man is just, then he keeps every promise" is a necessarily true proposi-

tion. But Plato's example of the unwisdom of returning a danger-
ous weapon to a man who has become a homicidal maniac, even
though a promise has been made to return it, shows that, when
we deliberate carefully, we frequently conclude that a particular
promise ought *not* to be kept.

Precisely at this point Plato must be using the undeclared
assumption that "x is a good man" entails "x is a just man." By
Cephalus' definition, if a man is just, then he keeps every promise; hence, by the undeclared assumption, if a man is good, he
keeps every promise. But it is false (and Cephalus admits this)
that if a man is good, he keeps every promise. Thus, Cephalus'
definition entails the contradiction: it is true that, if a man is
good, he keeps every promise, and it is false that, if a man is
good, he keeps every promise. The assumption that being a good
man entails being a just man is correct. It is also true that there
are times when a good man would not keep a promise. In conjunction with these true propositions, Cephalus' definition yields
a contradiction. The only way to avoid the contradiction is to
reject Cephalus' definition.

No one can consistently define 'just man' in Cephalus' way and,
at the same time, judge that in certain circumstances one ought
not to keep a promise. Similar points tell against the principle
that one ought always to tell the truth. At the very least, then,
Plato is right in maintaining that one cannot consistently accept
Cephalus' definition as a correct account of the nature of a just
man, and yet also believe that there are times when it isn't right
to tell the truth or to keep a promise. But Plato's argument seems
to prove more than this. There appears to be no reason for doubting that there are times when one ought not to tell the truth, and
there are times when one ought not to keep a promise. Hence,
Cephalus' definition is inconsistent with some ought-judgments
that we have no reason for doubting to be true.

We can ask Cephalus another rhetorical question: "Are these
acts—telling the truth and keeping promises—the only acts that
one can do rightly or wrongly?" The answer is obviously "No."
There are many other kinds of acts that we can do or fail to do
as we ought. One ought to be kind and considerate, for example,
but one can be kind without having to tell the truth or keep a
promise. One can be kind simply by helping a blind man across
the street. Cephalus' definition has, therefore, the further defect

of being too restrictive. It excludes from consideration many kinds of actions that are judged to be done rightly or wrongly.

Recall my argument against the principle that all promises ought to be kept. If that argument is correct, and I believe that it is, then the proposition "All promises ought to be kept" is false. But Cephalus' definition of 'just man', and the assumption that being good entails being just, together entail that a good man is one who keeps all his promises (i.e., "All promises ought to be kept"). Hence, Cephalus' definition is incorrect.

Section 3

THE ARGUMENT WITH POLEMARCHUS

NEXT POLEMARCHUS comes into the discussion to propose the following definition:

Df. II: A just man = Df. a man who gives every man his due.

This is an improvement over Cephalus' definition. "Giving every man his due" suggests being fair and impartial, and fairness and impartiality have a close connection with justice. But when Socrates asks Polemarchus what he has in mind when he speaks of giving every man his due, Polemarchus replies: What is due to a man is benefit, if he is a friend, and harm, if he is an enemy. Df. II gives way, accordingly, to

Df. III: A just man = Df. a man who does good to friends and harm to enemies.

Df. III and the immediately following Df. IV[8] are unacceptable

8 See p. 42.

for a reason that Plato seems to have overlooked. Mankind cannot be divided exhaustively into those who are one's friends and those who are one's enemies. Between those two poles, there are total strangers as well as nodding acquaintances. Both Df. III and Df. IV leave such strangers and acquaintances entirely out of consideration. According to those definitions it is not possible for a man to act either well or badly, either rightly or wrongly, either justly or unjustly, toward strangers and mere acquaintances. This consequence is counterintuitive. Many believe, and I think truly, that it is mean and contemptible and unjust to insult in a spirit of frivolity the idols of a strange tribe. There are also those who believe that one ought to be polite to one's acquaintances. Anyone who believes such things as these cannot accept Df. III and Df. IV. Besides, inasmuch as Df. III does not accord with commonly held ought-judgments, it cannot be a correct account of what it is to be a just man. For, once again, from the assumption that "x is good" entails "x is just" and Df. III, we can deduce that a good man is one who would always do good to his friends and harm to his enemies, i.e., one ought always to do good to one's friends and harm to one's enemies. But it is false to say that one ought always to do good to friends and harm to enemies. It is false that I ought to do harm to an enemy of mine who has come to me of his own accord and sincerely wishes to set aright all past grievances between us. Surely I should be doing a grievous wrong if I killed him before he even had a chance to explain the object of his visit. An exactly parallel criticism can be made of Df. IV.

Plato's first objection to Df. III is that it misclassifies justice. This definition makes it appear that a just man is a man who possesses a specialized skill, or that it is impossible to be just if one does not possess such a specialized skill. It classifies justice along with such specialized skills as doctoring, farming, shoemaking, when in fact being a just man is not a specialized skill at all. It is, rather, being a man of a certain state of character.

Imagine a poet who is not a good judge of horses. For all his poetic ability, he would not know how to give useful advice to a friend who wanted to buy a particular horse. Or imagine a brain surgeon, the best in the world, who does not know how to do something else that requires a specific skill.

Now according to Df. III, (1) and (2) below would be necessarily true statements.

(1) The poet cannot act as *justly* toward those of his friends who are in need of brain surgery as can the brain surgeon.

(2) The surgeon, being the one who is most competent to treat those who need brain surgery, is the one who can treat most *justly* those of his friends who come to him in need of brain surgery.

But (1) and (2) are false by any ordinary standards. Hence, Df. III cannot be a correct account of what people who make ought-judgments mean by 'just man'. By ordinary standards and contrary to (1), the poet could treat the friends in question as justly as could anyone else. And the surgeon, even though he can be of use to the friends who need his skill, to the point of being able to save their lives, can still treat them unjustly. He may perform the operation beautifully, yet he may overcharge the patient who can afford to overpay, and hence is not in the least harmed by overpaying. Nevertheless, it is surely unjust to overcharge.

The second objection to Df. III is that implicit in it is the assertion that a just man would do anything to help a friend and harm an enemy. He would even lie, steal, cheat, kill. Surely it is contrary to our familiar notions to say that a man is a just man because he lies, steals, cheats, kills in order to help a friend, or to harm an enemy. We would judge a man who did such things to be an unjust man.

There is a third argument against Df. III. (Cornford, p. 12.)* First, I shall formulate the argument, and then discuss its merits.

(1) x is a friend of y = Df. x believes that y is a good honest person.

(2) x is an enemy of y = Df. x believes that y is a rogue.⁹

* Plato, *The Republic*, F. M. Cornford, ed. and trans. (Oxford: Clarendon Press, 1941). All quotations from *The Republic* cited within the text refer to this edition.

⁹ There is another difficulty with Df. III that Plato does not mention. As soon as these definitions of 'friend' and 'enemy' are assumed, Df. III yields the following:

Df. III A: A just man = Df. a man who does good to those who he believes are good honest people and harm to those who he believes are rogues.

Now Df. III A is viciously circular. The *definiendum* recurs in the *definiens*. For being a good honest person either comes to the same thing as being a just person, or being a just person is a necessary condition for being a good

(3) It is possible that x believes that y is a good honest man when in fact y is a rogue.

(4) It is possible that x believes that y is a rogue when in fact y is a good honest man.

Assume that:

(5) x believes that y is a good honest man.
(6) y is in fact a rogue.
(7) x believes that z is a rogue.
(8) z is in fact a good honest man.

By (1) and (5):

(9) x is a friend of y.

By (2) and (7):

(10) x is an enemy of z.

Assume that:

(11) "x is a good man" entails "x is a just man."

By Df. III and (11):

(12) x is acting as a good man ought to, if, and only if, he benefits y and injures z.

But by (12) and (6) and (8):

(13) x is acting as a good man ought to if, and only if, he benefits y (who is in fact a rogue) and injures z (who is in fact a good honest man).

But

(14) It is not right to injure a man who does no wrong = A man ought not to injure a man who does no wrong.

---

honest person. Likewise, being a rogue either comes to the same thing as being an unjust person or being a rogue entails being unjust. In both cases, the concept of being a just man recurs in the *definiens* either directly or by implication. Df. III A is an example of the sort of definition that does not enable us to eliminate the *definiendum* from any context. It is like: a curved line = Df. a line that curves.

The same is true of Df. IV, which is stated in the immediately following paragraph.

(15) A man ought to injure those who do wrong.

(16) A man ought to benefit those who are good and honest.

But (13) is inconsistent with (14), (15), and (16). We have deduced a contradiction from (1), (2), (3), (4), (11), (14), (15), (16), and Df. III. Hence, at least one of them must be false.

Polemarchus suggests that the trouble must be with (1) and (2). He proposes to work with a new definition of friend and enemy. Now, x is a friend of y = Df. x believes that y is a good honest man and y is in fact good and honest. x is an enemy of y = Df. x believes that y is a rogue and y is in fact a rogue. Accordingly, we have

> Df. IV: A just man = Df. a man who does good to those who are good honest men (and he believes them to be good and honest men), and harm to those who are rogues (and he believes them to be rogues).

The new definition of 'friend' and 'enemy' does get around Socrates' last argument against Df. III. Let us note, in passing, that neither the earlier nor the later definition of 'friend' and 'enemy' is an accurate report of what these terms mean, as we use them. The standard dictionaries define friendship in terms of mutual affection, esteem, trust, and they define enmity in terms of dislike, hostility, mistrust. As we use the terms, two criminals may be friends. But neither the first nor the second definition of Polemarchus would allow for this. The first definition requires that, if I am to be a friend to you, I must believe that you are an honest man. Now, because I know that, like me, you are a notorious criminal, I cannot believe that you are an honest man. If I trust you, esteem you, like you, confide in you, I am certainly your friend: you may be perfectly honorable in my eyes. There is, after all, "honor among thieves." But that doesn't make you an honest man. Polemarchus' second definition also rules out the possibility of two crooks being friends, which shows that the definition is not an accurate transcription of what 'friend' means, as we use it.

Socrates' last argument against Df. III is valid even if we replace the incorrect definitions of 'friend' and 'enemy' with the correct ones. For it is possible for me to be your friend even though you are a thoroughly disreputable person. Hence, by Df.

III and (11) I ought to help you, although you are a villain; yet by the principle (15) that a man ought to injure those who do wrong, it is not the case that I ought to help you; and again we have derived a contradiction.

The central question at this juncture, is this. Is it true that a man ought to injure those who do wrong? This is precisely the question that Socrates raises as soon as Polemarchus proposes Df. IV. If the answer is in the negative, then Df. IV is discredited because Df. IV implies that injuring wrongdoers is a necessary condition of being just; or, in other words, if a man acted justly, he would always injure rogues.

Thus, Plato's tactic against Df. IV is to prove that ought-judgment (15) is false. Once again, the logical picture is this: if (15) is false, Df. IV is incorrect, but if (15) is not false, then Df. IV may still be incorrect, for some other reason.

Let us now look at Plato's argument against (15), which is the judgment that a man ought to injure those who do wrong. Plato is trying to prove that no man is ever justified in doing injury to any human being. He begins his argument by asking: ". . . does not harming a horse or dog mean making it a worse horse or dog, so that each will be a less perfect creature in its own special way?" (Cornford, p. 13.) Plato believes that the obvious answer to this question is "Yes." That answer is the major premise of his argument.

    (a) Harming a creature is making it a less perfect creature in its own special way, i.e., by the standard of excellence special to that kind of creature.

∴ (b) To harm a man is to make him a worse man by the standard of human excellence.

    (c) Justice is a peculiarly human excellence.

∴ (d) To harm a man is to make him less just.

    (e) But it is impossible that a good man's goodness would involve him in making another human being less good than he is.

∴ (f) The goodness (excellence) of a man cannot involve his doing harm to anyone, even to a wrongdoer.

∴ (g) Df. IV is incorrect.

Step (f) is equivalent to the proposition that no one is ever justified in harming another, i.e., that there is never any good reason why one man may (is permitted to) injure another. Df. IV cannot be correct unless it is true that a good man must harm some people who do wrong. Df. IV must therefore be abandoned if it turns out that there is never a good reason why one man may harm another.

Plato's conclusion (f), that there never is a good reason why one may harm another follows from (a), (c) and (e). An argument proves its conclusion true if, and only if, the premises validly imply the conclusion and they are true. (a), (c), and (e) validly imply (f). (c) seems to be true. Are (a) and (e) also true? If one or both are false, the argument will not have succeeded in proving its conclusion true. As a matter of fact, (a) is false, *if we understand its terms in their ordinary sense.* If someone maliciously spread false rumors about a good man and the public thereafter believed the worse of him, the good man will have been harmed in any ordinary sense of 'harm'. But it is false that the good man would necessarily have become a less good man. It will not help Plato's case to suppose that (a) is an arbitrary definition of 'harm'. Refutation by arbitrary definition is absurd, for it would refute every truth. For example, let someone say: "By 'brother' I shall henceforth mean 'a female sibling'. Hence it is false that one is a brother if, and only if, he is a male sibling." Such an argument is clearly invalid.

The fact that one of the premises of the argument is false if it is understood in its ordinary sense, which is the only relevant sense under the circumstances, proves that the argument has not succeeded in proving the truth of (f). The fact that one of the premises of (f) is false does not prove that (f) itself is false. Nevertheless, there are reasons for thinking that it is false. And premise (e) is also false for the same reasons.

There are two good reasons why a man may harm another: self-defense and defense of some third person against aggression. The law requires one to run away from an attacker. But if you can prove that it was impossible under the circumstances to defend yourself or your wife or child or a stranger without, let us suppose, wounding the attacker, the law will absolve you as having exercised your legitimate right of self-defense or of defense of another. Now of course one may question the goodness of the law itself. What is legally permitted may still be wrong by some other standard. Uncompromising pacifists would insist that it is never right to save one's own life by killing another, or even by wounding another. Still there is a strong case, on the face of it, for the legitimacy of self-defense. Why should a man not have the right to defend himself against unprovoked assault?

For the same reason that (f) is, in all probability, false, (e) is also false. It is conceivable that, in exercising your right of self-defense, you had to inflict a wound on your attacker, and he happens to be the sort of person who becomes a worse man as a result of having received such a wound. Still, there seems to be no reason to suppose that, in defending yourself, you acted wrongly.

Recall that Plato's reason for wanting to prove (f) is that thereby he would be disproving (15), and hence disproving Df. IV. I think I have said enough to show that (f) is, in all probability, false. But, in order to prove (15) false, we do not really need (f). (15) says that a man ought *always* to injure those who do wrong, (f) says that a man ought *never* to injure those who do wrong. (15) and (f) are *contraries*,[10] and in this particular case each is false. But the *contradictory* of (15) is, in all probability, true—namely that it is not the case that a man ought always to injure those who do wrong. This seems to be an eminently sensible principle. For example, in order to be a good man, a private citizen does not have to wound an escaped convict when the convict is already in the custody of the police; on the contrary, he would be acting wrongly if he did. Hence, Df. IV is, after all, incorrect: it is inconsistent with many ought-judgments whose truth we have no reason to doubt.

[10] Two propositions are *contraries* if it is possible that both are false, e.g., "My eyes are brown" and "My eyes are blue." My eyes may be violet. Two propositions are *contradictories*, if it is impossible for both to be true, and impossible for both to be false, e.g., "My eyes are brown" and "It is not the case that my eyes are brown."

THE ARGUMENT
WITH THRASYMACHUS

NEXT WE come to Thrasymachus' definition:

Df. V: A just man = Df. a man who serves the interest of the stronger.

Thrasymachus is at first incoherent as to what he means to say. He assents to two propositions at the same time:

(1) Whatever the $\left\{ \begin{array}{l} \text{ruler} \\ \text{strong} \end{array} \right.$ decrees, the $\left\{ \begin{array}{l} \text{subject} \\ \text{weak} \end{array} \right.$ ought to obey

(2) The subject is acting as he ought if, and only if, his action is in the interest of the ruler.

But Thrasymachus admits that it is possible that a ruler may decree a law which, if obeyed, is against the interest of the ruler, even though the ruler believes otherwise.

Now assume that L is such a law. Then, by (1), it follows that every subject ought to obey it. But, knowing what sort of law L is, we know that, if the subject obeys it, he will be acting against the interest of the ruler. Hence, it appears that a subject would be acting rightly by acting against the interest of the ruler. But this is inconsistent with (2). Hence, Thrasymachus must give up either (1) or (2) or else he must deny that a ruler can make a law such as L. He now denies that a ruler can make a law such as L by defining 'ruler' in the "strict" sense. A ruler is, by definition, supposed to be incapable of making a mistake about what is to his own interest.

Socrates now tries to prove that a ruler, as "strictly" defined, cannot be serving his own interest. Hence, as ruler, he cannot

make laws that are intended to benefit him. Hence, even if what-
ever the $\left\{ \begin{array}{l} \text{ruler} \\ \text{strong} \end{array} \right.$ decrees ought to be obeyed by the $\left\{ \begin{array}{l} \text{subject,} \\ \text{weak} \end{array} \right.$
still it is not true that right action on the part of the subject is in
every case action in the interest of the ruler.

Let us examine Socrates' argument, in which he tries to prove
that no ruler can legislate in his own interest.

The argument is deceptively simple:

(1) Every art serves the interest of its subject.
(2) Ruling is an art.
∴ (3) Ruling serves the interest of its subject.

This is a deductively valid argument. Hence, if its premises are
true, so is its conclusion.

Let us, however, examine the premises for truth. (1) is a generalization from such examples as this:

A physician's business is to treat his patients.
A ship's captain's business is to command the crew to run the
ship.
A groom's business is to care for the horses.
A shepherd's business is to care for the sheep.

Now the examples suggest that by 'subject' we are to understand
a thing that is not brought into being by exercising the art but
something upon which the art is practiced. Thus, a doctor
practices his art on sick people or people who want to stay well.
A ship's captain practices his art upon the ship. The shepherd
practices his art upon the sheep.

But if this is what we are to understand by 'subject', then (1)
is not true. There are many arts that do not serve the interest of
their subjects: a slaughterer of sheep, for example, is not serving
the interest of the sheep. A front-line soldier is not serving the
interest of the enemy he kills, yet killing the enemy is precisely
what the front-line soldier's art demands at times. Moreover,
there are many arts whose subjects, in the sense of 'subject' that
is under review, are not what the art strives to serve. Leather,
wax, string, nails, glue are among the subjects of the cobbler's
art, but the cobbler is not seeking to serve the interest of these
materials; he is seeking to produce shoes.

Confronted with such examples, we are forced to look for another definition of 'subject'. We must see whether we can find
another interpretation of 'subject,' one that does not turn (1) into
a fairly obvious falsehood.

Let us note that the physician's art aims at healing the sick and
at keeping the healthy in continuing good health. The ship's
captain's job is to exercise ultimate authority in the running of
the ship. The groom's job is to groom the horse in his charge. The
slaughterer's job is to produce a properly slaughtered animal. In
each case the interest of the art is to bring about a state of affairs
and in no case is that state of affairs the same as the practitioner's
looking after himself. By the 'subject' of an art we now understand that product or state of affairs that the art is meant to
realize. Accordingly, premise (1), which originally said: Every
art serves the interest of its subject, now reads: Every craft is
practiced with a view to producing a certain object or state of
affairs, and those who practice the craft are, strictly speaking,
interested only in producing that object or state of affairs. Now
(1) becomes more plausible. It is no longer vulnerable to the
earlier counter-examples, viz., the slaughterer and the soldier.

But another difficulty now arises. Note that, in the examples of
the physician, the captain, the groom and the slaughterer, the
object or state of affairs to be brought about is *implied* by the
concept of the art in question. It is impossible for someone to be
a physician but not a healer, just as it is impossible for something
to be food but not to nourish, or for something to be a clock but
not a timepiece. What a physician, a ship's captain, a groom, a
slaughterer, and a shepherd are supposed to do is clearly implied
by the meaning of 'physician', 'ship's captain', 'groom', 'slaughterer', and 'shepherd.' Is what a ruler is supposed to do similarly
implied by the meaning of the word 'ruler'? Yes; but what is
thus implied is far short of what Plato wants. To be a ruler implies being in a position of the highest executive authority in
some body politic. But among rulers there are public servants
and there are tyrants. What being a public servant implies is just
the opposite of what being a tyrant implies. From the meaning
alone of 'ruler', nothing follows as to whether or not a ruler is a
shepherd or a wolf to his subjects. So that even if we allow, as
we must, that governing a body politic is a distinct job, and that
it is implied by the very meaning of the word 'ruler,' we still

cannot get out of all that what Plato is after—namely, that the function of a ruler must be to look after the well-being of the governed.

Plato is actually raising the question: What is the proper function of government? Most writers have answered this question by saying that the proper function of government is to try to ensure the well-being of the body politic that it governs.[11] But this is an ought-judgment that, in this instance, does not follow from the meaning of 'ruler' or from that of 'government'. Thus, Plato's argument to prove that no ruler, strictly speaking, can be serving his own interest is valid, yet he has not proved that his major premise, premise (1), is true. Hence, he has not proved his conclusion that it is impossible to be a ruler and not to serve the interest of the ruled. Even if Jefferson were right that what a government ought to do is self-evident, Jefferson's is frankly an ought-judgment: A government ought to serve the people. Plato's conclusion appears to be about what is *logically* impossible: it is impossible for a man to be a ruler and not to serve the interest of the ruled. Almost everyone will agree with Jefferson that a government ought to serve the interest of the governed, whereas it seems clear that Plato's logical claim is false.

The point of establishing the conclusion that it is impossible for someone to be a ruler and not to serve the interest of the ruled was that it would be inconsistent with the proposition that a ruler, strictly speaking, is out to look after himself and no one else. This proposition Thrasymachus couples with his notion that there is no right or wrong apart from laws, and no laws apart from the decrees of a person or a group with the power to enforce them. But if a ruler (a man with power to enforce) is bound to decree laws that are in his own interest, then it follows that the

---

[11] An unequivocal statement of this view occurs in the second paragraph of *The Declaration of Independence*: "WE hold these Truths to be self-evident, that all Men are created equal, that they are endowed by their Creator with certain unalienable Rights, that among these are Life, Liberty, and the Pursuit of Happiness—That to secure these Rights, Governments are instituted among Men, deriving their just Powers from the Consent of the Governed, that whenever any Form of Government becomes destructive of these Ends, it is the Right of the People to alter or abolish it, and to institute new Government, laying its Foundation on such Principles and organizing its Powers in such Form, as to them shall seem most likely to effect their Safety and Happiness."

duty of a subject consists in his doing that which is to the interest of the stronger.

Now Socrates is not successful in attacking the premise that a ruler, strictly speaking, is out to look after his own interest. However, Thrasymachus' definition of what constitutes justice in a subject may be criticized by attacking his notion that *there is no right or wrong apart from enforced laws*. The plain fact is that, even in a democracy where laws are supposedly the reflection of the wishes and judgments of the majority, it makes sense to suppose that some laws are bad laws, and that it is not the business of a good man to obey them, but the contrary. By breaking this link in the chain, we can show the weakness of Thrasymachus' argument.

Finally, we can ask the same question about Thrasymachus' definition as we did about Cephalus'. Can we say that just and right action consists in nothing more or less than serving the interest of the stronger? Are not these very actions sometimes right and sometimes wrong, sometimes just and sometimes unjust? The fact that the answer to the question is definitely "Yes" is another way of bringing out the fact that a just or a good man cannot be, by definition, a man who serves the interest of the stronger.

But this is by no means the end of the matter. Glaucon and Adeimantus amplify the case for Thrasymachus. The old question "What is a just man?" remains. But in amplifying Thrasymachus' case, Glaucon and Adeimantus also introduce some new questions.

(1) Is justice a matter of nature or one of convention?
(2) Is being just a thing that is good in itself, as well as good for the external rewards it brings? Or is it merely good for the external rewards?

Thrasymachus' and Plato's differences about these questions explain their different conceptions of justice and, ultimately, of what a good man is.

Let us amplify the case for Thrasymachus, as Plato does it.

Man is naturally a wholly self-centered creature. For him to be selfish, inconsiderate, grasping, greedy, vain, jealous, lazy, lecherous, gluttonous is easy—these things come naturally to him. If a man had the ring of Gyges, he would stop at nothing to gain his own ends, regardless of the desires, interests, wishes, or opinions of others.

Why then are men generally restrained? Why don't they exercise unlimited self-seeking? Because they don't have the ring of Gyges—i.e., because they "can't get away with it." They would, if they could; but they can't, so they won't. The vast majority of them can't because that vast majority are weak; their power is very much less than their natural appetites. With their small power, if they tried living a life of inconsiderate self-seeking, they would lose more than they would gain. That much they have sense enough to see. When a strong man takes charge of the state, therefore, the weak ones are ready to submit to him because without a ruler there can be no organized state, and without an organized state life is a Hobbesian jungle. But the man who takes charge is necessarily the one whose strength consists not of muscular power but of cunning intelligence. Such men are very few, and they represent the ideal of human excellence. They are men who act in accordance with nature; theirs is the true natural morality. Their excellence consists in their ability to exercise unlimited self-seeking. These are the ways in which their self-seeking is unlimited: they care nothing for others; no one has the power to oppose them, to expose them, to make them pay for what they do to others; they have no pangs of conscience. The only limitations on their self-seeking are those that their own intelligence imposes on them. For the strong, in the strict sense, make no mistake about what is to their interest. If it is not to their interest to kill someone, they control themselves and do not kill him, even if they want to very badly.

Against this *natural* excellence of the few strong ones, we have the *conventional* goodness of the multitudes who are weak. In actuality, then, the "genuine article," the true human excellence, is found only in those whom convention would condemn. For convention says: do not kill outside the law; do not take what belongs to someone else, etc. But these rules are contrary to the natural desires of man: the multitude live by them because there is nothing they can do that is better; the ruler enforces them, but he does not obey them himself. *All* principles of conduct are brought into being by the fiat of a ruler who is himself above the law he creates. He lays down laws that, if they are obeyed, will serve his own interest—and he has the power to enforce them.

The weak have two good reasons then to obey. If they don't, they will be punished; on the other hand, if there are no laws at all, they will hardly survive, for they will then be living in a human jungle.

Are justice and goodness in a man then matters of nature or of convention? It is a matter of nature if we are thinking of the ruler's excellence. It is a matter of convention if we are thinking of the subject's justice and goodness. And, of the two, the ruler's excellence is better, because it is what *everyone* would like to have, if he could.

Are being just and good, good in themselves or only externally rewarding? They are both, if we are thinking of the ruler's excellence. They are only externally rewarding, however, if we are thinking of the subject's justice and goodness.

A good man serves his own self-interest. That is true of both ruler and subject. But the excellence of the ruler consists in his power to pursue his own interest with no limitations except those of self-imposed prudence, while the goodness of the subject consists in his serving the interest of the ruler and thereby enjoying some degree of security that he would not otherwise have.

Being a good man is also a characteristic of the strong, the ruler, the man who has the cunning intelligence to secure for himself the means of unhindered self-seeking.

According to Thrasymachus, common decency, the ordinary human virtues, are against the grain. They are against nature. Genuine excellence, the excellence of the man of power, is the only type of excellence that comes naturally, that is not against the very nature of man.

PLATO'S OWN DEFINITION OF A GOOD MAN

PLATO, TOO, believes that man's goodness is connected with strength and is a matter of interest, but he disagrees with Thrasymachus on vital matters. Thrasymachus extols the opposites of such ordinary human virtues as honesty, fairmindedness, considerateness, and kindness. He thinks that not these but their opposites are in accordance with nature. Plato thinks otherwise.

Implicit in Plato's answer to Thrasymachus, there are two ideas of nature. On the one hand, 'natural' means 'in accordance with the nature of man'. On the other hand, 'natural' means 'in accordance with nature around us'. Plato's defense of ordinary virtues is that they are natural in both ways.

Plato begins with the second sense of 'natural'. First, it is a biological fact—hence, a fact of nature around us—that no individual is self-sufficient. Unlike many other animals, the human infant is helpless. It would not survive if no one took care of it. Again, unlike that of many other animals, a man's body is not equipped for the struggle to survive. Man is naked; in some parts of the world, he would die without clothes. Man needs shelter. He needs food. Above all, man is not born with "built-in responses," the way other animals are. A gorilla in captivity builds a nest exactly like the ones that gorillas build in their natural habitat. A salmon's migratory habits are exactly predictable; they are explained entirely by his body chemistry. The first major fact of nature around us, then, is that man is not biologically self-sufficient.

The second fact of nature around us is that men are differently endowed. They are not built alike: some are short, some tall;

some stocky, some frail; they develop different talents and propensities.

The third fact of nature around us is that the work that is needed to sustain mankind can best be accomplished by a division of labor. A man has rudimentary physical needs: food, shelter, clothing. A man who tries to be his own carpenter, shoe-maker, and farmer will do none of these jobs well. For one thing, not all men have the same talents. For another, nature around us does not wait upon our convenience. The wheat has to be harvested at the right time. If your house needs a new roof just at harvest time, you must neglect either your house or your crops. The only sensible thing to do is to divide the work among specialists, according to natural talents and propensities.

One thing we must be clear about at this point. Plato is not taking nature around us indiscriminately as a model of what we ought to be. There are wolves and earthquakes, and he is not in-viting us to imitate the predatory habits of wolves or the fury of earthquakes. He is focusing attention on those features of nature around us that are relevant to the way individuals and states ought to be. No reasonable man could deny the need for a division of labor; the facts of nature around us leave no alternative. But division of labor implies cooperation. Thus, both human solidarity and division of labor are natural, not conventional, requisites of human existence. And the truth of this is known by any reason-able and reflective man.

This is, however, only half the story. We have looked at man as a creature in nature around us. Now it is time to look at man as he is in himself. Underlying the differences that distinguish this man from that, there is something that is the same in all men: their characteristic of being human. What is it to be human? This is a crucial question, because Plato believes that we can have no satisfactory understanding of human excellence unless we have a clear idea of what it is to be human. The excellence of a man is unique; it differs from the excellence of a dog or of a hammer or of anything or any creature other than man. To be human is unique and peculiar to man. If one is human, one is, to be sure, an animal, but a human animal is a special sort of one: he is the only animal that reasons, and is capable of acquiring a per-sonality, of being a person with certain character traits. And, like all animals, he has appetites and passions.

Natural excellence in man, then, has to accommodate his animal appetites, his personality, and his capacity to reason. This threefold distinction corresponds to Plato's threefold division of the soul into reason, spirit, and appetite. That these are distinct features of being human is evident from almost every common experience. Take a dramatic case. A drug addict has an irresistible craving for his particular drug. If his reason is not impaired, he will soon come to know that indulging himself is suicidal. And he doesn't want to die. His craving for the drug is therefore incompatible with his craving for life. So far, then, we have two cravings that cannot be satisfied simultaneously. In a brute animal, these two cravings would have to "fight it out." The "stronger" would be the craving that won. But in the case of man, this is not a brute fight between two cravings. What a man knows, or believes, what ideals he has, make a difference as to which craving will win. Moreover, a man of strong character is more likely to "listen to reason" than a weak man. Here we have an illustration of Plato's doctrine. First, Plato holds that reason, spirit, and appetite are distinct features of being human. Second, he ranks reason, spirit, and appetite, in that order, to indicate that reason has a guiding function; then comes spirit, the element of character, which is allied to reason; the lowest are the passions, which need to be ordered and directed. Let me repeat: for Plato the passions or appetites are to be ordered and directed, not repressed or denied out of hand.

Now combine the natural facts about what man is in himself together with the natural facts about what man is, as a creature in nature. The principle of the division of labor applies to man as he is in himself and also as he is a creature in nature. The good man is like the good car. Each is in good repair to do its own work well. A man is in good repair if his reason is in control of his passions, and his character traits are such as to dispose him to listen to reason. Justice = Df. that state of man in which reason controls and guides, spirit disposes a man to listen to reason, and the passions are controlled by reason. In Plato's words, justice = Df. each part of the soul doing the job that it is best suited to do by its own intrinsic nature. Thus, justice is a special case of the division of labor and just as natural, just as independent of anyone's fiat, as are the facts that show the need for the division of labor on the economic level. A man's goodness is made up of justice, wisdom (knowledge of good and evil), courage (knowledge of what to fear and what not to fear) and temperance (acceptance of the rule of reason). (Cornford, pp. 140–141.)

Moreover, that each man should work honorably with others is not a convention imposed upon the weak by the strong but a natural requirement. There is honor even among thieves. It is impossible for a band of thieves to operate efficiently, if there is no unity and loyalty among them. It is natural, therefore, that there be trust and loyalty; without these, there can be no cohesive society, and without cohesive society human life is impossible. For a human being emerges only within a culture; there is no human life outside human society. Thus cooperation, mutual respect of life and other rights are not conventions imposed upon the weak in the interest of the strong; they are to the interest of everyone. Those who strike at social order as such are destroying the foundations of human life.

This completes Plato's answer to the two questions: (1) Is human excellence a matter of nature or convention? (2) Is it intrinsically good, or is it good only because of its external rewards?

Two closely related issues remain. Is Plato's definition of 'good man' correct? And has he succeeded in proving that a life of injustice is one that no man could prefer on rational grounds?

Plato's definition of 'good man' assumes certain things about human reason. According to Plato, reason is not only man's capacity to apprehend the good; it is also a passion for the good, a love of the good. Human depravity is not a matter of perversity: it is not a matter of knowing full well what the good is, and yet loving evil. For Plato, human depravity is at bottom a matter of ignorance; it is not knowing what the good is. Given these assumptions about reason as both a faculty of apprehending, and a yearning for, the good, the famous Platonic dictum follows: To know the good is to do the good. It follows that a good man—a man who is just, wise, temperate, and courageous—will know, hence love, and do the good, and he will hate and avoid evil. For in a good man reason rules.

If reason is what Plato says it is, then his definition of a good man is unassailable. It is reducible to the truism that a good man is a man who knows right from wrong, and never does anything that he ought not do. In fact, Plato's good man is like the God of theism: he is perfectly good. This is what lends plausibility to Plato's theory that in the best form of government the ruler is a philosopher-king, a perfectly good man who exercises absolute authority in running the affairs of the body politic. One obvious objection to this is that there are in fact no perfectly good people, and hence Plato's ideal form of government is not practicable.

Plato is on solid ground when he singles out (i) man's capacity to reason and (ii) his capacity to become a person with distinctively human character traits, as unique to man. He is also right that governing one's life in the light of reason is a necessary condition of being a good man. But he is on shaky ground when he assumes that the good must be the same for all men—in other words, that however individuals may differ temperamentally, still, if they exercise their reason, they are all bound to agree on what the good is. That, I believe, is a questionable assumption. Why should a man believe that sacrificing his life—say for the sake of making the world a better place for his children—is reasonable, if he does not care one whit about how his children live after him? Why should a man believe that he ought to do whatever he can to make the social order more just and fair, if he does not have the slightest tendency to feel indignant at injustice and unfairness, just as long as he himself is left alone? The ring of Gyges makes Gyges invisible at will. It is an allegorical symbol for a number of things, among them of immunity from detection and punishment, and a lack of concern for the weal or woe of others. It is a symbol of the absence of shame, of immunity from self-blame. Imagine a man who felt no shame, no remorse, no guilt—who would, on the contrary, be perfectly content to rob, to rape, to kill at will, and who could go undetected and unpunished—what reason could such a man have for believing that he ought not to rob, to rape, to kill at will? Plato argues that he ought not because, if he did, his life would be wretched on the whole. But his life would not be wretched, if he had the immunities of Gyges. Plato pictures the man who would rob, rape, and kill as being necessarily at the mercy of his passions and appetites. But this is not so. Gyges could exercise rational self-control by stealing, raping, and killing only when doing these things were sure not to hurt him. In fact, Thrasymachus has made it quite clear that his ideal man is a man who knows what is to his own interest and unerringly acts so as to realize it. Plato's fundamental error is his assumption that, however individuals may differ temperamentally, still, if they use their reason, propositions like "I ought not to rob," "I ought not to rape," "I ought not to kill whomever I please" will be believed by anyone. Yet it is quite possible to imagine a man who enjoys the immunities of Gyges and who is not swayed by his passions and appetites. Quite the contrary: he is so constituted as to govern himself by reason.

The notion of a man governing himself by reason is crucial to the whole discussion. I doubt that there is any such thing as reason, if by 'reason' we mean what Plato means. He sees reason as an ability to deliberate, and to discover the truth about what to cherish and what to reject. He takes it that, by exercising his reason, each human being, regardless of his emotional and temperamental differences from other human beings, will know with certainty, and unfailingly act upon, such propositions as that he himself ought not to cheat, steal, rape, rob, kill, or lie, even if doing these things is the only way he can get what he wants, and even if he can do them in such a way as to make sure that he himself will not be hurt in any way.

The implausibility of 'reason' in Plato's sense leaves us with two possibilities. A cool and calculating man may be said to govern himself by reason, if he acts according to the dictates of sound thinking—that is, in accordance with thinking that leads from true or the most probably true premises to conclusions that they imply either demonstratively or to a high degree of probability. A man who enjoys the immunities of Gyges may very well be "governed by reason," in this sense of the phrase. He may know what is to his own interest, and, caring for nothing else, he may unerringly act so as to realize it. There is another sense in which a man is said to be governing himself by reason. This is by being a reasonable man. Such a man is fair-minded; can see the other man's side; is tolerant, kind, considerate. In fact, the expression 'reasonable man' is a synonym or a near-synonym of 'good man'. Gyges is surely not a reasonable man.

If I am right in having rejected Plato's own conception of reason on the grounds that it corresponds to nothing in reality, then we are left with the notion of cool, calculating reason and with the notion of being a reasonable man. Will either notion justify Plato's claim that he has given us an explicative explicit definition of "good man," and that he has once and for all proved that the worst calamity that can befall a man is to be a bad man? If Plato defines 'just man' and 'good man' in terms of cool, calculating reason, he can argue convincingly that to be a bad man is against one's own interest. But then his definitions of 'just man' and 'good man' turn out to be incorrect. If, on the other hand, Plato defines 'just man' and 'good man' in terms of the notion of a reasonable man, then he does not have an explicit definition of 'good man'. This may not be serious. But then he cannot prove that the life of injustice and evil is the worst thing that can happen to a man. And this is a serious gap in Plato's argument. I shall now justify these propositions.

If in Plato's *definiens* of 'just man' the word 'reason' means what Plato wants it to mean, then there are no just men. And if the word 'reason' is to mean cool, calculating reason, then Gyges or anyone like him in relevant respects would satisfy the conditions of being a just man. This implication would be unacceptable to anyone who has what to us is a normal sense of right and wrong. Thrasymachus himself admits that from the normal or "conventional" point of view, Gyges is neither just nor good.

Moreover, Plato sees that "x is a good man" entails "x is a just man." If Gyges could be classified as just, then a man who is a good man could be a man like Gyges in all relevant respects. That is, a man like Gyges could satisfy one of the logically necessary conditions for being a good man. This implication too would be unacceptable to people who have a normal sense of right and wrong. A man like Gyges in all relevant respects could satisfy one of the logically necessary conditions for being a good man, the condition of being just, because the other logically necessary conditions—namely, being wise, courageous, and temperate—do not rule out this possibility. Any man relevantly similar to Gyges is a man who knows exactly what is to his own interest, and whose appetites and emotions are controlled by his cool, calculating reason; such a man unerringly acts so as to serve his own interest always. Still under the assumption that reason is cool, calculating reason, by Plato's definition of 'just man' such a man would be just. His reason is in control and he is disposed to listen to the dictates of reason. Now to be wise is, by Plato's definition, to know what is good and what is evil, what to do and what not to do. Let us assume that Gyges is "wise." From this assumption it does not follow that Gyges knows that he ought not to rob, even when robbing would be the only way of safely serving his own interest. Similarly, let Gyges be "courageous": that is, he knows what to fear and what not to fear. From this it does not follow that Gyges knows that robbing in order to serve your own interest, even if you can do so with impunity, is something to be feared. Lastly, let Gyges be "temperate": he cheerfully accedes to the rule of reason over his passions and emotions. From this it does not follow that Gyges will think that it is wrong for him to rob when robbing is the only way of serving his own interest with impunity.

If the definitions of 'just man' and 'good man' could be correctly articulated in terms of cool, calculating reason, then it would be easy enough to prove that it is to one's interest to be a good man. Not to be a good man would then be not to govern oneself by sound thinking. But a man who does not act in accordance with sound thinking is, to say the least, a very poor insurance risk. No one would be surprised if he did not survive very long; if he did survive, by some improbable chance, no one would be surprised to discover that he had "made a mess" of his life. But this argument is academic. The reason why Plato does not use it is that reason in the sense of cool, calculating reason, is not all that 'reason' means in the *definiens* of his definition of a good man.

This conclusion should surprise no one who reads Plato with care. By 'reason' Plato obviously means much more than cool, calculating reason. Reason in the sense of being reasonable is closer to Plato's notion and can be a constituent of his definition of a good man. Since 'good man' and 'reasonable man' are synonyms or near-synonyms, it is perfectly safe to define a good man as a man who is reasonable. But now Plato cannot maintain that he has an explicit definition—one that provides logically necessary and sufficient conditions. This the present definition cannot do in any illuminating way. We can, if we wish, say that the logically necessary and sufficient conditions for being a good man are to be a reasonable man. But this is rather like saying that the logically necessary and sufficient conditions for being a father are to be a father—which is not very illuminating. Now we *can* say illuminating things about being just and being good. In order to be a just man, a man has to be more than a self-possessed person who governs himself by cool, calculating reason; he has to be fair, unbiased, judicious. And in order to be a good man, a man has to be not only just, but also habitually kind, and considerate, even when being unkind, inconsiderate, and unjust would be to his own advantage. But that is still not enough. If he is to fit our notion of a good man, a man must have, in addition, enough self-esteem to value himself no less than he values anyone else, and yet enough humor not to take himself too seriously. These are matters of fine balance and discrimination; they cannot be precisely defined. The list of virtues that we think are essential to being a good man is too long and complex for exhaustive cataloguing. Besides, there may be as yet uncatalogued virtues which, when thought of, might be found to belong among the essential conditions for being a good man.

The point I am making is that the notion of a reasonable man—hence, the notion of a good man—cannot be defined explicitly, that is, in terms of a set of logically necessary and sufficient conditions that exhaust the meaning of the *definiendum*. Perhaps this fact is not too important. After all, Plato may be quite satisfied with finding agreement on the proposition that a good man is a reasonable man, in the ordinary sense of 'reasonable man'. We may not have found the *essence* of a good man, but we may have found enough to be instructed and illuminated.

On the other issue, however, there is no possible defense of Plato. That issue has to do with proving that the bad man is his own worst enemy. Once we characterize a good man as a man who is reasonable, it becomes impossible to prove to Gyges or to Thrasymachus that the life of injustice is the worst calamity that can befall a man. What can one say to a cool, calculating villain, who is perfectly happy, to prove to him that the life of cool, calculating villainy he leads is against his own interest? Gyges and Thrasymachus will ask: "Why should I be reasonable? What is there in it for me?" I do not see that anything can be said in answer to this question along Platonic lines. If I do not want to be reasonable, and if not being reasonable carries no penalties; on the contrary, if it makes me happy, as no other way of living can, why should I be reasonable? Why, all things considered, should I be good? This is an unanswerable challenge.

SELECTED BIBLIOGRAPHY

[1] Cross, R., and A. D. Woozley. *Plato's Republic*. New York: St. Martin's Press, Inc., 1964.

[2] Demos, R. "A Fallacy in Plato's *Republic?*" *Philosophical Review*, LXXIII (1964), 395–398.

[3] Joseph, H. W. B. *Essays in Ancient and Modern Philosophy*. Oxford: The Clarendon Press, 1935. Chaps. I–V.

[4] Prichard, H. A. "Does Moral Philosophy Rest on a Mistake?" *Mind*, XXI (1912), 21–37; reprinted in W. Sellars and J. Hospers, eds., *Readings in Ethical Theory*. New York: Appleton-Century-Crofts, Inc., 1952.

[5] Sachs, D. "A Fallacy in Plato's *Republic*," *Philosophical Review*, LXXII (1963), 141–158.

[2] is a rejoinder to [5]

PART II

Descartes and the Theory of Knowledge, Meditations on First Philosophy, I-II

THE DREAM ARGUMENT

René Descartes (1596–1650) is the father of modern philosophy, which is the historical successor to medieval philosophy. Although in many ways Descartes is a medieval thinker, he gave philosophy a radically new direction. Medieval philosophers believed that by means of our senses we come to know with certainty that there exists a material world, and that we also know with certainty some important facts about it. These philosophers used statements about the material world as premises in their philosophical arguments and deduced from them metaphysical conclusions. For example, this is how St. Thomas Aquinas begins the first of his five arguments for the existence of God: "It is certain, and evident to our senses, that in the world some things are in motion." This proposition entails, to begin with, that there exists a world. It says further that in it some things are in motion, and that we know that fact with certainty and as "evident to the senses."

Descartes would say that if "S knows with certainty that p" implies that S cannot be mistaken about p, then assertions like St. Thomas' are false. The issue is whether or not we can be mistaken about what is evident to the senses. It is evident to the senses that there are material objects, e.g., trees and birds, and physical phenomena, e.g., thunderclaps and rainbows. It is evident to the senses that the tree is standing still and that the thunderclap made a tremendous crash. These things are "evident to the senses" in that some of his own experiences would lead a normal adult to believe them automatically and irresistibly. Descartes wants to argue, however, that if we rely on the testimony of the senses alone, we may be mistaken in believing anything that is evident to the senses. He recalls that his senses have sometimes deceived him, and that he ought, therefore, to withhold assent from anything that the senses tell him, until he has discovered the conditions under which he can infallibly trust them. Yet Descartes is in no position, at the very beginning of the *Meditations*, to use any assumptions, that are based on memory. For him, memory is also fallible. Accordingly, until we have a way of determining which among our memory impressions are true, we must not assume that we know anything merely by recollecting it.

Descartes has another argument, however, which does not rest on knowledge by recollection. There is a famous passage early in the First Meditation in which Descartes seems to be arguing that, because it is possible that I am now dreaming, I may be mistaken in believing what is evident to the senses. But exactly what that argument is, and what it proves, Descartes does not make clear. The passage itself provides clues and hints, but no precise indicatiohs. Under the circumstances, the best we can do is to construct an argument that is suggested by the relevant clues and hints. What I shall henceforth call 'the dream argument' is not to be found in that form in Descartes, but every one of its premises, except one, is a proposition that one can attribute to Descartes, with powerful support from the text. The exception is premise (6) below. Descartes needs a somewhat more flexible criterion of knowledge than the one given in (6). We will discuss this matter in considerable detail later.

The dream argument yields some interesting conclusions. There is a good deal of textual justification for thinking that Descartes himself may have intended to demonstrate somewhat milder conclusions. I suspect that Descartes may not have been absolutely clear in his own mind as to exactly what he wanted to say on these issues. I shall, at any rate, begin with an interpretation of Descartes' dream argument, the premises and conclusions of which I believe to be true[1] and philosophically important, and therefore worth knowing for their own sake. After I have explained this interpretation, I shall consider another which may be closer to Descartes' intent, but which, as we shall see, yields highly questionable results.

The dream argument has three parts. The premises and the conclusions of all three parts require for their formulation two technical terms, 'p is a perceptual proposition' and 'p is incor-

---

[1] Premise (6) may be too restrictive as a general criterion of knowledge, but it is perfectly good as a criterion of incorrigible knowledge, as we shall later see.

rigible for S'. Of these, the second is by far the more crucial. In it I propose to capture one thing that Descartes might have meant by 'indubitable' in its "logical" sense. In the *Meditations,* one finds at least two distinguishable senses of 'indubitable'. There is the "psychological" sense, in which an indubitable proposition is one from which we are unable to withhold assent. There is also the "logical" and profoundly important sense in which a proposition is indubitable for me only if it is one that I am fully justified, and cannot be mistaken, in believing, solely on the basis of the evidence that I have right now.

These two senses of 'indubitable' correspond to a genuine distinction. For example, I look in a certain direction and am unable to withhold assent from the proposition that there is a wall in front of me. You may easily convince me that this proposition might have been false. But to believe that the proposition might have been false is not the same thing as to doubt it now. I cannot at the same time be certain that there is a wall in front of me and doubt that there is one there. That is a logical impossibility: doubt and certainty about the same proposition are mutually exclusive. Yet I can grant, while still being certain that there is a wall in front of me, that there might not have been one there. What is more, while still being certain that there is a wall in front of me, I can readily grant that my believing that there is does not entail that there is. Thus, "psychological" indubitability is incompatible with doubt, but not with the belief that what I am now certain of might have been false, nor with the admission that my now believing it to be true is not enough to guarantee that it is true.

Compare this with an instance of "logical" indubitability. I am certain that I exist. I grant that I might not have existed. If I did not exist, then I would not be believing that I exist. This is equivalent to saying that, from my believing that I exist, it follows that I exist. In other words, my believing that I exist is itself the guarantee that I do exist. My believing that there is a wall in front of me is not enough to guarantee that there is a wall in front of me: that belief could be mistaken. My belief that I exist, however, could *not be* mistaken. The proposition that I believe about the wall is an example of a proposition that is *for me* indubitable psychologically, but not logically. The proposition that I believe when I believe that I exist is an example of a proposition that *for me* is logically indubitable. Thus, there can be no doubt that inability to withhold assent and logical indubitability are two different things.

But what exactly does Descartes mean by 'indubitable' in the logical sense? Descartes' own words provide some grounds for thinking that he means *incorrigible,* a concept that I shall define presently. But other things that he says suggest that he means something more inclusive than that. The three parts of the dream argument assume that logical certainty (= logical indubitability) is identical with incorrigibility. This concept and the dream argument based upon it are philosophically interesting and sound, but it is almost certainly too narrow to suit Descartes' own philosophical strategy.

The dream argument, then, is only a partial interpretation of Descartes' own dream argument. The second interpretation is exegetically more accurate. But I shall first give the first interpretation (= the dream argument) because it is philosophically important and able to stand on its own, and is, therefore, worthy of separate treatment.

I shall try first to explain the concept of a perceptual proposition and then the concept of an incorrigible proposition. Then I shall formulate the premises of the dream argument, and give reasons for believing that these are propositions that may plausibly be attributed to Descartes. After that, I shall give the dream argument itself, in three parts. Finally, I shall try to determine to what extent the conclusions implied by the dream argument agree with Descartes' asserted or implied philosophical aims in the *Meditations.* That will be where I shall consider the second interpretation of Descartes' dream argument.

Definition of 'Perceptual Proposition'

I SHALL define 'perceptual proposition' as meaning a proposition that ascribes to physical objects (e.g., tables and chairs) or to physical phenomena (e.g., claps of thunder, flashes of lightning, rainbows, flames, afterimages) visual, tactual, gustatory, auditory, or olfactory properties or relations. These, in turn, I shall define as being properties or relations whose presence in, or absence from, the objects or phenomena to which they are ascribed, it is logically possible to ascertain at any given time by looking, touching, tasting, listening, or smelling.

The following are examples of perceptual propositions: This is a ball. The book is to the left of the pen. That cigar has a pronounced aroma. The animals in that cage are stuffed. The figure on the blackboard is a triangle. The figure on the blackboard is a chiliagon. This liquid is sour. The bell in the clock tower is ringing. There is a liquid in that jug. That was a clap of thunder. That was a flash of lightning. There is a rainbow. The flame is hot. I see an afterimage.

The following are examples of propositions that are *not* perceptual: Methane is a hydrocarbon. This liquid has a pH of +6. Jones is a manic depressive. My brother is a creative individual. Lightning is an electrical discharge.

Defined as it is above, 'perceptual proposition' is a philosopher's technical term. It is not a term we would find defined in this way in any standard dictionary of the English language. I have deliberately defined the term in this way because the propositions that are perceptual by my definition are the ones with which the dream arguments are exclusively concerned. It is these propositions, together with whatever logically depends upon their being true or upon their being known to be true, that the dream arguments are meant to prove corrigible and not capable of being known incorrigibly. In Descartes' own words, the question is to determine the reliability of what "I have learned either from the senses or through the senses." (Haldane and Ross, Vol. I, p. 145.[*]) The dream arguments are in part a broadside attack on the presumption that what I learn either from the senses or through them is something that I am fully justified, and cannot be mistaken, in believing, solely on the basis of the perceptual evidence that presents itself to me now.

[*] *Philosophical Works of Descartes*, E. S. Haldane and G. R. T. Ross, trans. (London: Cambridge University Press, 1931). All quotations from the *Meditations* cited within the text refer to this edition. Copyright 1931, by Cambridge University Press. Reprinted by permission.

Definition of 'p is incorrigible for S'

THE DEDUCTIONS in all three parts of the dream argument require a definition of 'p is incorrigible for S' that will capture the logical sense of 'indubitable' in the *Meditations*. This is, however, a difficult and complicated matter. To begin with, Descartes himself does not provide a clear definition of the logical sense of 'indubitable'. Second, one gets a very strong impression that he himself did not have a single, consistent view. The propositions "I think" and "I exist" are important paradigms of propositions that are incorrigible for me. It is not only that I cannot withhold assent from them, but also that I am fully justified, and cannot be mistaken, in believing them solely on the basis of evidence present to me now. Thus, early in the Second Meditation, Descartes says: ". . . having reflected and carefully examined all things, we must come to the definite conclusion that this proposition: *I am, I exist,* is necessarily true each time that I pronounce it or mentally conceive it." (Haldane and Ross, Vol. I, p. 150.) Here Descartes flatly says that "I exist" is "necessarily true" and that I know that it has to be true every time I think it or assert it. This amounts to saying that I am fully justified, and cannot be mistaken, at any time, if at that time I believe that at that time I exist. But early in the Third Meditation Descartes says: ". . . perhaps a God has endowed me with such a nature that I may be deceived even in respect of the things which seem to me the most manifest of all. . . . It is easy for Him, if he wishes it, to cause me to err even in those matters which I believe myself to be intuiting in the most evident manner." (Haldane and Ross, Vol. I, p. 158. The above translation is faithful to the original Latin; the Haldane and Ross version is not.) Since "I exist" is one example Descartes gives of a proposition that I "intuit in the most evident manner," what he is saying here is that even "I exist" may be logically doubtful. This is inconsistent with his earlier statement in the Second Meditation. It cannot be, however, that the same belief both is and is not logically dubitable. I believe that Descartes is right in the earlier statement. Not only "I think" and "I exist" but also many other propositions are such that it is logically impossible to believe them and to be mistaken in so doing. I shall argue for this in detail later. Here I shall simply assume the validity of this assertion, and make it a basis for suggesting a definition of incorrigibility that is, philosophically and up to a point exegetically, the most useful I can think of.

According to the defensible view of Descartes, "I exist"—a paradigm of an incorrigible, logically indubitable proposition—is a proposition whose truth is known "intuitively." This suggests that generally an incorrigible proposition is one whose truth is known "intuitively." In his early work, *Rules for the Direction of the Mind,* Descartes defines intuition as follows: ". . . intuition is the undoubting conception of an unclouded and *attentive* mind, and springs from the light of reason alone." (Haldane and Ross, Vol. I, p. 7. My italics.) Although Descartes seems to change his mind from time to time as to whether all intuitions certify their own truth, he is consistent throughout in what he means by 'intuition'. Moreover, he relates incorrigibility both to intuition and also to the logical impossibility of being wrong in some instance.

The connection with intuition suggests, therefore, that incorrigibility should be defined in terms of an *attentive* attitude of mind. The connection with the logical impossibility of being wrong suggests that the *definiens* should also include a reference to *knowledge.* For it is impossible to know a false proposition.

At the same time, we must recognize a distinction between necessarily true, necessarily false, and contingent propositions. If a proposition is necessarily true, it is true no matter what the perceptual facts are. If a proposition is necessarily false, it is false no matter what the perceptual facts are. But a contingent proposition is a proposition that is neither necessarily true nor necessarily false. The following are examples of necessarily true propositions: "Red resembles orange more closely than it resembles green." "Every red object is colored." "An uncle is a male." "Every uncle is a brother." "All squares are four-sided." "In baseball the team that scores more runs wins." The negation of a necessarily true proposition is necessarily false. Thus, "Some squares do not have four sides" and "There are uncles who are not brothers" are examples of necessarily false propositions. Examples of contingent propositions are the following: "Malaria is not an infectious disease." "That is a red ball." The negation of a contingent proposition is also contingent. We shall see later on that some logically indubitable propositions are necessarily true, some are contingent. Here I shall assume that this assertion is true and regard it as a condition for which any adequate definition of logical indubitability (incorrigibility) must find a place.

Descartes himself recognizes, although not always, that among logically indubitable propositions some are necessarily true, while some are contingent. Moreover, not all necessarily true propositions are incorrigible for us.[2] The need is to define incorrigibility in such a way that a proposition's being necessarily true is neither a necessary nor a sufficient condition for its being incorrigible.

Furthermore, many contingent propositions are incorrigible, although not incorrigible for everyone. The proposition that I feel pain is incorrigible for me, but not incorrigible for anyone else. We ought, therefore, to define incorrigibility in such a way as to include in the class of incorrigible propositions all those contingent propositions that are incorrigible for one person at one time. These considerations make it reasonable for us to offer the following two definitions:

Df. A: p is incorrigible for S = Df. (i) It is possible that S believes attentively that p, and (ii) "S believes attentively that p" entails[3] "S knows that p."[4]

Df. B: S believes incorrigibly that p = Df. (i) S believes attentively that p, and (ii) "S believes attentively that p" entails "S knows that p."

[2] See pp. 125–133.

[3] Where p and q are propositions, p entails q = Df. It is impossible for p to be true and q to be false. This amounts to saying that necessarily q follows from p.

[4] Something like Df. A may be found in H.-N. Castaneda's "Behavior and Consciousness: Their Logical Connections," in *Intentionality, Minds, and Perception*, H.-N. Castaneda, ed. (Detroit: Wayne State University Press, in press). See also Castaneda's "The Private Language Argument," in *Knowledge and Experience*, C. D. Rollins, ed. (Pittsburgh: University of Pittsburgh Press, 1964). The clause (i) is included in order to make sure that no proposition turns out to be incorrigible for the absurd reason that it is impossible for S to believe it attentively.

Definition of 'S believes attentively that p'

THE PROVISO that S believes *attentively* that p is important both for understanding Descartes and for keeping the philosophical issues straight. Let me first give the reader some idea of what attentive belief is. We must begin by distinguishing occurrent belief from dispositional belief. Of a man in deep and dreamless sleep we may correctly say: He believes that his wife loves him. At the time that this is being truly said of him, he is not thinking that his wife loves him; in fact, being in deep and dreamless sleep, he is not thinking at all. Yet it may be truly said of him that he believes that his wife loves him. These are examples of dispositional belief. However, if a man is at a given time actually thinking that his wife loves him, then at that time he has an occurrent belief. S dispositionally believes that p = Df. If S were to have an occurrent cognitive attitude with respect to p, it would normally be one of belief.

The distinction between attentive and inattentive belief is a distinction within the class of occurrent beliefs and not of dispositional beliefs. Those of us who have had eye tests and hearing tests have had the experience of strenuously attending to an experience: "What is it that I see? Is it an 'A'? Is it a 'B'? Or do I see an indistinct shape that no amount of concentration on my part will transform into an identifiable letter?" Or else, the examiner will ask you to tell him exactly when the two vertical lines merge into one. This request "sets you up," as it were, to attend with care so that you can "catch" the phenomenon as soon as it occurs in your visual field. And, during a hearing test, the fainter the signals become, the more strenuously we attend to them in order to make sure that we hear every sound that we can possibly hear and that we do not report hearing sounds that we do not actually hear. These are familiar examples of being attentive to one's own experience.

One example of an attentive belief is my consciously, actively thinking that I am in pain, at a time when I am aware of being in pain. A necessary condition for my believing attentively that I am having (or not having) a certain experience is that I pay attention to an experience of mine, such as an itch, a pain, a pressure, a sound, a smell, etc. Do I now feel pain? If I consider the question attentively, I may find either that I am now feeling pain, or that I am not. Do I now feel itchy? Sometimes a person who considers this question attentively will find an itch somewhere, an itch that he did not notice, while writing or thinking about other things. For believing attentively that I have an itch, it is necessary and sufficient that, while paying attention to my experiences, I both feel an itch and at the same time believe (occurrently) that I have an itch. These two conditions are, in fact, distinct. It is logically possible that there are creatures who can attend to their itches yet cannot be said to believe that they have an itch, simply because, in order to *believe* that it has an itch, an organism must have the concept of an itch, while in order to *feel* an itch, an organism does not have to have any concepts at all. It is also possible for a man, who can do both, to feel an itch without consciously, actively thinking that he is itching.

Another example of an attentive belief is my believing (occurrently) that I am conscious, while paying attention to any one of a number of my own mental goings-on. Among mental goings-on are mental activities (e.g., calculating, planning, solving a problem) or mental occurrences (e.g., believing occurrently, randomly associating ideas) or mental episodes (e.g., my having thought of yesterday's lunch while I was planning tomorrow's dinner, my feeling depressed or moody). I may be paying attention to something without my noticing that I am paying attention to it. But if, while noticing that I am being attentive—say, to my pain—I believe occurrently that I am being attentive, then I attentively believe that I am being attentive. Yet I know that I cannot be attentive if I am not conscious. If, while being aware of my being attentive, I think to myself that I am conscious, then I believe attentively that I am conscious. In general, if I am paying attention to one of my own mental goings-on, and while doing so I believe occurrently that I am conscious, or that the relevant mental going-on is going on, then I believe attentively that I am conscious or that the relevant mental going-on is going on.

Another example of believing attentively is believing occurrently that all squares have four sides while one is focusing attention on the defining properties of a square. A square is, by definition, a plane figure, bounded by four equal straight lines that form four internal right angles. Anyone who, while focusing his attention on these defining characteristics, believes occurrently (is actually thinking at that time) that every square has four sides, is believing attentively that every square has four sides.

These examples suggest that we should define attentive belief as follows:

Df. AB: at t S believes attentively that p = Df. (i) At t S is paying attention to matters that are relevant to the truth or falsity of p, including attention to his own sensations, if they are relevant, (ii) among them stands revealed and open to S evidence for p, and (iii) at t S occurrently believes that p.

Some Cases of Attentive Belief Do, and Others Do Not, Entail Knowledge

IF I BELIEVE attentively that I am in pain, or that I am conscious, or that a square has four sides, I know that I am in pain[5] or that I am conscious, or that a square has four sides.[6] But not every attentive belief is such that having it entails knowing what is believed. I may attentively believe that I am now awake. I pay strenuous attention to the sounds I hear, the things I see, the smells I smell; I very carefully notice that I am sitting in front of a desk, writing with a pen on blue-lined sheets of yellow paper. I could, in fact, write a description of my desk that would give in words as exact an idea of it as would a clear photograph. In paying strenuous attention to all these experiences and objects, I believe that I am aware of them while being awake—which is sufficient for saying that I attentively believe that I am awake. But it does not follow from this that I know that I am awake. For, if "I attentively believe that I am awake" entails "I know that I am awake," then, because "I know that I am awake" in turn entails "I am awake," "I attentively believe that I am awake" would entail "I am awake." But this is not so. It is possible that I attentively believe that I am awake while in fact I am dreaming.[7]

[5] See pp. 78–79.
[6] See pp. 119–120.
[7] This is a controversial statement. There are influential philosophers who have denied it, e.g., Gilbert Ryle, Norman Malcolm, possibly Ludwig Wittgenstein. This is one of the key issues that divides pro-Cartesian philosophers from the anti-Cartesians.

"I am dreaming" entails "I am sleeping," and "I am sleeping" entails "I am not awake." Thus, it is possible that I attentively believe that I am awake when I am actually not awake. In fact, this conclusion is an instance of the assumption we shall attribute to Descartes—namely, that for any contingent proposition, p, if p entails that S is not dreaming, then it is possible that S attentively believes that p, while S is dreaming. Thus, there are many contingent propositions that one can believe attentively and yet not know. "I am now perceiving a book in a waking moment" entails "I am not dreaming"; but I can attentively believe that I am now perceiving a book in a waking moment and not know so. Nevertheless, there are at least three classes of attentive belief that entail knowledge. They concern one's own present experiences, or one's own present relevant mental goings-on, or conceptual necessities—e.g., that all squares have four sides.

The Philosophical and Exegetical Importance of Attentive Belief

Is BELIEF in the definientia of Df. A and Df. B (p. 72, above) attentive or inattentive belief—or does it matter which? There are really two questions here. Since we are trying to understand what Descartes meant by logically 'indubitable', which of these two kinds of belief should we decide that he meant? On the other hand, insofar as we want to get at the truth concerning the philosophical issues themselves, does it matter which concept we choose? The answer to both questions is that it does matter, philosophically as well as exegetically, and that for both purposes we need the notion of believing attentively.

It is fairly clear that Descartes himself was thinking in terms of attentive belief. In Principle XLV, Part I, of *The Principles of Philosophy*, Descartes says: "I term that clear which is present and apparent to an *attentive* mind. . . . But the distinct is that which . . . contains within itself nothing but what is clear." I have italicized the word 'attentive'. It is a key word in the passage. For Descartes "clarity and distinctness" are marks of "indubitability," while being "present and apparent to an attentive mind" is a mark of clarity. Because clarity is a necessary condition for distinctness, attention is a necessary condition for achieving distinctness. A root notion in the explanation of "indubitability" is, therefore, the notion of attention.

Furthermore, Descartes' special paradigms of indubitably true propositions are "I am conscious" ("I think"), and "I exist." Descartes says such things as this: "I am, I exist, is necessarily true each time that I pronounce it, or that I mentally conceive it. . . . I am, I exist, that is certain. But how often? Just when I think; for it might possibly be the case that if I ceased entirely to think, that I should likewise cease altogether to exist." (Haldane and Ross, Vol. I, pp. 150, 151–152.) Descartes is here saying that there is no logical possibility of my being mistaken when I believe occurrently that I exist. For if I believe occurrently anything at all, then I am thinking, and if I am thinking, then I exist.

There is an important time factor in Descartes' notion of logical indubitability. If I am now thinking that I now exist, then I am now fully justified, and cannot now be mistaken, in believing that I now exist, solely on the basis of the evidence now present to my attentive mind. The evidence is the fact that I now believe that I now exist. But if I am now fully justified, and cannot be mistaken, in believing that I now exist, then I now know that I now exist. Generally, for any person, S, and for any time, t, if at t S believes occurrently that he himself exists at t, then at t S knows that he himself exists at t.

It is important to keep straight the back-references to times. Suppose I am *now* thinking (I am now believing) that *yesterday* I existed. It follows that I cannot *now* doubt that *yesterday* I existed. But it does not follow that I *now* know that *yesterday* I existed. In contrast to this, from "I *now* believe that I *now* exist," it does follow that I now know that I now exist. Inasmuch as we are doing Cartesian exegesis, it seems fairly clear that Df. A and Df. B should be expanded as follows:

Df. A: p is incorrigible for S at t = Df. (i) It is possible that at t S believes attentively that p, and (ii) "At t S believes attentively that p" entails "At t S knows that p."

Df. B: at t S believes incorrigibly that p = Df. At t S believes attentively that p, and "At t S believes attentively that p" entails "At t S knows that p."

If we set aside for the moment the problem of faithfully explaining Descartes' doctrine, and turn instead to the philosophical issues themselves, again it is fairly clear that the concept of p being incorrigible for S, defined in terms of attentive belief, is a useful concept for explaining central issues in the theory of knowledge and metaphysics, particularly in that branch of metaphysics that is known as the philosophy of mind. Let me give a simple illustration. The proposition that S is in pain and its negation, as well as the proposition that S's pain has a certain quality are generally regarded as paradigms of propositions incorrigible for S. Now a definition of 'p is incorrigible for S' is adequate only if it is a consequence of that definition that:

> If p is incorrigible for S, and S occurrently believes that p, then S is fully justified, and cannot be mistaken, in believing that p, solely on the basis of evidence present to his attentive mind.

This condition of adequacy is met only if we define 'p is incorrigible for S' in terms of attentive belief. For suppose 'p is incorrigible for S' to be defined in terms of belief without qualification. But, "S believes that he himself is not in pain" does not entail "S is not in pain." I may be in pain, although I am not aware of it. My attention may be diverted by my total concentration on a philosophical problem. An instant before I attend to my pain again, the thought may flash through my mind that I am not in pain, and at that instant I may believe that I am not in pain. But my belief is false: I am in pain. I am just not aware of my pain. The fact that I am not attending to my pain entails that I am not fully justified in believing that I am not in pain, and, consequently, it entails that I am not fully justified in that belief solely on the basis of evidence present to my attentive mind. I am fully justified only if I believe attentively that I am not in pain. Thus, to account for the incorrigibility of "I am not in pain" or "I do not have a pain" as being a paradigm case of incorrigibility, attentive belief seems to be essential.

When a philosopher asserts that someone may be having a pain that he is not aware of, he assumes that a man can have a pain and not feel it. A philosopher may, however, make the contrary assumption. He may assume that having a pain entails feeling a pain. (Everyone is agreed that feeling a pain entails having it.) But even if we assumed that having a pain entails feeling it, my assertion would still remain true. We would still have to define incorrigibility in terms of attentive belief, in order to accommodate paradigm cases of incorrigible propositions. If having a pain entails feeling it, then no matter how faintly one may feel it, there is no possibility of one's having a pain without being to some degree conscious of it. Then, if a man has a pain and, at the time he has it, occurrently believes that he has a pain, it seems safe to suppose that at that time he *knows* that he has a pain. And he knows it in the manner required. He is fully justified, and cannot be mistaken, in believing that he has a pain, solely on the basis of evidence present to his mind. One does not have to define incorrigibility in terms of *attentive* belief, in order to secure the incorrigibility for me of "I am in pain," if it is assumed that having a pain entails feeling it.

But this will not do for other paradigms, e.g., "The pain I now have is just noticeably throbbing." Under the supposition that having a pain entails feeling it, I feel the pain I now have. But the quality it has of being just noticeably throbbing is one that I may not notice without a special effort of attention. Hence, if I should happen to believe inattentively that the pain I have is not a throbbing pain, I am not fully justified in believing it, because my belief is not based upon evidence that is present to my attentive mind. Thus, I am fully justified, and cannot be mistaken, in believing that my pain has this or that quality only if my belief is *attentive*. Once again, even assuming that having a pain entails feeling it, in order to account for the incorrigibility of such paradigm cases as "I now have a pain that is just noticeably throbbing," or "I now have a pain that comes and goes in quick intervals," we must define incorrigibility in terms of attentive belief. Hence, philosophically as well as exegetically, the concept of incorrigibility is best defined as we have defined it—in terms of attentive belief.

Incidentally, this harmony of philosophical and exegetical considerations is evidence of the fact that Descartes has certain true and important insights in the area in which theory of knowledge and philosophy of mind shade into each other. However, the present concept of incorrigibility is much more rigorous than anything we find in Descartes. What he says in many places only suggests this definition. The rigorous concept fits all of Descartes' own examples, but it also makes for tensions within the Cartesian system. For example, with the help of this concept of incorrigibility and the criterion of incorrigible knowledge that I shall elicit from things that Descartes says, we will prove, in the third part of the dream argument, that no one knows incorrigibly a perceptual fact. This conclusion seems to be inconsistent with things that Descartes says elsewhere. It may be that these tensions arise because neither the rigorous concept of incorrigibility nor the criterion of incorrigible knowledge faithfully represent what Descartes meant. Or it may be that, had Descartes been clearer in his own mind, he would have refrained from making certain assertions that he does in fact make.

It is important to keep in mind that, from what has been said about attentive belief, it does not follow that it is impossible to believe a perceptual proposition attentively and not to know it. We shall soon prove, in the first part of the dream argument, that no perceptual proposition is incorrigible for anyone, and this conclusion would be false, if it were impossible to believe a perceptual proposition attentively and not to know it. But there is nothing in the conception of attentive belief that entails that this is impossible.

For example, my believing attentively that there is a pig in front of me does not entail my knowing that there is a pig in front of me. I believe attentively that I have a pain if, and only if, while being attentive to my feelings or to my sensations, I both feel a pain and believe occurrently that I have a pain. In a fashion parallel to this, I believe attentively that there is a pig in front of me if, and only if, the following conditions are satisfied. I am having certain experiences; I carefully note that they all "hang together"—for example, I hear a piglike grunt coming from the place where I see a piglike configuration of colors and shapes. Nothing in my present experience suggests to my vigilant mind that I am not seeing a pig. I am thus led to believe that there is a pig in front of me. Now these conditions of my attentively believing that there is a pig in front of me can be fulfilled even if there is no pig in front of me. It is logically possible that they all happen when I am under the influence of a drug, or they may happen in a dream. This latter possibility is the sort of thing that is envisaged in the dream argument.

We could have still another concept of incorrigibility—call it 'incorrigibility₁'—as given in the following definition:

Df. C: p is incorrigible₁ for S = Df. "S believes that p" entails p, and "S believes that not p" entails not p.

This, in turn, could be paired with a fourth definition, Df. D, of 'S believes p incorrigibly₁', which is analogous to definition B. But definition C and definition D would be of no use to us either philosophically or for understanding Descartes. A faithful exposition of the *Meditations* is possible only if we take "I think" and "I exist" to be either incorrigible for me or to be believed by me incorrigibly. "I think" and "I exist" are not incorrigible₁ for me. "I believe that I am not thinking" does not entail "I am not thinking." Quite the contrary; it entails that I am thinking. The same is true of "I believe that I do not exist." It entails that I exist, not that I do not exist. Hence, both "I am thinking" and "I exist" are not incorrigible₁. For similar reasons, definition D would be useless both philosophically and for understanding Descartes. The trouble with both definition C and definition D is that they do not make adequate provision for the incorrigibility of some contingent propositions—e.g., "I think," "I exist."

Either definition A or definition B will do for understanding what Descartes has to say about the philosophically interesting properties of the propositions "I think" and "I exist." I shall use definition A in the forthcoming proofs of the three parts of the dream argument, as well as in the forthcoming proofs of the two evil demon arguments because it is easier to manipulate than B.

According to definition A (and also Df. B), a contingent proposition (i.e., a proposition that is neither necessarily true nor necessarily false) may be incorrigible for S, and a proposition may be both necessarily true and corrigible for S. For example, "I exist" is a contingent proposition, yet it is incorrigible for me for reasons that we shall see in Section 3 of this Part. "I am drinking water" is both contingent and corrigible for me. And, as the next section will show, there are mathematical propositions that are corrigible for us. But, because they are mathematical propositions, if they are true, they are necessarily true, and, if they are false, they are necessarily false.

The reader would do well to keep in mind that 'contingent'

and 'corrigible' are not synonymous terms. Moreover, they do not even apply to the same entities: not every corrigible proposition is contingent. Similarly, 'necessary' and 'incorrigible' are not synonymous terms, and they do not apply to the same entities: not every incorrigible proposition is necessarily true.

The Essentially Cartesian Character of the Premises of the Dream Argument

WE ARE now in a position to formulate the premises of the dream argument.

(1) If a man dreams that he is attentively perceiving that p (where p is a perceptual proposition), then he attentively believes that p.

(2) It is possible that a man is dreaming that he himself is attentively perceiving that p (where p is a perceptual proposition), when in fact p is false.

(3) If a contingent proposition entails that a certain man is not dreaming, then it is possible that in his dream that man attentively believes that that proposition is true.

(4) It is possible that p is false, and in a dream a man has a clear and distinct intuition that q (where p is a perceptual proposition and q is a proposition incorrigible for him).

(5) If in a dream a man has a clear and distinct intuition that q (where q is a proposition incorrigible for him), then he attentively believes that q.

(6) A man knows incorrigibly a proposition that is corrigible for him, only if there is a proposition incorrigible for him that entails the proposition that is corrigible for him.

Next we must see whether these premises can be justifiably ascribed to Descartes. I shall discuss them in this order: (6), (2), (3), (1), (4), (5).

I shall refer to (6) as "the criterion of knowledge," although strictly speaking it is only a partial criterion. The full criterion would include the clause: If p is incorrigible for S, and S believes attentively that p, then S knows incorrigibly that p.

There are many passages in Descartes that would seem to justify attributing to Descartes the view that (6) is a criterion of knowledge. There are, however, other passages that would not. In fact, these other passages suggest a more inclusive criterion of knowledge. I shall propose the other criterion when I come to offer the second interpretation of the dream argument. Even though exegetically it may not be altogether accurate to attribute (6) to Descartes, formulating (6) for use in the dream argument makes good philosophical sense. For the conclusions of the three parts of the dream argument are absolutely correct, if the criterion of knowledge (6) is regarded as a criterion of incorrigible knowledge. From the exegetical point of view, also, it makes sense to formulate (6) and to find such justification for it as exists in the text. For even if (6) is not the whole of the criterion that is suggested by everything that Descartes says, it forms a part of the more inclusive criterion. (I believe, it is needless to say, that (1)–(5) can be attributed to Descartes without qualification.)

The main justification for saying that Descartes would accept (6) comes from his rule of provisional doubt. This is a methodological rule to the following effect: treat no proposition as a piece of knowledge if it is not logically indubitable for you, unless it is entailed by a proposition that is logically indubitable for you, and remember that a proposition is not logically indubitable for you unless it survives every possible doubt, no matter how tenuous, including the doubt that perhaps you are being deceived by an evil demon. The criterion of incorrigible knowledge seems to be a precise and clear counterpart of Descartes' methodological rule.[8]

According to the above methodological rule, then, a necessary condition for knowing a proposition that is itself corrigible is that it be entailed by a proposition that is incorrigible for the knower. This is required by Descartes' assumption that we know either by intuition or by deduction. I am supposing Descartes to be saying that if a proposition is corrigible for a man, then there is only one way in which he can know it: he must be able to deduce it from a proposition that is itself incorrigible for him.

[8] This formulation of the criterion I owe to Edmund L. Gettier. The formulation of premises (1) and (2), above, I owe to Hector-Neri Castaneda. Both helped me to set up the deductions in all three parts of the dream argument.

And in order for him to be able to make the deduction, the corrigible proposition must be entailed by the incorrigible one. Knowledge acquired by deduction may be called "mediate knowledge." A proposition that can be known only by deduction is one that can be known only mediately. Intuition, on the other hand, is an immediate apprehension. But of what? Descartes never deviates from the view that intuition is of "clear and distinct" ideas and propositions. But he sometimes talks as if all clear and distinct apprehensions might be false—which is a deviant view, one that leads to absurd results, as I hope to show later on. On the other hand, Descartes often says that not all clear and distinct apprehensions can be false. In some of his writings, for example in *Rules for the Direction of the Mind* and in *The Principles of Philosophy,* he repeatedly says that there is an inexhaustible number of propositions that are known to be true by intuition. This is the correct view, as I shall argue; in line with it, intuition is a faculty by the proper exercise of which we have an immediate apprehension of the truth of certain propositions. Thus, I have an immediate apprehension of the truth that I cannot be deceived (or undergo any other mental experience) if I do not exist; I have an immediate apprehension of the truth that I cannot be aware of a pain, if I am not conscious. These are truths whose denials are self-contradictory. But I can know intuitively that I am in pain, and the denial of that proposition ("I am not in pain") is not self-contradictory. One knows intuitively that one is in pain simply because it is impossible to believe attentively that one is in pain and not to know that one is in pain. "I am in pain" is contingent and incorrigible for me, and I know it intuitively. There are many other contingent propositions that are incorrigible for me and which I know intuitively. Thus, according to the view that Descartes ought to have held consistently, intuition apprehends immediately the truth of those propositions that are incorrigible for the man who is intuiting them. Deduction, on the other hand, proceeds by steps, each of which can be, in principle, simple enough to be intuitively clear. But this does not destroy the distinction between immediate and mediate knowledge. I know whatever I know immediately, without making inferences. I know anything else that I know, by making inferences. So much for premise (6).

Premise (2) is unquestionably a proposition that Descartes would accept. It is an immediate consequence of Descartes' conception of dreaming, although the reason that Descartes himself gives for accepting (2) is not this, but a reason that he cannot give at this stage of the argument without ceasing to abide by his own procedural rules. First, let us see why (2) is an immediate consequence of what Descartes understands a dream to be. Descartes assumes what is commonly assumed—namely, that dreams are, or consist of, impressions, thoughts, feelings, sensations, images, or any of the other mental phenomena that occur during sleep. It is, moreover, part of this conception of dreaming that it is possible to have a very vivid and lifelike dream that we are attentively perceiving that, say, the walls are yellow, when in fact there are no yellow walls to be perceived. This is premise (2). Since it is an immediate consequence of what is meant by 'dreaming', premise (2) is necessarily true, provided that this conception of dreaming is not self-contradictory or otherwise incoherent.[9]

Descartes could have introduced premise (2) this way, and he should have done so. Instead, he writes as follows:

> At this moment it does indeed seem to me that it is with eyes awake that I am looking at this paper; that this head which I move is not asleep, that it is deliberately and of set purpose that I extend my hand and perceive it; what happens in sleep does not appear so clear and distinct as does all this. But in thinking over this I remind myself that on many occasions I have in sleep been deceived by similar illusions, and in dwelling carefully on this reflection I see so manifestly that there are no certain indications by which we may clearly distinguish wakefulness from sleep that I am lost in astonishment. (Haldane and Ross, Vol. I, p. 146.)

The excerpt asserts that in a dream we seem to have "clear and distinct"—or, at least, very vivid and lifelike—perceptual experiences. So far this is only a part of the commonly accepted conception of dreams. But having said this, Descartes then goes on to invoke memory "to remind [himself]" that "on many occasions [he has] in sleep been deceived by similar illusions." From this assumption, (2) follows readily enough. However, this way of

[9] The most extended and tenacious attack on such premises as (1)–(5) and the conception of dreams underlying them is to be found in Norman Malcolm's book, *Dreaming* (New York: Humanities Press, 1959). The reader will benefit from coming to grips with Malcolm's arguments. In this connection the reader should study items [2], [3], [7], [13], [15], [18], and [26], listed in the selected bibliography at the end of Part II.

substantiating (2) is not open to Descartes at this stage of the proceedings. According to Descartes, we are not to assume that we have knowledge by recollection. On Descartes' view, beliefs based on memory are just as much in need of justification as the belief that there is a world of material substances. By the restrictions he has imposed on himself, Descartes is prevented from defending his initial assumptions through appeal to memory impressions. To be consistent with his own procedural rules, Descartes should have introduced premise (2) without appealing to memory at all, as he could easily have done.

Premise (3) is what I think we should take Descartes to be assuming when he says that ". . . there are no certain indications by which we may clearly distinguish wakefulness from sleep." What might these "certain indications" be? The most natural interpretation is that they are premises that entail that we ourselves are awake, and that we know how to make the inference from those premises. Now "I am awake" is a contingent proposition, and we must therefore suppose that the required premises are contingent. We do not want to trivialize the inference by allowing necessarily false premises, for necessarily false premises entail any conclusion you please. And we must have premises that are not necessarily true, because no necessarily true premise entails a contingent proposition. Now why is any contingent premise that entails that I am not asleep not a "certain indication" of my not being asleep? Again, the natural interpretation of Descartes' assumption is that it is possible at one and the same time to believe attentively any such premise, to infer from it that one is not asleep, and yet to be dreaming. If this is true, then it is possible to believe attentively any such premise while one is dreaming. This last possibility is what is assumed in premise (3), and it is a perfectly reasonable assumption for anyone to make who subscribes to the everyday conception of dreams. For, like (2), (3) is an immediate consequence of that conception.

We have next to justify attributing premise (1) to Descartes. We know that the first part of the dream argument is intended to prove that all perceptual propositions are doubtful. Given our interpretation that 'p is indubitable (for S)' means that p is incorrigible for S and our definition of 'p is incorrigible for S', and given that premise (2) is clearly implied by what Descartes assumes about the nature of dreams, what is the minimal assumption that, when added to premise (2) and the definition of incorrigibility, will formally imply the intended conclusion that all perceptual propositions are doubtful? The needed minimal assumption is premise (1). This in itself is a weighty reason for believing that Descartes would accept this premise. The case for attributing (1) to Descartes becomes conclusive when we note that (1) is just what one would expect Descartes to say, given his theory of perception and given that his conception of a dream is the ordinary one. I have already said that the ordinary, everyday conception is that dreams are, or consist of, thoughts, impressions, feelings, images, or any other mental phenomena that occur during sleep. It is this conception that Norman Malcolm questions. I am persuaded by Malcolm's critics, however, that his arguments have by no means demolished that conception of dreams. We are, as far as we know, under no rational compulsion to give up the Cartesian conception of dreams.

According to that conception, dreaming that one is attentively perceiving that p, where p is a perceptual proposition, involves the occurrence of certain mental phenomena while one is sleeping. What phenomena specifically? The answer to that lies in Descartes' theory of perception, which assumes that perception is judgmental. It thus comes to three propositions: first, that we perceive that such and such is the case; second, that perceiving that such and such is the case entails believing that such and such is the case; third, that perceiving a thing or a collection of things entails perceiving that such and such is the case. Now Descartes is pretty obviously of the opinion that "S is perceiving that p" entails three propositions: (i) p, (ii) S is having certain visual, tactual, auditory, olfactory, or gustatory sensations, and (iii) on the basis of these sensations, S believes that p. Exactly what is meant by 'on the basis of these sensations' is not altogether clear, but that problem need not detain us here. Suffice it to say that the belief instigated by the sensations need not involve an inference on the part of the perceiver. On Descartes' view of dreaming and of perceiving, the difference between S's perceiving that p and S's dreaming that he is perceiving that p is that the latter entails (ii) and (iii) *and* that S is asleep, but does not entail (i), while "S is perceiving that p" entails (i) and (ii) and (iii), but does *not* entail that S is asleep. Accordingly, the following two entailments would seem to be axiomatic for Descartes: "S is attentively perceiving that p" entails "S attentively believes that p," and "S is dreaming that he attentively perceives that p" entails

"S attentively believes that p." The latter entailment is our premise (1).

Told another way, the story is this. According to Descartes, perceiving is not a purely mental phenomenon. There is no perceiving anything unless there are physical objects. Yet perceiving cannot occur without the occurrence of two purely mental phenomena. He who is perceiving must be having certain experiences, and on their basis he must be believing that a certain perceptual proposition is true. Further, according to Descartes, the purely mental features of perceiving that p must occur in anyone's dream (i.e., whenever anyone is dreaming), that he himself is perceiving that p. How else, Descartes might pertinently ask, can we explain the difference, say, between dreaming that I was perceiving something and dreaming that I decided to stop smoking? Finally, according to Descartes, "S is dreaming at t that he himself is attentively perceiving that p," is the same proposition as "S is asleep at t, at t S is having certain experiences, and on their basis he attentively believes at t that p." From this it follows that "S is dreaming (at t) that he himself is attentively perceiving that p" entails "S attentively believes (at t) that p." The latter entailment is premise (1).

In the Third Meditation, and elsewhere, Descartes says things that lead me to believe that he means to affirm premise (4). He writes:

> . . . I have before received and admitted many things to be very certain and manifest which yet afterwards I recognised as being dubious. What then were these things? They were the earth, sky, stars and all other objects which I apprehended by means of the senses. But what did I clearly [and distinctly] perceive in them? Nothing more than that the ideas or thoughts of these things were presented to my mind. And not even now do I deny that these ideas are met with in me. But there was yet another thing which I affirmed, and which, owing to the habit I had formed of believing it, I thought I perceived very clearly, although I did not perceive it at all, to wit, that there were objects outside of me from which these ideas proceeded, and to which they were entirely similar. And it was in this that I erred, or, if perchance my judgment was correct, this was not due to any knowledge arising from my perception. . . . Of my thoughts some are, so to speak, images of the things, and to these alone is the title 'idea' properly applied. . . . Now as to what concerns ideas, if we consider them only in themselves and do not relate

them to anything else beyond themselves, they cannot properly speaking be false; for whether I imagine a goat or a chimera, it is not less true that I imagine the one than the other. (Haldane and Ross, Vol. I, pp. 158–159.)

Descartes is saying that purely phenomenal reports, e.g., "I am now seeing a red surface next to a blue surface," "I now feel pain," "I seem to see a blue canopy overhead," are "indubitable," or, in my terminology, incorrigible for me. And about such judgments he writes as follows: ". . . everything which anyone clearly and distinctly perceives is true, although that person in the meantime may doubt whether he is dreaming or awake, nay if you want it so, even though he is really dreaming or is delirious." (In his reply to Father Bourdin, *Objections and Replies,* in Haldane and Ross, Vol. II, p. 267.) In the Second Meditation he writes:

> But it will be said that these phenomena (that I hear noise, that I see light) are false and that I am dreaming. Let it be so, still it is at least quite certain that it seems to me that I see light, that I hear noise and that I feel heat. That cannot be false; properly speaking it is what is in me called feeling; and used in this precise sense that is no other thing than thinking. . . . (Haldane and Ross, Vol. I, p. 153.)

Here again Descartes is distinguishing purely phenomenal reports such as "It seems to me that I see light," "I seem to be hearing a noise," from perceptual propositions, and saying of the former that they are incorrigible for me, although every one of them is contingent. He is saying that, in the case of some contingent propositions that are incorrigible for me (viz., propositions that describe or report my own immediate experiences), it is possible that in my dream[10] I attentively believe them while I am not perceiving that p, where p is a perceptual proposition.

---

10 In idiomatic English the two assertions, "In my dream I solved a problem" and "I dreamt that I solved a problem," come to much the same thing. Neither of them clearly entails that I did solve a problem. For a precise formulation of premises (4) and (5) of the dream argument, it is useful to stipulate that "In my dream I attentively believed that p" is to entail "I attentively believed that p," and that "In my dream I had a clear and distinct intuition that q" is to entail "I had a clear and distinct intuition that q." The locution 'I dreamt that so and so' we shall continue to use in its idiomatic sense.

And if it is possible that in my dream I have a "clear and distinct" intuition that a certain contingent proposition is incorrigible for me even while I am not perceiving that p, then it is also possible that in my dream I have "a clear and distinct" intuition that a certain contingent proposition is incorrigible for me even while p is false. But if this is possible for some contingent propositions that are incorrigible for me, then there is no reason why it should not be possible for *all* contingent propositions that are incorrigible for me. That takes us half way to premise (4).

We go the rest of the way when we find Descartes leaving no doubt that in his opinion contingent propositions that are incorrigible for me are not necessarily the only incorrigible propositions that satisfy the condition in question. For it is possible that there are necessarily true propositions, q, that are incorrigible for me, and for any perceptual proposition, p, it is possible that, while p is false, in my dream I have a clear and distinct intuition that q. In the *Discourse on Method*, Descartes writes: "For even if in sleep we had some very distinct idea such as a geometrician might have who discovered some new demonstration, the fact of being asleep would not militate against its truth." (Haldane and Ross, Vol. I, p. 105.)

Certain passages in the *Meditations* may seem to be incompatible with the one just quoted from the *Discourse on Method*. But they are not really incompatible. Early in the Third Meditation (Haldane and Ross, Vol. I, pp. 158–159), Descartes seems to be saying that none of my clear and distinct intuitions guarantees its own truth. This includes my intuition of my own existence, as well as my intuition of even the simplest mathematical propositions—e.g., that a square has four sides. In this passage, Descartes seems to be saying that the ultimate guarantee of the truth of all clear and distinct intuitions must be a God who is not a deceiver. As long as I remain unsure that such a God exists, I have reason for doubting even that I exist[11] or that a square has four sides. In other words, if God does not exist, then it is possible that no clearly and distinctly intuited proposition is true. But if that is

[11] This passage cannot be taken as stating Descartes' firm opinion. Elsewhere in the *Meditations* and in his other writings, he says things that are incompatible with this. He is, I think, wrong here and right in the other passages. The matter is even more complicated. For the above passage is susceptible of yet another interpretation—namely that, although if I intuit a proposition clearly and distinctly, then I know it, I do not know that I know it, so long as I am ignorant of God's existence.

possible, then it is also possible that I clearly and distinctly intuit a proposition without knowing it. For a proposition cannot be known unless it is true. Now Descartes has defined intuition to be the undoubting conception of an unclouded and attentive mind (see p. 71, above). Hence, I cannot be intuiting that p unless I believe attentively that p. Therefore, if my intuiting that a square has four sides is not sufficient for my knowing so, then my attentively believing that a square has four sides is not sufficient for my knowing so. In other words, if there is no God, then all mathematical propositions are corrigible for anyone.

Nevertheless, it seems clear that Descartes is prepared to admit that, if there is any mathematical proposition, q, that is incorrigible for me, then for any perceptual proposition, p, it is possible that, while p is false, in my dream I have a clear and distinct intuition that q. The same would be true, one would suppose, of any necessarily true proposition that was not mathematical. If any necessarily true non-mathematical proposition, q, was incorrigible for me, then for any perceptual proposition, p, it would be possible that, while p is false, in my dream I had a clear and distinct intuition that q. Since the class of propositions that are incorrigible for me is made up of all contingent propositions that are incorrigible for me and all necessarily true propositions that are incorrigible for me, (4) is clearly a proposition that Descartes would have to be taking for granted.

Premise (5) is analogous to premise (1). In connection with premise (1), I said that the following two entailments are axiomatic for Descartes: "S is attentively perceiving that p" entails "S attentively believes that p," and "S is dreaming that he himself attentively perceives that p" entails "S attentively believes that p." The analogous entailments relevant to premise (5) are: "S clearly and distinctly intuits that q" entails "S attentively believes that q," and "In his dream, S clearly and distinctly intuits that q" entails "S attentively believes that q." The latter entailment is premise (5), when q is any proposition incorrigible for S. Premise (5) entails that for any proposition, q, that is incorrigible for S, "In his dream S clearly and distinctly intuits that q" entails that S knows that q. This is as it should be. Descartes says, for example, that "I think" and "I exist" are incorrigible for me; whether I am awake or dreaming, each time that the thought that I am thinking or the thought that I exist occur to me clearly and distinctly I know that I think and that I exist.

The conclusion of the first part of the dream argument is deducible from (1) and (2). The conclusion of the second part is deducible from (3), and (6); and (1), (2), (4), (5), and (6) entail the conclusion of the third part.

The Three Parts of the Dream Argument

We are now in a position to formulate the three parts of the dream argument. Their rigorous versions are given in Appendix I. Here they are given informally.

The first part of the dream argument proceeds from two premises: (1) If a man is dreaming that he is attentively perceiving that p (where p is a perceptual proposition), then he attentively believes that p, and (2) It is possible that a man is dreaming that he himself is attentively perceiving that p (where p is a perceptual proposition), when in fact it is not the case that p. It follows from these two propositions that it is possible at one and the same time that a man believes attentively that p and that p is false. But if p is false, then no one knows that p. Therefore, it is possible at one and the same time that a man attentively believes that p and does not know that p. But this entails that it is false that a man's attentively believing that p entails his knowing that p. And, by our definition of 'p is incorrigible for S', it follows that no perceptual proposition is incorrigible for anyone.

The second part of the dream argument begins with the assumption that, if a contingent proposition entails that a certain man is not dreaming, then it is possible that in his dream that man attentively believes that proposition to be true. Now let there be a contingent proposition that entails that a certain man is not dreaming. From this and our original premise it follows that it is possible at one and the same time that the man in question attentively believes that proposition and that the proposition is false. But if the proposition is false, the man in question does not know it. Therefore, it is possible at one and the same time that the man attentively believes that proposition but does not know it. That entails that his attentively believing it does not entail his knowing it. That in turn entails that the proposition is corrigible for that man. The result is true of any man and of any contingent proposition that entails that he is not dreaming.

In other words, we have deduced so far that (i) any contingent proposition that entails that a man is not dreaming is corrigible for that man. But because "S is not dreaming" is a contingent proposition, no necessarily true proposition entails it. It is true that every necessarily false proposition entails it, but no necessarily false proposition is incorrigible for anyone. Hence, there is no non-contingent incorrigible proposition that entails it. But we have already deduced in (i) that no contingent incorrigible proposition entails it. Therefore, *no* incorrigible proposition entails it. Moreover, the proposition that S is not dreaming is corrigible for S, and, like every proposition, entails itself. Hence, by (i), the proposition "S is not dreaming" is itself corrigible for S. Hence, there is no proposition incorrigible for S that entails that S is not dreaming. It follows, by the criterion of incorrigible knowledge, that no one knows incorrigibly that he himself is not dreaming.

The third part of the dream argument begins with the conclusion of the first part, namely, that a perceptual proposition is corrigible for anyone. Consequently, given the criterion of incorrigible knowledge (premise (6)), a man would know that a perceptual proposition was true only if he could deduce it from a proposition incorrigible for him. But according to premise (4), it is possible at the same time that in a dream a man has a clear and distinct intuition that q and that p is false (where p is a perceptual proposition and q is a proposition incorrigible for him). However, by premise (5), if in a dream a man has a clear and distinct intuition that q (where q is a proposition incorrigible for him), then he attentively believes that q. Now let there be a man, S, and a perceptual proposition, p, such that S knows incorrigibly that p. We know immediately that p is corrigible for S, because every perceptual proposition is corrigible for anyone. Also, from the assumption we have made, namely, that S knows incorrigibly that p, it follows that there is a proposition, q, that is incorrigible for S and entails p. And now from the assumptions we have made we deduce that, if a man knows incorrigibly that a perceptual proposition is true, then his attentively believing that q does and does not entail the perceptual proposition in question. But the consequent (the *then* part) of this hypothetical is self-contradictory, and therefore its antecedent (its *if* part) is necessarily false. Hence, it follows that no one ever knows incorrigibly that a perceptual proposition is true.

Let us now summarize our results. The conclusion of the first part of the dream argument asserts that every perceptual proposition is corrigible for anyone. The conclusion of the second part is that no one knows incorrigibly that he himself is not dreaming. The conclusion of the third part is that no one knows incorrigibly that any given perceptual proposition is true.

The second part of the dream argument is important for two reasons. First, it is interesting in its own right: it is an arresting fact that no one can know incorrigibly that he himself is not dreaming. Second, the second part of the dream argument provides an explanation of Descartes' affirmation that "there are no certain indications by which we may clearly distinguish wakefulness from sleep." (Haldane and Ross, Vol. I, p. 146.)

Descartes nowhere seems to be saying or implying that we have no conceptual distinction between dreaming and waking. We know very well that "S is dreaming" entails "S is asleep," whereas "S is awake" does not entail "S is asleep." On the contrary, it entails that S is *not* asleep. What Descartes seems to be saying is that, at any given moment no one can know incorrigibly that he himself is awake and not dreaming, by appeal to evidence that consists of propositions incorrigible for him. And this, I think, is necessarily true.

As to the conclusion of the third part of the dream argument, all its basic premises, except the criterion of incorrigible knowledge, are assumptions about dreaming. That is to say, the assumptions about dreaming and the criterion of incorrigible knowledge are enough to entail the conclusion that no person ever knows incorrigibly any perceptual proposition to be true. From this it follows that no one knows incorrigibly that he himself is perceiving a physical object.

The Inconsistency of Some of These Conclusions with Some of Descartes' Final Pronouncements

We HAVE so far deduced, from premises that we have attributed to Descartes, three conclusions: (1) that every perceptual proposition is corrigible for anyone; (2) that no one knows incorrigibly that he is not dreaming; (3) that no one ever knows incorrigibly that any preceptual proposition is true. A corollary of this third conclusion is that no one can prove, from perceptual premises alone, that he himself is perceiving a material object. Did Descartes *mean to prove* all three of these propositions? We are not asking a question of the sort that can be answered only by mind readers or mediums. The question, rather, is partly exegetical and partly logical. The exegetical part is: does the total textual evidence say or imply clearly which, if any, of these conclusions Descartes wanted to prove or thought that he had proved? The logical part of the question is: given that all three of the above mentioned conclusions follow deductively from premises that we have attributed to Descartes, are the conclusions implied by them consistent with Descartes' asserted or implied aims?

Descartes ultimately wants to be able to say, among other things, it seems to me, that we know "with certainty" a perceptual fact, if we perceive it clearly and distinctly, and that we know "with certainty" that we ourselves are awake, if our senses, our memory, and our understanding together corroborate the proposition that we are awake. The conclusion of the first part of the dream argument, taken by itself, is not in conflict with either one of these assertions. The proposition that all perceptual propositions are corrigible does not, by itself alone, rule out the possibility of finding a suitable criterion of clarity and distinctness for perceptual propositions. And if such a criterion could be found, then clarity and distinctness would be a criterion of the truth of clear and distinct perceptual judgments. And eventually Descartes will claim to have proved that all clearly and distinctly perceived propositions are true. So far, then, we have no reason to suspect that Descartes did not mean to prove that all perceptual propositions are corrigible for everyone.

It is otherwise with the conclusion of the second part of the dream argument. The text gives no clear indication that Descartes meant to arrive at it. From premise (3), but without (6), the criterion of incorrigible knowledge, we deduce that no proposition that is incorrigible for anyone entails that he himself is not dreaming. This is the weaker conclusion, and it may be all that Descartes means to imply when he says that he sees "manifestly that there are no certain indications by which we may clearly distinguish wakefulness from sleep." (Haldane and Ross, Vol. I, p. 146.) But this quotation is also compatible with the stronger conclusion that no one knows incorrigibly that he himself is not dreaming. This we deduce from the conjunction of (3) with (6), the criterion of incorrigible knowledge. Now the stronger conclusion gives every appearance of being inconsistent with Descartes' assertion, at the end of the Sixth Meditation, that God's goodness guarantees that it is possible to know "with certainty" that one is not dreaming. There appears to be a flat contradiction between the proposition that we can never know incorrigibly that we are not dreaming and the proposition that God's goodness guarantees that we can know with certainty that we are not dreaming.

If there is a contradiction here, then the premises of the second part of the dream argument are inconsistent with any premises that Descartes might assume in order to prove that God's goodness guarantees that we can know we are not dreaming. If it were not for this apparent inconsistency, it would not be too rash to suppose that Descartes did mean to imply that no one knows incorrigibly that he himself is not dreaming. For that conclusion is entailed by six premises, the first five of which are either assumptions or implications of assumptions that he makes. The possible exception is the criterion of incorrigible knowledge. Because there is an apparent inconsistency here, we ought to see whether there may not be strong clues in Descartes as to how the criterion of knowledge should be modified so as to avoid inconsistency.

Is this apparent inconsistency a genuine one? Even a somewhat abbreviated examination of this question requires that we refer to passages in the Fourth, Fifth, and Sixth Meditations. These are the passages that strongly suggest a different criterion of knowledge from the one we have been using, and with it a different interpretation of Descartes' dream argument.

The plan of the *Meditations* makes it clear that the dream argument (and the evil demon argument discussed in the next section) are to lead to a limited scepticism. We believe many propositions as a matter of course; without ever having given the matter a thought, we take it for granted that, even without a knowledge of God, we are fully justified in believing them. Descartes' dream argument is intended to shake us out of our dogmatic assumption that we are fully justified in believing, solely on the basis of present perceptual experiences and without a knowledge of God, that we are perceiving a physical object, and in believing that this or that perceptual proposition is true or that we ourselves are awake. And, as we shall see, the evil demon argument is meant to perform a similar function with respect to our uncritical assumption that, even when we are ignorant of God's existence, we are fully justified in believing mathematical propositions. In neither case is it Descartes' intention to prove such radically sceptical theses as that no one ever knows "with certainty" that a perceptual proposition is true, or that there are physical objects, or that he himself is awake, or that no one ever knows "with certainty" a mathematical proposition to be true.

Descartes himself does not seem to think that there is any inconsistency between the premises and conclusions of his dream argument and the claims he makes in the last three *Meditations*. We must therefore look into the likely reasons why Descartes does not see such an inconsistency. (It may turn out that we see an inconsistency because we have begun with a somewhat distorted view of what Descartes means to say.) In the Fourth Meditation, Descartes thinks that the principle of clarity and distinctness has been demonstrated. This is the principle that whatever we perceive clearly and distinctly is true. Hence, if I clearly and distinctly perceive that I am not dreaming, then I know that I am not dreaming. This principle of clarity and distinctness is supposed to follow from God's goodness.

My first interpretation of Descartes' dream argument requires two assumptions. The first is that a logically indubitable proposition is one that is incorrigible for the knower. The second assumption is that (i) according to Descartes, knowledge is incorrigible knowledge, and that (ii) Descartes' criterion of knowledge requires that, if a proposition is corrigible for someone, then that person knows that proposition to be true only if he can deduce it from a proposition that is incorrigible for him. If the three parts of the dream argument are accurate reconstructions of Descartes' dream argument in the First Meditation, then two conclusions of Descartes' dream argument are incompatible with his final pronouncements. For, according to this interpretation of his dream argument, in the First Meditation Descartes is saying that no one knows with certainty that he himself is awake, and no one knows with certainty any perceptual facts. Yet in the last three Meditations he concludes that, whenever I perceive clearly and distinctly that I am awake, I know with certainty that I am awake, and also that any perceptual proposition that I perceive clearly and distinctly to be true I know with certainty to be true.

The fact that these final pronouncements are clearly stated, and that there can be no doubt that Descartes means to assert them as final conclusions, strongly suggests what I earlier referred to as the second interpretation of Descartes' dream argument. The conclusions of this version must be consistent with Descartes' final pronouncements. An interpretation that satisfies this condition and also accords with the text is easy to find. We need only relax the criterion of knowledge in a certain way.

The Second Interpretation of the Dream Argument

LET US, THEN, begin to formulate the second interpretation of the dream argument as part of a more comprehensive theory. Our objective will be to see how successfully Descartes has worked out the details of that theory. For all we can tell, the theory that we are about to construct is internally coherent. If it has weaknesses, and we shall find that it does, they lie elsewhere.

We begin by relaxing the criterion of knowledge in a certain way. Assume that there are propositions that I perceive clearly and distinctly to be true because they are incorrigible for me—for example, "I exist," "I am in pain." Some that are corrigible for me I perceive clearly and distinctly to be true because I can deduce them from propositions that are incorrigible for me. For instance, "Somebody is in pain" is not incorrigible for me, but if I deduce it from "I am in pain," then I perceive clearly and distinctly that somebody is in pain. And some that are neither incorrigible nor deducible from any proposition that is incorrigible for me, I perceive clearly and distinctly in the sense that my senses, my memory, and my understanding corroborate them. The relaxed criterion of knowledge then becomes: if a proposition is corrigible for someone, then he knows it with certainty only if (1) it is entailed by a proposition that is incorrigible for him, or (2) his senses, his memory, and his reason corroborate it (i.e., he perceives it clearly and distinctly through sense, memory, and reason).

The clause (2) that follows the word 'or' is the escape-hatch. The second part of the dream argument has the intermediate conclusion that "I am awake" is corrigible for me and that no proposition that is incorrigible for me entails it. From this, by the criterion of incorrigible knowledge, it follows that I do not know incorrigibly that I am awake. The escape-clause, however, makes it possible for me to know with certainty that I am awake even though "I am awake" is corrigible for me and is not entailed by any proposition that is incorrigible for me.

The third part of the dream argument, as we have seen, proves that no perceptual proposition is ever known to be true. This conclusion does not follow, however, if the criterion of incorrigible knowledge is replaced by the one that contains the escape-clause.

Before making a detailed appraisal of the escape-clause, let us observe that the relaxed criterion of knowledge that we are now attributing to Descartes is a significantly different interpretation of Descartes from the one I have been working with up to now. If this new criterion of knowledge replaces the old, the second and third parts of the dream argument must be revised. The final conclusion of the second part would now be that no one knows that he himself is awake, *unless his senses, his memory and his reason corroborate that proposition*. This conclusion is consistent with Descartes' later assertion that we *can* know that we ourselves are awake. It is also consistent with the view, which we have held all along, that Descartes introduces his dream argument in order to discredit the supposition that what I learn either from the senses or through the senses is something that I am fully justified, and cannot be mistaken, in believing solely on the basis of perceptual experiences that I am now having.

The conclusion of the third part of the dream argument would now be that no one knows a perceptual proposition to be true, unless his senses, his memory, and his reason corroborate it. This too is consistent with Descartes' later conclusion that we can know that a perceptual proposition is true. And it too is consistent with our belief that Descartes introduces the dream argument in order to discredit the supposition that what I learn from the senses is something that I am fully justified, and cannot be mistaken, in believing solely on the basis of perceptual experiences that I am now having. Note, however, that the criterion of knowledge has now been relaxed to the point where a man can know with certainty that a certain proposition is true, *even if it is corrigible for him and not entailed by a proposition that is incorrigible for him.*

The system itself in outline goes this way: we can deduce that God exists; from His nature we can deduce that He is not a deceiver; from that we can deduce that all clear and distinct perceptions are true. Some propositions are clearly and distinctly perceived because they are incorrigible for us. Some are corrigible for us, yet are capable of being clearly and distinctly perceived because they are entailed by propositions that are incorrigible for us. Finally, there are propositions that are not of either of these two kinds, yet we perceive them clearly and distinctly in the sense that our senses, our memory, and our understanding corroborate them. I can, in this sense, clearly and distinctly perceive certain perceptual facts, as well as the fact that I am awake. Hence, I can know with certainty that I am awake, and I can also know with certainty a number of perceptual facts.

The Shortcomings of this Theory

THIS SYSTEM incorporates the relaxed criterion of knowledge and with it the second interpretation of the dream argument. I shall now argue that Descartes does not succeed in working out the details of this system. If I am right about this, then, even though the system is internally consistent, it is still not a satisfactory answer to the sceptic who denies all possibility of perceptual knowledge.

The focus of our attention will be the escape-clause. According to it, there are propositions that I perceive clearly and distinctly in the sense that my senses, my memory, and my understanding corroborate them.

A case in point is my attentive belief that I am awake. Reason tells me that our memory can never connect our dreams one with another, or with the whole course of our lives, as it unites events which happen to us while we are awake . . . when I perceive things as to which I know distinctly both the place from which they proceeded, and that in which they are, and the time at which they appeared to me; and when, without interruption, I connect the perceptions which I have of them with the whole course of my life . . . (Haldane and Ross, Vol. I, p. 199.)

then I can be perfectly certain that these are waking perceptions. Thus, I sometimes clearly and distinctly perceive that I am awake. I know at those times that I am awake, because whatever I perceive clearly and distinctly cannot fail to be true.

This is what Descartes is saying at the end of the Sixth Meditation. The first difficulty with it is that it relies on memory. In order to tell that I am now having a waking experience, I must be able to "connect [without interruption] the perceptions which I [now] have . . . with the whole course of my life." But in order to make such a connection, I must remember what my life has been up to now. But, in order to know that I am remembering correctly, I must know that my present memory impressions as to what my life has been up to now are *correct* memory impressions. And to be able to know that, I must be able to distinguish among my memory impressions the ones that are veridical from those that are not. Descartes is fully aware of the need to provide a reliable criterion for making the required distinction. At this point in the Sixth Meditation, he would be assuming that he has already vindicated reliance on memory. The supposed vindication comes at the end of the Fifth Meditation, in the following argument. (The text is in Haldane and Ross, Vol. I, p. 184):

> (1) God exists. All things depend on Him. He is not a deceiver. (Supposedly proved in earlier Meditations.)
>
> ∴ (2) Whatever [at some time or other] I perceive clearly and distinctly cannot fail to be true. (The argument for this is at the end of the Fourth Meditation, and I shall discuss it presently.)

But   (3)   If I recollect having clearly and distinctly
                  perceived that p[12] [and God exists], then no
                  contrary reason can be brought forward that
                  could even cause me to doubt that p is true.

Assume that (4)   I recollect having clearly and distinctly per-
                  ceived that p.

∴ (5)   No contrary reason can be brought forward
                  that could even cause me to doubt its truth.

∴ (6)   I know that p is true.

The crucial assumption is (4). How can I know with certainty
that something I recollect is true? Premise (2) applies only if
I have a *clear and distinct* recollection of having clearly and
distinctly perceived that p. But that calls for an independent
criterion or test for distinguishing my clear and distinct recollections from their opposites. Descartes sees that he must provide a
criterion for this, and he does. At the end of the Sixth Meditation,
he says that the test is the corroborative testimony of the senses,
memory, and reason. In short, Descartes proposes a coherence
test for distinguishing clear and distinct recollections from the
rest.

The theory under examination supposes that the coherence
criterion will guarantee that we know *with certainty* any proposition that we clearly and distinctly remember having clearly and
distinctly perceived. Now this certainty cannot be explained in
terms of incorrigibility. For the theory assumes that the clarity
and distinctness of a memory impression that p consists neither
in the proposition "I remember that p" being incorrigible for me,
nor in its being entailed by a proposition incorrigible for me. The
revised criterion of knowledge is in part based upon that assumption. Therefore, knowing with certainty that I truly remember
that p cannot be explained in terms of incorrigibility. In other
words, to know with certainty in this instance is not the same
thing as to know incorrigibly.

We therefore need another explanation of 'knowing with cer-

12 In the argument in the text, Descartes is specifically talking about
theorems, i.e., propositions that are conclusions of deductive arguments.
But there is no reason why he should not admit the generalized principle
(3), if he admits special cases of it. Indeed, he thinks he has proved, and
frequently appeals to, the principle that *all* clearly and distinctly perceived
propositions are true.

tainty'. And what we need is implied by the liberalized criterion of knowledge itself. According to the liberalized criterion, if a proposition is corrigible for someone, then he knows it (with certainty) only if (1) it is entailed by a proposition that is incorrigible for him, or (2) his senses, his memory, and his reason corroborate it. Hence, a man knows with certainty that something is the case only if he knows it incorrigibly, or if he knows it, let us say, infallibly.

Infallibility is meant to be different from incorrigibility. It is also meant to preserve Descartes' original intent that we know (with certainty) that p only if we are fully justified, and cannot be mistaken, in believing that p, solely on the basis of evidence to which we are attentive now.

The notion of infallibility is, I think, strongly suggested by certain passages in Descartes. It is as if, instead of there being two senses of 'indubitable' in Descartes, there are three. In addition to "psychological" and "logical" indubitability (= incorrigibility), which we have already encountered, there seems to be a second logical property. This is the one that I am calling 'infallibility'. We have found that at times Descartes talks as if he thought that even the most clearly and distinctly intuited propositions are not known with certainty to be true, except by those who know that God exists, and that He cannot be a deceiver. At other times he talks as if he thought that *some* but not all clearly and distinctly intuited propositions can be known with certainty only by those who know that God exists. The propositions "I think" and "I exist," for instance, do not require a knowledge of God. Perceptual propositions and propositions of the form "I remember that p" do require it.

Any proposition, knowledge of whose truth requires knowledge of God's existence is known to be true, only if it is known that God guarantees its truth. Descartes assumes that no one can have *any reasonable* grounds for doubting that which God guarantees to be true. God guarantees the truth of all propositions that we perceive clearly and distinctly to be true. Hence, no one could have any reasonable grounds for doubting a certain memory impression, if it is clear and distinct. To know a proposition infallibly is to know that it needs, and has, God's guarantee.

Accordingly, infallibility is not a psychological property. It is, rather, a second logical property, alongside incorrigibility. We might say that an incorrigible proposition is one that, whether or not there is a God, one cannot reasonably doubt, given the evidence now present to one's attentive apprehension. An infallible proposition is one that one cannot reasonably doubt because it is a proposition whose truth is known to be guaranteed by God. In order to be known, incorrigible propositions do not need knowledge of the existence of God; infallible ones do. But in either case the property is a logical one. Whether or not a proposition is either incorrigible or infallible depends upon facts that have nothing to do with psychological facts about me. A proposition is incorrigible for me, if, and only if, my believing it attentively entails my knowing it, and it is possible that I believe it attentively. This is so whether I believe the proposition attentively or not; whether I do so or not is a psychological fact about me.

Infallibility is also different from inability to withhold assent, no matter how hard we try. Inability to withhold assent is a psychological fact about us in relation to a certain proposition. A proposition, on the other hand, is infallible if, and only if, it is a proposition whose truth can be known only by those who know that God exists. Consequently, no one who knows that God exists could have any reasonable grounds for doubting it. None of these conditions is about anyone's psychology.

We now have an explanation of what, in the theory we are expounding, we are to understand by 'knowing with certainty'. It means knowing either incorrigibly or infallibly. But knowing incorrigibly that I remember something or other is ruled out by the theory. For memory needs God's guarantee. So knowing with certainty that I remember that p comes to knowing it infallibly.

According to the theory, a memory impression is known infallibly to be true only if the impression is clear and distinct. It is clear and distinct only if sense, memory, and reason corroborate it. In other words, the memory is clear and distinct only if it passes the test of coherence.

But the coherence test cannot guarantee infallibility. For, however much what I now remember "ties in" or "hangs together" with my present perceptual experiences, and however much what I remember itself "hangs together," "makes a coherent story," it is logically possible that a part of what I seem to remember, or even the whole of it, is not true recollection.

Suppose, for instance, that five different eyewitnesses agree that the pedestrian stepped off the curb against a red light. This agreement makes it highly probable that that is what happened. But it is not enough for us to be able to say that we are now fully justified, and cannot be mistaken, in believing that that is what happened.

Take an example in which, in place of different eyewitnesses, we have the different memory impressions of the same man at a given time. Suppose I have an impression that the following things happened this morning: I asked my wife to boil me an egg for breakfast; I saw her boiling an egg; I sat at the table reading the morning paper while waiting for my breakfast; I ate breakfast; I pushed some eggshells from a plate into a garbage bag. I do not remember having eaten an egg, but I do seem to remember that I paid no attention to what I was eating, because something in the paper totally absorbed my attention.

All these memory impressions corroborate the proposition that I ate an egg for breakfast. Their "agreement" or "coherence" makes it highly probable that I ate an egg this morning. Nevertheless, no amount of such "agreement" would entitle me to assert that I cannot possibly be mistaken in believing that I ate an egg for breakfast.

This is true even when we find perceptual evidence that "agrees" with all the memory impressions. We could find traces of egg in my stomach. Or my wife could tell us that I ate an egg for breakfast. All this favorable evidence would increase the probability of the proposition that I ate an egg for breakfast. I may even reach a point at which, in the face of the evidence, I am no longer capable of withholding assent from that proposition. But I would never reach a point at which I could justifiably say that I now have all the evidence that fully justifies my believing that I ate an egg for breakfast and completely precludes my being mistaken in believing so.

In short, the coherence test can, at best, guarantee highly probable knowledge. It cannot guarantee that a particular memory impression is one that I am fully justified, and cannot be mistaken, in believing to be true. But if it cannot guarantee that, then it cannot guarantee that I know infallibly that that memory impression is true. For a necessary condition of my knowing infallibly that p is that if I believe that p, then I am fully justified, and cannot be mistaken, in believing that p, on the basis of evidence present to my attentive apprehension here and now.

Here someone may suggest that, if coherence did not guarantee infallible knowledge, God would be a deceiver. But surely this is not necessarily so. Suppose that, by exercising my God-given reason, I clearly and distinctly perceive that probable knowledge is different from certain knowledge. Moreover, probable knowledge seems to be enough for me to be able to conduct my daily life quite satisfactorily. Thus let perceptual propositions, the proposition that I am awake, and all my knowledge by recollection be knowable, not with certainty, but only to a high degree of probability. This would in no way conflict with the supposition that God is good and not a deceiver. If I have natural propensities to believe that I know with certainty propositions that reason tells me I can know only to a degree of probability, then I have to see to it that my natural propensities do not subvert my reason.

I conclude that the alternative theory we are attributing to Descartes has not shown how I can know with certainty whether a present memory impression is veridical. That being the case, the theory has not provided an account of how I can know with certainty that I am awake. For the theory asserts that I can know with certainty that I am awake, only if I can know with certainty that some things I seem to recollect are true. Let my senses, my memory, and my reason corroborate to a high degree of probability the proposition that I am awake. I can never know it with certainty (infallibility). I can know it only to a degree of probability; this, however, is not what Descartes wants.

There is a second difficulty in the theory. The theory says that I can know with certainty that I am awake because I can perceive clearly and distinctly that I am awake. And whatever I perceive clearly and distinctly is true. But how do I know that whatever I perceive clearly and distinctly is true? Descartes has no convincing answer to that question.

Do I know the principle of clarity and distinctness incorrigibly, or do I know it because, once I have a clear and distinct intuition that God is not a deceiver, I am simply unable to imagine what conceivable reason there could be to shake my conviction that all clear and distinct perceptions are true? This question forces us to look into the deduction of the principle of clarity and distinctness itself. There is a relevant deduction at the end of the Fourth Meditation. (The text is in Haldane and Ross, Vol. I, p. 178.)

(1) Every clear and distinct perception is something.

∴ (2) Every such perception cannot have nothing for its cause. It must have God for its cause.

But (3) God is not a deceiver.

∴ (4) Every clear and distinct perception is true.

Obviously, this argument is as incomplete as it is ineffectual. It is ineffectual because, by the same form of argument, we can prove that every unclear and indistinct idea is also true. For, they, no less than the clear and distinct ones, are something; hence they, too, must have God as their cause.

There are even more serious problems when we try to complete the argument. The crucial step is from (3) God is not a deceiver, to (4) Every clear and distinct perception is true. Why is this so? Is it because God has created me in such a way that I am incapable of withholding assent from whatever I perceive clearly and distinctly? But this is a proposition that is not incorrigible for me. It is not a proposition that I am fully justified, and cannot be mistaken, in believing, solely on the basis of evidence now present to my attentive apprehension. For, the proposition that I am incapable of withholding assent from certain kinds of propositions relies on memory and involves a prediction.

Is it then the case that the principle of clarity and distinctness follows from God's goodness, because God must have given me the means of telling truth from falsehoood (assuming that God created me with the capacity to tell them apart and intended that I should exercise that capacity)? But then why should clarity and distinctness be the infallible mark of truth? Why not something else?

We have been exploring a possible interpretation of Descartes in which there is no inconsistency between the dream arguments and Descartes' final claims about knowing perceptual propositions with certainty, and knowing with certainty that we ourselves are awake. I have so far argued that the theory is unsuccessful as an attempt to show how we can know with certainty (infallibly) that we are awake. Now I shall argue that the theory is equally unsuccessful as an attempt to show how we can know perceptual propositions with certainty.

The theory attempts to show this, once again, by appealing to a coherence test. This appeal to a coherence test is clear in Descartes' explanation of what it is to perceive a perceptual fact clearly and distinctly. It is summed up at the end of the Sixth Meditation, just before Descartes proposes the coherence criterion of memory:

> . . . For knowing that all my senses more frequently indicate to me truth than falsehood respecting the things which concern that which is beneficial to the body, *and being able almost always to avail myself of many of them in order to examine one particular thing*, and, besides, *being able to make use of my memory in order to connect the present with the past*, and of my understanding which already has discovered all the causes of my errors, I ought no longer to fear that falsity may be found in matters every day presented to me by my senses . . . (Haldane and Ross, Vol. I, p. 198. My italics.)

There is a double reliance on coherence here. The first is in the first italicized phrase, where Descartes may plausibly be interpreted as saying that one necessary condition for discerning clarity and distinctness (the mark of truth) in a perceptual proposition is that all the relevant senses agree in its corroboration. Thus, I perceive a book only if my sight, smell, hearing, touch, and taste would all agree that the thing in front of me is a book.

The second reliance on coherence is in the second italicized phrase. There Descartes appeals to memory again, and hence to the coherence test of its reliability, in order to provide a way of determining which of my perceptual judgments are clear and distinct. For example, in order to be perceiving clearly and distinctly that there is a book in front of me, I must be able to "connect the perceptions which I have of [it] with the whole course of my life . . ." (Haldane and Ross, Vol. I, p. 199.) If I could not, then neither could I be certain that my present visual, tactual, auditory, olfactory, and gustatory experiences were not occurring in a dream. And if I could not be certain that they were not, I could not be certain that there was a book in front of me. And if I could not be certain of that, then I would not be perceiving clearly and distinctly that there is a book in front of me.

I have already argued that the coherence criterion for memory cannot provide for infallible knowledge by recollection. By similar reasoning, one could argue that the coherence of the relevant senses cannot provide for infallible perceptual knowledge. Let the testimony of all my senses converge on the proposition that there is a book in front of me. It is logically possible that I am having these experiences under the influence of a drug, or because of an unusual quantum jump in my brain, or because of pure chance. The probabilities for these are very low indeed; very low probability is not the same, however, as logical impossibility.

The probability of the proposition that there is a book in front of me, relative to the combined evidence of sense and memory, may be greater than its probability relative to the evidence of either alone. But no matter how close to certainty this probability came, it would not ever become infallible certainty.

I have come to the end of my argument that the system or theory we have been considering is not worked out satisfactorily by Descartes. The proof of the principle of clarity and distinctness is unconvincing. The coherence test for the reliability of memory and for the clarity and distinctness of perceptual propositions provides only for probability, not for certainty. There is no argument in Descartes to show that if coherence did not guarantee infallible—that is, not just probable—knowledge, then God would be a deceiver. There are further difficulties that we have not yet mentioned. We shall see in Part III that Descartes' arguments for the existence of God are inconclusive. Hence, the system we have been discussing is radically incomplete.

Summary and Assessment

AT THIS POINT, it will be useful to offer a summary of what we have found so far. We have found that there are two possible interpretations of Descartes' dream argument. The first commits us to the proposition that no one knows incorrigibly that he himself is awake, and that no one knows incorrigibly any perceptual facts. These conclusions are in conflict with Descartes' final pronouncements, in which he wants to be able to say that we can know with certainty that we ourselves are awake, and that we can know with certainty that certain perceptual propositions are true. The conclusions of the first interpretation of the dream argument follow from six premises, and from the concept of incorrigibility that enters into the formulation of some of them.

We can avoid the conclusions of the dream argument if we deny at least one of its assumptions. The concept of incorrigibility is inviolable; it is philosophically indispensable. It marks a distinction between those propositions that we are fully justified, and cannot be mistaken, in believing—whether or not God exists —solely on the basis of evidence present and "open" to our attentive mind, and propositions that are not of that kind. It is one of Descartes' fundamental contributions to philosophy to have recognized this distinction and its importance.

The first five premises of the dream argument are immediate consequences of the everyday conception of what dreams are, together with the judgmental theory of perception. I believe that these five premises are incontrovertibly true propositions because the conceptions from which they follow are sound. A number of philosophers have tried to discredit them. Their arguments seem to me to be faulty, but this is not the place to debate that issue. At any rate, I shall proceed on the assumption that premises (1)–(5) of the dream argument are true.

The remaining premise is (6), the criterion of incorrigible knowledge. I think that Descartes would not be altogether at ease with that as a criterion of knowledge in general. The places at which he introduces the coherence criterion show that he did see, however imprecisely, that some corrigible propositions that he wants to be able to say we know with certainty are not deducible from incorrigible ones. Examples of such propositions are: "I am not dreaming," "That thing is a book," "I remember that I had an egg for breakfast." Descartes is aware that scepticism stands unrefuted as long as propositions of that kind are not shown to be knowable. But they cannot be shown to be knowable unless the criterion of knowledge is liberalized.

The Cartesian system or theory that we considered as an alternative to the first interpretation of the dream argument incorporates a liberalized criterion of knowledge, which allows for the knowability of propositions that are not incorrigible and not deducible from any incorrigible premises. But we found that this system is incomplete. Moreover, the theory encounters further difficulties which we shall discuss in Part III. These are of such a nature as to suggest that this way of answering the sceptic is doomed to failure.

We could avoid the conclusions of the first interpretation of the dream argument by simply dropping the criterion of incorrigible knowledge that is assumed in that interpretation. But that would be an unwise move. The wiser move would be to liberalize the criterion in a manner different from the one that is assumed in the theory we have just been discussing.

It would be unwise to drop the criterion of incorrigible knowledge because it is a useful one. There are beliefs that satisfy it and there are also beliefs that fail to satisfy it. Like the concept of incorrigibility, it marks a distinction where there is a real and philosophically important difference, the difference between propositions that are known incorrigibly and those that are known but not incorrigibly. All propositions that are believed incorrigibly are known incorrigibly. A proposition is believed incorrigibly by someone if, and only if, that person believes it attentively, and also if his believing it attentively is logically sufficient for (entails) his knowing it. "I am in pain," "I have a throbbing pain," "I exist," "I am conscious," "A square has four sides"—these are all examples of propositions that it is possible to know incorrigibly. Moreover, some propositions that are corrigible can be known incorrigibly, but only if they are entailed by incorrigible premises.

For example, the proposition "Somebody is in pain" is corrigible for anyone. But there are two circumstances under which I can know that that proposition is true. One is by observing another person's behavior and circumstances. On the basis of such observations, I can know "beyond reasonable doubt," "with practical certainty," "with moral certainty," that somebody, namely, the person I am observing, is in pain. But I do not know this incorrigibly. No behavioral evidence now available to me entails that I cannot be mistaken in believing that somebody is now in pain.

But there is another way in which I can know that somebody is in pain. If I believe attentively that I am in pain, I know incorrigibly that I am in pain. And if, when I believe attentively that I am in pain, I also believe attentively that somebody is in pain, then I know incorrigibly that somebody is in pain—namely, myself. In order that I may know incorrigibly the corrigible proposition that somebody is in pain, that corrigible proposition must be entailed by a proposition that is incorrigible for me.

Thus it is possible to know incorrigibly many propositions in a manner that conforms to the criterion of incorrigible knowledge. "I am in pain" can be known incorrigibly by me because it is incorrigible for me. "Somebody is in pain" can be known incorrigibly by me because it is a corrigible proposition that is entailed by a proposition that is incorrigible for me.

In contrast to propositions that satisfy this criterion, however, there are many that fail to satisfy it. There are many propositions that it is possible to know, but not incorrigibly. "I am not dreaming," "He is in pain," "That thing is a book," "I had an egg for breakfast," can be known "with certainty," "beyond reasonable doubt," "with practical certainty," but they cannot be known incorrigibly. God's existence and His veracity will not change that fact. Nor are they likely to explain how one can be fully justified, and cannot possibly be mistaken, in believing, even attentively, propositions that are not known incorrigibly.

There is nothing wrong with the criterion of incorrigible knowledge. Therefore, the conclusions we have reached in the three parts of the dream argument are absolutely true. All perceptual propositions are corrigible for anyone. No one can know incorrigibly that he himself is awake. No one can have incorrigible knowledge of any perceptual proposition whatever.

We get into difficulty only if we treat the criterion of incorrigible knowledge as if it were a criterion for *all* knowledge. Descartes' way of trying to get out of this particular difficulty is by way of God, the principle of clarity and distinctness, and the relaxed criterion of knowledge involved in this system. But this system is not successfully worked out, and I submit that the prospects of working it out successfully are very dim indeed.

There is a way out that Descartes never considers seriously. It is to admit that perceptual propositions and, hence, the propositions of the empirical sciences (e.g., physics, chemistry, biology, behavioristic psychology) are not known to be true relative to the criterion of incorrigible knowledge. They do not constitute incorrigible knowledge. Nevertheless, there appear to be significant differences between careful empirical judgments and irresponsible guesswork. Descartes' attempts to explain these differences are unsatisfactory, as we have seen and will have further occasion to see. We would do better, I think, to admit that there are at least three distinct classes of propositions: (1) those that are either incorrigible for someone, or corrigible for him but entailed by propositions that are incorrigible for him; (2) those that the available evidence would confirm to some degree of probability; (3) those for or against which there is no evidence whatever. We would have, correspondingly, incorrigible knowledge, probable knowledge, and faith, if we chose to extend belief to propositions for or against which there is no evidence whatever. Whether we used the word 'knowledge' in such a way that in order to know we have to know incorrigibly, or in such a way that in order to know we have to know either incorrigibly or to some degree of probability, would be, from a strictly logical point of view, a verbal matter. The substantive distinctions will have been made.

Section 2

THE EVIL DEMON ARGUMENT

Comparison of the Dream and Evil Demon Arguments

THE CONCLUSIONS of the three parts of the dream argument follow from premises that in no sense refer to an evil demon. These same conclusions could be deduced by assuming that a malicious demon could have made it his business to deceive me. What if a demon who is no less deceitful than he is powerful causes me to believe that I am perceiving perceptual facts, when there are in fact no perceptual facts to be perceived? Such a demon could have created in me an ineluctable propensity to believe any number of perceptual propositions and at the same time not have created any physical objects at all. In that case, there would be no perceptual facts for me to perceive, and I would then be systematically deceived. No matter what perceptual proposition I believed to be true, that proposition would be false. Suppose I believe that there is a red ball in front of me. The proposition that I believe to be true entails that there exists a physical object. But if it is false that a physical object does exist, then the proposition that I believe to be true is false. And so for any perceptual proposition. Hence, I would not be fully justified, and could be mistaken, in believing any given perceptual proposition, no matter how much evidence I possessed, as long as I could not be certain that an evil demon was not deceiving me. From the fact that I would not be fully justified, and could be mistaken, in believing any perceptual proposition, it would follow that I do not know any perceptual propositions incorrigibly.

The evil demon can be deceiving me about perceptual facts even when I am awake. But he can also make me believe that I am awake when the fact is that I am dreaming. He may have created me in such a way that I was born asleep and have never waked up since I was born. And he causes me to dream frequently, and makes me believe, in my dream, that I am awake. As long as I do not know for certain that an evil demon is not deceiving me, I can never know for certain that I am not dreaming. But the circumstances that prevent me from knowing incorrigibly that I am not dreaming also prevent me from knowing incorrigibly that I am perceiving a perceptual fact. For, in order to know incorrigibly that I am perceiving a perceptual fact, I have to know incorrigibly that I am not dreaming. Hence, as long as I do not know that an evil demon cannot be deceiving me, I cannot know incorrigibly that I am perceiving a perceptual fact. In other words, I cannot know incorrigibly that a given perceptual proposition is true.

It is thus that the possibility of an evil demon can lead us to the same conclusions as the dream arguments did. But this does not mean that the dream arguments are superfluous. If Descartes can prove that God exists and that His goodness entails that He is not a deceiver, then we can know that an evil demon cannot be deceiving us. That, however, is still not enough to prove that it is possible for me to know that I am perceiving a perceptual fact. This is so because my knowing that it is impossible for me to be an evil demon's dupe is a necessary but *not* a *sufficient* condition of its being possible for me to know that I am perceiving a perceptual fact. It is not sufficient because in order for it to be possible for me to know incorrigibly that I am perceiving a perceptual fact, it must be possible for me to know incorrigibly that I am not dreaming. But to know incorrigibly that I am not dreaming, I must know more than simply that it cannot be that I am a demon's dupe. In order to overthrow the conclusion of the second part of the dream argument, I must know more than simply that I am not being deceived systematically. I must be able to know, and know incorrigibly, *when* it is that I am not dreaming. This shows that, as far as perceptual knowledge is concerned, the dream arguments are not performing quite the same function as, and are not merely a dispensable adjunct to, the evil demon arguments.

Furthermore, if my arguments toward the end of the preceding section are correct, Descartes has not succeeded in describing the conditions that are sufficient for our knowing infallibly that we are not dreaming and for knowing infallibly that we are perceiving a perceptual fact. Thus, the dream arguments are not only important in their own right; it is also true, unless I am mistaken, that Descartes has not succeeded in answering them.

The evil demon arguments, in turn, are not simply a duplication of the dream arguments in matters pertaining to the senses. They are relevant to other fundamental questions in the theory of knowledge. The dream arguments are specifically relevant to the problem of what we can know "from the senses or through the senses." The evil demon arguments are specifically concerned with whether or not we can know propositions that, if they are known at all, are not known "from the senses or through the senses," e.g., mathematical propositions.

Now there can be no question in anybody's mind, because Descartes is quite clear on the point, that Descartes wants to prove that God exists and that He is not a deceiver. Descartes needs the existence of God so that he can deduce the principle of clarity and distinctness. But there is a good deal of confusion as to what Descartes wants to do with the principle of clarity and distinctness itself. The confusion exists because Descartes himself is not clear on the point. Is he saying that anyone who does not know that he is not an evil demon's dupe cannot know that even his clearest and most distinct perceptions are true? There are places in the *Meditations* where that is what he seems to be saying or implying.

> For whether I am awake or asleep, two and three together always form five, and the square can never have more than four sides, and *it does not seem possible* that truths so clear and distinct can be suspected of falsity. . . . how do I know that I am not deceived [by a malignant God] every time I add two and three, or count the sides of a square, or judge of things yet simpler, if anything simpler can be imagined? (Haldane and Ross, Vol. I, p. 147. My italics.)

Two comments are in order on this passage. First, the question of the fallibility of such a judgment as that a square has four sides would arise even if I were making that judgment in a dream. Thus, my inability to tell whether I am awake does not pose a problem here. Second, note the shift from "The square can never have more than four sides" to *counting* the sides of *a square*. The first is a proposition of geometry. The second may involve a perceptual fact. Descartes could be saying that, whenever I count the sides of a figure on a blackboard or on a piece of paper, in order to determine whether or not the figure is a square, I may be caused by the demon to count four sides, when in fact the figure has some other number of sides. The quotation, therefore, does not in itself support unambiguously the hypothesis that what Descartes meant to say was that this simple geometrical proposition—that a square can never have more than four sides—can be reasonably doubted by anyone who does not know that he is not being deceived by a malignant demon.

But one passage early in the Third Meditation, which I have already cited, says unambiguously that an all-powerful God can easily "cause me to err even in those matters which I regard myself as intuiting in the most evident manner." (Haldane and Ross, Vol. I, p. 158. Cf. p. 70, above.) And this includes the very paradigms of incorrigibility, "I think" and "I exist"! In this passage Descartes is implying that anyone who is ignorant of the true God can never know infallibly even his own existence;

a fortiori, he can never know even such an absolutely evident mathematical truth as that a square has four sides. Now Descartes is badly mistaken here, and a little farther on I shall devote some time to explaining why this is a bad mistake.

But this erroneous doctrine is not a persistent theme in Descartes. In other passages he flatly asserts that there are some things that we can know incorrigibly, even if an evil demon is deceiving us. We can know, for example, that we ourselves exist. For how can the evil demon deceive me, if I do not exist? According to this, we do not need the principle of clarity and distinctness so that we can certify the truth of all our clear and distinct perceptions. For some of them are self-certifying and incorrigible for us. It is true, according to Descartes, that we must disprove the existence of the demon (by proving the existence of the true God) so that we can arrive at the principle of clarity and distinctness; and we do need that principle for various reasons, but not in order to validate our conviction that we know with certainty the truth of such clear and distinct propositions as "I exist."

In some passages, Descartes talks as if we need the principle in order to have "scientific" knowledge of theorems, that is, of deduced propositions. In passages outside the *Meditations,* Descartes distinguishes scientific knowledge (*scientia*) from mere persuasion (*persuasio*), as follows: When any reason whatever exists over and above what reasons we already possess that could impel us to doubt, we have mere persuasion. True knowledge (*scientia*) is persuasion from reasons so powerful that no reasons more powerful can shake them. And no one who is ignorant of God possesses such reasons as these.[13]

In still other passages Descartes talks as if we need the principle of clarity and distinctness in order to provide the warrant for our claims to knowing propositions that we *remember* having clearly and distinctly perceived by having proved them, but the proof of which we do not now have before our minds. He says this sort of thing toward the end of the Fifth Meditation. (Haldane and Ross, Vol. I, p. 184.)

Finally, according to Descartes we can know that we are not

[13] In a letter to Regius, dated May 24, 1640. See *Oeuvres de Descartes,* Charles Adam and Paul Tannery, eds. (Paris: Léopold Cerf, 1899), Vol. III, p. 65, 1. 4–7.

dreaming only if we can know the true God. For, as we saw in the preceding section, we can know that we are not dreaming only if we can distinguish our correct memory impressions from the erroneous ones. And we need God to guarantee memory. No one, therefore, who does not know that he cannot be a dupe to an evil demon can have ultimately unshakable grounds for his perceptual beliefs and for everything that is entailed by them.

Thus, although disproving the demon's existence is not a sufficient condition for countering the sceptical arguments against the senses, it is a necessary condition in Descartes' philosophical scheme. But the evil demon idea touches on matters that are not affected by the dream arguments. For, as Descartes says, whether I am asleep or awake when I believe that a square has four sides, my belief is true, unless I am being duped by an evil demon.

I have already given reasons for thinking that Descartes did not demonstrate either that we know the principle of clarity and distinctness to be true or that we have an incorrigible way of telling which of our memory impressions are veridical. There will be more to say on these issues in Part III, when we take up the problem of God's existence in some detail. But insofar as these two centrally important Cartesian claims about the principle of clarity and distinctness and about memory are not demonstrated, simply to have proved the impossibility of an evil demon will not accomplish what at various points Descartes hopes to accomplish. It will not prove, for example, that there is a real difference between *scientia* and *persuasio*. It will not provide the final reason why we know a proposition that we remember having perceived clearly and distinctly by virtue of our having proved it, yet the proof of which we do not now have before our minds.

In the rest of this section I shall discuss in some detail Descartes' questioning of the reliability of all our mathematical beliefs, including the simplest ones, e.g., that a square has four sides. The evil demon argument yields interesting conclusions about the corrigibility of certain mathematical propositions. But it simply does not affect the status of some mathematical propositions, namely, the simplest ones, e.g., that a square has four sides. Descartes is wrong whenever he shows signs of thinking otherwise.

Some Mathematical Propositions Are Incorrigible and Can Be Known Incorrigibly

I WANT FIRST to make clear why Descartes is mistaken whenever he says or implies that even the simplest mathematical propositions, such as that a square has four sides, are corrigible for us. Then I shall explain what is sound in Descartes' view of our knowledge of mathematical propositions.

Given our definition of incorrigibility, we can agree with Descartes that not all mathematical propositions are incorrigible for us. But our definition allows the possibility that some are, whether or not God exists, and it is here that we are in disagreement with Descartes. For, in the erroneous passages, Descartes is saying that, without God, no mathematical proposition can be known incorrigibly. The truth is that, whether or not we know that God exists, the proposition that a square has four sides is incorrigible for us and can be known incorrigibly.

That proposition is incorrigible for anyone who has the relevant concepts because (1) it is logically impossible for a man to believe attentively that all squares have four sides without knowing it, and (2) it is logically possible for a man to believe attentively that all squares have four sides. Whenever a man is attending to the features that define being a square, and at the same time believing occurrently that all squares have four sides, he is believing that proposition attentively. It is a fact, attested to by any standard dictionary, that having four sides is one of the defining characteristics of being a square. Moreover, it is logically impossible to believe attentively that all squares have four sides and not to know it. This is a consequence of the fact that it is logically impossible for a man to believe *simpliciter* that all squares have four sides and not to know it. The supposition that a man believes that all squares have four sides without knowing it entails a contradiction. For "S believes that all squares have four sides" entails "S has the concept of a square." This, in turn, entails "S knows that all squares have four sides." The supposition, therefore, entails the contradiction that S does and does not know that all squares have four sides. Hence, it is logically impossible to believe, without knowing, that all squares have four sides. Therefore, it is logically impossible to believe attentively, without knowing, that proposition. This and the fact that it is possible for a man to believe attentively that all squares have four sides is logically equivalent to the proposition that "All squares have four sides" is incorrigible for anyone. Hence the proposition about the square can be known incorrigibly by anyone. In order for a man to know incorrigibly that p, it is sufficient that at one and the same time he be believing attentively that p and that p be incorrigible for him.

We ought to be clear that the incorrigibility for anyone of "A square has four sides" and the possibility of knowing it incorrigibly do not depend upon linguistic factors. I may misspeak my thought that a square has four sides by expressing it through uttering the sentence, 'A triangle has four sides'. The property upon which I am focusing attention is the property of being a square. The thought that I am thinking is the thought that a square has four sides. What I call the object of my thought does not change that fact. I may even mistakenly believe that the correct word in English for a square is the word 'triangle'. But this is only a mistake about what a word means in a certain language. It is not a mistake about what a square is. Either because of a slip of the tongue or because of a misapprehension about the meaning of the word 'triangle', I may utter the sentence 'A triangle has four sides' to express my attentive belief that a square has four sides. But in those circumstances what I mean by the sentence 'A triangle has four sides' is that a square has four sides. And my belief is that a square has four sides.

All of this refutes the claim that Descartes sometimes makes, to the effect that, without a disproof of the evil demon through a proof of the true God, even our simplest mathematical beliefs may be false. I have given in detail a counter-example to that claim. And it is interesting to note that, in my counter-example, every argument I have used and every assumption I have made is strictly Cartesian, either in the letter or in the spirit. That is to say, everything one needs in order to correct Descartes' mistakes in these matters one can find in Descartes himself, at least by implication. Descartes is simply not of one mind about these things.

The Impossibility in Principle of Being Deceived About Every Mathematical Proposition

I HAVE REFUTED by means of a counter-example Descartes' erroneous doctrine that *no* mathematical proposition is incorrigible for anyone. This doctrine is true only if one may be mistaken about *any* mathematical proposition at all. The evil demon is a metaphor for this possibility. In aberrant moments, Descartes assumes that this is a real possibility. I shall now try to explain why this assumption is *necessarily* false. We do not need this further examination, if our sole objective is to prove the falsity of the doctrine that *no* mathematical proposition is incorrigible for anyone. The counter-example has already done that (assuming, of course, that it is a good counter-example). The value of showing that the assumption entailed by the doctrine *cannot* be true is that, by seeing *why* this is so, we ourselves may learn much that is worth knowing.

We have already noted that, in the opening paragraphs of the Third Meditation, Descartes confesses to an ambivalence. He admits that, if he concentrates on the things that he conceives clearly and distinctly, there is absolutely no doubt in his mind that they are true:

> . . . when I direct my attention to things which I believe myself to perceive very clearly, I am so persuaded of their truth that I let myself break out into words such as these: Let who will deceive me. He can never cause me to be nothing while I think that I exist, or some day cause it to be true to say that I have never existed, it being true to say now that I exist, or that two and three make more or less than five, or any such thing in which I see a manifest contradiction. (Haldane and Ross, Vol. I, pp. 158–159.)

Descartes does not here mention the proposition "A square has four sides." But from the context here and from his earlier juxtaposition of that proposition with the arithmetical one, "Two and three make five," in the First Meditation (Haldane and Ross, Vol. I, p. 147) it is quite clear that "A square has four sides" is one of the cases in point. On the other hand, says Descartes, when I think that perhaps an omnipotent God is deceiving me,

"I am constrained to confess that it is easy for Him, if He wishes it, to cause me to err, even about matters which I regard myself to be intuiting in the most evident manner." (Haldane and Ross, Vol. I, p. 158. With corrections in the translation.) Descartes makes it clear that the doubt is a second-order doubt. It is not directly a doubt concerning such a proposition as "A square has four sides." The doubt is "tenuous" and "so to speak, metaphysical," says Descartes. It is a doubt that may be better understood by reference to the distinction between *scientia* and *persuasio,* which was mentioned earlier. *Scientia* is a technical term in Descartes (Fr. *science*); it is used only in connection with theorems. But in the present context Descartes is doubting even clearly and distinctly intuited "axiomatic" propositions. He is here saying that our conviction of their truth is shakable; it is only *persuasio.* It becomes unshakable knowledge only if the principle of clarity and distinctness is deduced from God's existence and veracity. The doubt about such a proposition as "A square has four sides" is a second-order doubt, in that *it does not arise about the proposition directly.* I may doubt that I shall live to be one hundred and fifty years old, and this is a reasonable doubt, given actuarial facts. The doubt about a square having four sides arises only when it is suggested that perhaps even our most evident intuitions are false. To allay that doubt, Descartes thinks that we need to prove God's existence and from that the principle of clarity and distinctness.

According to Descartes, the geometrical proposition "A square has four sides" may be reasonably doubted for one last-ditch reason alone, namely, that it may be that an all-powerful God is deceiving us, even about such manifest truths. The second-order doubt is in the question: Have I blocked all avenues to any possible reasonable doubt of even the most manifest truths? As long as I have not answered that question, I may reasonably doubt such first-order propositions as the one about squares, no matter how indubitable they seem to be in themselves.

To show that this second-order, "metaphysical" doubt is reasonable, Descartes must assume (1) that it is possible to be deceived even about such simple mathematical propositions as the proposition that every square has four sides, and (2) that if this is possible, then no mathematical proposition is either incorrigible for us or capable of being known incorrigibly by us. I shall show that both assumptions are necessarily false: there is a sense in which we can be deceived about certain necessarily true propositions, but there is no sense in which we can be deceived about such necessarily true propositions as "All squares have four sides." And, in any case, some mathematical propositions are incorrigible for us. In Section 7 of Part III I shall argue that the very possibility that Descartes envisages in (1) makes it impossible to prove anything. What I have called 'the erroneous doctrine in Descartes' is a form of intellectual hara-kiri.

What then, are we to understand by Descartes' assumption that perhaps an evil spirit, no less clever and deceitful than powerful, wills it that I be deceived even about such a simple and evident proposition as that a square has four sides? What are the ways in which one being, X, deceives another, Y, about a proposition, p? Ordinarily we assume that X deceives Y about p only if either (i) X intentionally brings it about that Y believes that p, when in fact p is false or (ii) X intentionally brings it about that Y believes that it is not the case that p, when it is the case that p.

But this ordinary conception of the logically necessary conditions for being deceived by someone does not make it possible to be deceived even about such propositions as "A square has four sides." We have proved that this proposition is of a kind that it is impossible to believe and not to know. This entails that it is impossible to believe it at a time when it is false. Therefore, it is impossible to be deceived about that proposition in the manner specified in (i).

The second way of being deceived, specified under (ii), requires that it be possible for a man to believe a very simple and evident contradiction. To believe that it is not the case that a square has four sides is to believe that there are squares that do not have four sides. This is a simple and evident contradiction, which can be detected by anyone who has the concept of square. And someone who does not have the concept can believe neither the true proposition that all squares have four sides nor its denial. Now it is by no means evident that a person can believe a simple and evident contradiction. On the contrary, it seems evident that he cannot. Thus, (i) and (ii) will not explain to everyone's satisfaction how a person can be deceived about such simple and evident propositions as the one about the square.

Therefore, in order to make room for the possibility of being deceived about at least some necessarily true propositions, the two clauses, (i) and (ii), which are part of what in everyday life we regard as ways of being deceived, have to be supplemented. The result is a *technical* concept, E(Z):

E(Z): "X deceives Y about p" entails either that (i) X intentionally brings it about that Y believes that p, although p is false, or that (ii) X intentionally brings it about that Y believes that it is not the case that p, although it is the case that p, or that (iii) X intentionally brings it about that Y believes that p, although it is not the case that Y knows that p.

Clause (iii) is perfectly suited to some propositions that are necessarily true. It is conceivable that a man may believe a proposition that is in fact necessarily true, and yet fail to know that proposition. He may not know because he believes it for the wrong reason, or for an inadequate reason, or for no reason at all. The addition of clause (iii) is sufficient to give sense to the notion of being deceived about some necessarily true propositions, without having to assume that a man can believe a simple and evident contradiction. This, in turn, enables us to consider the supposition that possibly one is never fully justified in believing certain necessarily true propositions.

We now have in E(Z) a concept that explains how one may be deceived about some necessarily true propositions. We need it for the evil demon arguments. However, before we formulate them, note that the addition of clause (iii) does not make it possible for us to be deceived about such propositions as "All squares have four sides." For we have already argued that it is impossible to believe that proposition and not to know it. In other words, it seems that there is no sensible explanation of how a person may be deceived about such simple and evident propositions as the one about the square.

Besides, even if it were possible for a person to believe a necessarily false proposition, such as "Not all squares have four sides," it would not follow that the necessarily true negation of it is corrigible for everyone. The assumption that it is logically possible for a person to believe that some squares do not have four sides is no reason whatever for saying that the proposition "All squares have four sides" is corrigible for everyone. The proposition is corrigible for me if it is logically possible that I believe attentively that it is true, without knowing that it is true. But we have already argued at length that this condition cannot be fulfilled in the case of "All squares have four sides." Hence, at any time when I believe attentively that a square has four sides, I know incorrigibly that a square has four sides.

Thus, while in E(Z) we have given a sense to the notion of being deceived about some necessarily true propositions, we have found that in that sense it is impossible to be deceived about certain very simple and evident necessarily true propositions—for example, the mathematical proposition "All squares have four sides."

The Evil Demon Arguments

THE TRUTH of the matter is this: some mathematical propositions are incorrigible for us, and some are not. There is an evil demon argument that proves that, if a mathematical proposition answers to a certain description, then it is not incorrigible for us. Let us call it 'Evil Demon Argument I'. The formal version of this argument is in Appendix II, along with the formal version of Evil Demon Argument II and what I call 'The Abortive Argument'. Here I give them informally.

Let 'p is M' mean: p is a mathematical proposition such that it is possible either to believe attentively that p is true when it is really false, or to believe attentively that p is false when in fact it is true. The first evil demon argument begins with the assumption that it is possible for a man to believe attentively that p (where p is M), while the evil demon is deceiving him about p. Now recall E(Z). If the evil demon is deceiving me in the manner of the first alternative, then I believe that p, while p is false. This entails that I fail to know that p. According to the second alternative, I believe that p is false, while p is true. Again, it follows that I fail to know that p.[14] There remains the third alternative,

14 In this step I am assuming that "S believes that p" entails "It is not the case that S believes that not p." I use this principle in the evil demon arguments. The principle I am assuming seems to be very basic. I am unable to think of any principle more evident than it from which to deduce it. I believe that the principle is logically connected with our conception of

according to which I believe that p, but fail to know it. This, too entails that I do not know that p. Hence, if the evil demon is deceiving me about p at all, it follows that I do not know that p. Hence, it is possible for a man to believe attentively that p and yet not know that p. Hence, any proposition that is M is corrigible for anyone.

Given this conclusion, if there are propositions that are M, then there are mathematical propositions that are corrigible for us. But there are propositions that are M. Here is an example. Add fifty numbers, n_1 to n_{50}, each number running into the billions. Check and recheck your addition. Let others check it. Let computers check it. Let all the checks tally. Still, it is possible to believe attentively that $n_1 + n_2 + n_3 \ldots n_{50} = m$, when in fact that equation is false. If the evil demon played his tricks on us, he could see to it that all of us, and the computers, made some mistake in addition, perhaps the same in every case or a different mistake for every different case. It does not matter, just as long as we all come out with the same wrong total, and are prevented from noticing the error. The fact that all the checks tally is a strong reason for believing that the answer is right, while, by hypothesis, it is wrong. Hence, in this instance, it is possible both to believe attentively that the answer is right and the answer to be wrong.

Or, the evil demon could let us all obtain the correct total, but make us think that the correct total is a wrong answer. He could do this by causing us to make two mistakes in addition, one of which cancels the other, and therefore the sum comes out right. But the demon allows us to notice only one of the mistakes. We

---

believing that p. As far as I have been able to determine, this principle is not deducible from the assumption that it is impossible for anyone to believe a proposition and its contradictory at the same time. But if we assume the principle that "S believes that p" entails "It is not the case that S believes that not p," we can deduce that no one can believe an explicit contradiction. For, "S believes that (p and not p)" entails "S believes that p, and S believes that not p." But, by my principle, "S believes that not p" entails "It is not the case that S believes that p." Hence, "S believes that (p and not p)" entails the self-contradictory proposition "S believes that p, and it is not the case that S believes that p." Hence, it is impossible that S believes that (p and not p). Although the principle I am assuming seems self-evident to me, there may be those who will find it questionable. My evil demon arguments will not persuade them.

then have grounds for believing that the sum is wrong, when in fact it is right. Hence, it is possible both to believe attentively that the sum is wrong and for the sum to be correct.

Thus, it is possible either for S to believe attentively that the sum is correct when it is not, or for S to believe attentively that the sum is incorrect when it is correct. Therefore, the equation for the sum is a proposition that is M. Hence, it is a mathematical proposition that is corrigible for anyone.

The conclusion of evil demon argument I is analogous to the conclusion of the first part of the dream argument. That conclusion is that any perceptual proposition is corrigible for anyone. Evil demon argument I proves the corrigibility for anyone of a certain class of mathematical propositions, namely, those that are M. Moreover, we know that there are propositions that are M.

The next evil demon argument, argument II, yields a conclusion that is analogous to the conclusion of the second part of the dream argument. Assume that: if p is a proposition of kind M, and a contingent proposition, q, entails that S knows that p, then it is possible at the same time that S believes attentively that q and that the evil demon is deceiving S about q. Let there be a proposition, p, which is M, and let there be a contingent proposition, q, which entails that S knows that p. Under these circumstances, it is possible at the same time that S believes attentively that q and that the evil demon is deceiving S about q. But by E(Z), if the evil demon is deceiving S about q, at least one of these situations must hold: S believes that q, but q is false, which entails that S does not know that q; or S believes that q is false, but q is in fact true. Again, it follows that S fails to know that q. Lastly, S believes that q but does not know that q, which again entails that S does not know that q. Thus, if the evil demon is deceiving S about q, then S does not know that q. Therefore, it is possible at the same time that S believes attentively that q and that S does not know that q. Hence, q is corrigible for S. Therefore, any contingent proposition is corrigible for anyone, if it entails that the man in question knows that a proposition of kind M is true.

This intermediate conclusion is analogous to an intermediate conclusion in the second part of the dream argument. That conclusion[15] is that there is no proposition that is incorrigible for anyone, from which he can deduce that he himself is not dream-

[15] See Step (12), Evil Demon Argument II, Appendix II.

ing. The analogous intermediate conclusion of the second evil demon argument is that no contingent proposition that is incorrigible for someone entails that he knows that p, where p is a proposition of kind M.

The second evil demon argument can be continued so as to yield a conclusion that is analogous to the final conclusion of the second part of the dream argument. That conclusion, you will recall, is that no one knows incorrigibly that he himself is not dreaming. We get an analogous conclusion that no one knows incorrigibly that he himself knows that a proposition of kind M is true. We have already proved that any contingent proposition is corrigible for anyone, if it entails that the person in question knows that a proposition of kind M is true. But "S knows that p" (where p is a proposition of kind M) is a contingent proposition that entails itself. Therefore, it is corrigible for anyone, and no necessarily true proposition entails it. Therefore, any proposition that entails it is either corrigible for S or necessarily false. But every necessarily false proposition is corrigible for S. Therefore, any proposition that entails "S knows that p" is corrigible for S. It follows by the criterion of incorrigible knowledge that no one knows incorrigibly that he himself knows that p (where p is a proposition of kind M). We have established a substantive point: namely, that no one has incorrigible knowledge that he knows a proposition of kind M.

We must be absolutely clear as to what we have proved and what we have not. We have proved that no one has incorrigible knowledge that he himself knows a mathematical proposition of kind M. We have *not* proved that no one knows a mathematical proposition of kind M. Indeed, as far as I can tell, there is no evil demon argument that is analogous to the third part of the dream argument. Either one of two evil demon conclusions would be analogous to the conclusion of the third part of the dream argument: either (1) no proposition of kind M is known to anyone, or (2) no proposition of kind M is known incorrigibly to anyone. If we could prove (1), we could prove (2) because (2) is an immediate consequence of (1). But (1) cannot be proved. The abortive argument will show this. And there seems to be no independent proof of (2) itself. The most we get out of the evil demon argument is that (a) no proposition of the sort M is incorrigible for anyone and (b) that no one has incorrigible knowledge that he himself knows a proposition of kind M.

Let me now explain why I believe that no evil demon argument can prove that no one knows a proposition that is M. We are stopped by the second and third disjunctive conditions entailed by a proposition of the form: X is deceiving Y about p. The second condition is that S believes that not p, although p is true. The third condition is that S believes that p, but it is not the case that S knows that p. Those clauses in E(Z) block any radically sceptical argument with respect to mathematical propositions. The best way to see this is to set into motion such an argument and see how far it takes us. I shall call this 'the abortive evil demon argument'. For the formal rendition of it, see Appendix II.

To get the abortive argument under way, we need a premise that is analogous to the premise of the first dream argument. Here it is: It is possible at the same time that a man believes attentively that he himself knows a mathematical proposition of kind M and that the evil demon is deceiving him about the proposition that he himself knows a mathematical proposition of kind M. Once again, if it is possible that the evil demon is deceiving the man about that proposition, at least one of the three conditions of E(Z) must be satisfied. And, in order to reach a radically sceptical conclusion, every one of the three conditions must entail that the man in question does not know that he himself knows a mathematical proposition of kind M. Now it is only the first necessary condition of the person's being deceived that entails that the person does not know a mathematical proposition of kind M. The second and third conditions do not entail this.

The relevant instance of condition (ii) of E(Z) is this. The man believes that it is false that he himself knows that p, when as a matter of fact he does know that p. But this does not entail that it is false that the man knows that p. "S believes that it is false that he himself knows that p" does not entail "It is false that S knows that p." Consider the case of a man who believes attentively that a square has four sides, but who is ignorant of the fact that his believing this attentively entails his knowing it incorrigibly. In his ignorance of this entailment, the man may actually believe that it is not the case that he himself knows that a square has four sides. Here we have a case of a man who believes that it is false that he himself knows that p, at a time when he does know that p, and knows it incorrigibly. Hence the abortive argument aborts first at this point. For in order for us to reach the conclusion that no one knows a proposition that is M, *every one* of the three alternatives of E(Z) must entail that the man does not know that p.

The argument is stopped again in connection with the third alternative of E(Z). The relevant instance of condition (iii) of E(Z) is: the man believes that he himself knows a proposition of kind M, but it is false that he knows that he knows that proposition. This entails that it is false that the man knows that he himself knows that proposition. If the argument is to go through, "S believes that S knows that p, but it is not the case that S knows that S knows that p" must entail that "It is not the case that S knows that p." But there is no such entailment, not even in the case of propositions of the sort M. It is false that for any proposition, p, "It is not the case that S knows that S knows that p" entails "It is not the case that S knows that p." A three-year-old child may know that candy is sweet, and yet not know that he knows that candy is sweet. He may not know that he knows because he does not know what it is to know that something is so.

Although it is granted that there is not, in every case, entailment from "It is not the case that S knows that S knows that p" to "It is not the case that S knows that p," it might be supposed that in some cases the entailment holds—for example, in the case of propositions that are M. The argument for this would run as follows:

First Step: If p is M, then
(1) a man knows that p
    if, and only if,
(2) he has a demonstrative proof that p is true.
Second Step: If p is M, then
(2) a man has demonstrative proof that p is true
    if, and only if,
(3) there is a proposition, q, not identical with p; the man knows that q is true; and he knows, without assuming that p is true, that q entails p.
Third Step: If p is M, then
(3) is true
    if, and only if,

(4) the man knows that (3) is true.

Fourth Step: Therefore, if p is M, then

(1) a man knows that p is true
   if, and only if,
(4) he knows that (3) is true.

Fifth Step: Therefore, if p is M, then

(1) a man knows that p is true if, and only if, he knows that (2) he himself has a demonstrative proof that p is true.

Sixth Step: Therefore, if p is M, then

(1) a man knows that p is true if, and only if, he knows that (1) he himself knows that p is true.

The sixth step entails that if p is M, then, if a man does not know that he himself knows that p, he does not know that p. In order to arrive at the conclusion that this is true, we must assume that the third step is true. But it is in fact false. For the man in question to know that (3) is true, he has to know that he himself knows that q is true, and also that he himself knows, without assuming that p is true, that q entails p. But surely in order to know that q is true, the man does not have to know that he knows it. He may know that q is true because (a) he attentively believes that q, and (b) attentively believing that q entails knowing incorrigibly that q. But he may not know that he knows that q because he lacks the concept of knowledge. Hence, even in the case of propositions that are such that to know they are true is the same thing as to have demonstrative proof that they are true, not knowing that one knows they are true does not entail not knowing that they are true. Because of this, the abortive proof aborts also in connection with clause (iii) of E(Z).

The abortive argument is one way of showing that there is no proof of the proposition: (1) No one knows a proposition of kind M. However, the abortive argument does not show that there is no way of proving that (2) no one knows incorrigibly a proposition of kind M. It simply seems to be true that no true evil demon premises together with the criterion of incorrigible knowledge will entail (2).

I have argued that Descartes is mistaken in those passages in the *Meditations* in which he thinks that any part of the evil demon argument proves that even the simplest mathematical propositions, such as the one about a square having four sides, are corrigible for anyone, and that the only way a person may be ultimately assured of their truth is by appeal to the veracity of the true God. I have argued also that Descartes is right only insofar as *some* mathematical propositions are corrigible for anyone, and that with respect to those particular mathematical propositions, it is impossible to find an incorrigible contingent proposition that entails that a person knows some particular mathematical propositions that belong in this category. Thus, while the criterion of knowledge is instrumental in yielding the conclusion that no one knows incorrigibly any perceptual facts, it has no analogous implications regarding our knowledge of mathematical propositions. The abortive argument thus aborts in two places. In the first, it aborts because of a condition that is part of what we ordinarily understand by being deceived. This is condition (ii) of E(Z). In the second, it aborts because we had to add a *technical* condition, (iii) of E(Z), in order even to consider the supposition that an evil demon might be deceiving us (i.e., that we could be mistaken) about necessarily true propositions. If it is agreed that Descartes cannot show, as indeed no one can, that even the simplest mathematical propositions, e.g., that a square has four sides, are corrigible for us; if it is agreed that Descartes simply made a mistake whenever he thought otherwise, then it must be conceded that the basic assumptions of the evil demon argument do not imply radical scepticism with respect to mathematics.

This result is in accord with Descartes' philosophical intentions. Descartes does not intend that his initial critical doubts should carry him to radically sceptical conclusions about perceptual propositions, or about propositions of the form: S is perceiving a physical object, or about mathematical propositions. His ultimate objective includes proving that, although they are themselves corrigible for us, contingent propositions such as "I am perceiving a material object" or "The object over there is oblong and brown and is exactly three yards away from the wall," as well as corrigible mathematical propositions, can be known either by being deduced from propositions that are incorrigible for us or because God guarantees their truth.

In the preceding section I suggested that Descartes has no sound argument to offer either for the principle of clarity and distinctness, or for the claim that that principle can help us deduce that, when the senses, memory, and reason corroborate each other, we know with certainty that we are not dreaming. Now we find Descartes talking as if, in order to know that certain mathematical propositions are true, we have to have demonstrated the principle of clarity and distinctness, starting from the proposition that God exists. But the appeal to God's veracity works no better in mathematics than it does in connection with perceptual judgments.

Again there is a way out. There are mathematical propositions that are incorrigible for anyone, e.g., "A square has four sides." There are, on the other hand, mathematical propositions that are corrigible for anyone. Fermat's so-called last theorem is one such proposition. The theorem states that $x^n + y^n = z^n$ is false for every positive integer value of x, y, z, and n, provided that $n > 2$. There is no known proof or disproof of it. However, a very large number of its instances have been found to be true, and none found to be false. Anyone who believed the theorem at a time when he had before his mind a number of the confirming instances and no disconfirming instance, would be believing the theorem attentively. But in this case attentive belief would not entail knowledge. Hence, Fermat's last theorem is corrigible for anyone. Believing it attentively but not knowing it are jointly possible. Mathematicians say that they would know Fermat's "theorem" to be true, if they were able to deduce it from incorrigible mathematical premises. God in that case is superfluous and irrelevant. Although Fermat's theorem is corrigible for anyone, it would be known incorrigibly if it were deduced from premises that are incorrigible for anyone. And for all we know, it may be deducible from such premises. However, nothing short of an actual mathematical proof or disproof of the theorem would be an acceptable justification for saying that we knew the theorem or its denial.

"I THINK, I EXIST"

WE NOW TURN to the propositions, "I think" and "I exist." Thus far we have found that in spite of some confusions Descartes can justly be credited with the correct insight that there are incorrigible propositions that are necessarily true and hypothetical. "A square has four sides" is a case in point. Descartes insists in several places in the *Meditations* that this sort of proposition neither says nor implies that there are actual square objects. It simply says that if a thing is a square, then it has four sides. Whether or not there are actual squares is not a question for the (pure) mathematician. "If there are squares, then every one of them has four sides" is an *hypothetical* proposition. "There are squares" is an *existential* proposition. "There are squares" is contingent and corrigible.

Descartes also believes that there is an incorrigible, necessarily true, and existential proposition, namely, "God exists." When we come to Descartes' ontological argument in Part III, Section 5, we shall see that Descartes believes that he can deduce the existence of God from the nature of God. Propositions that explicate the nature of an entity are necessarily true. Thus, "A square has four sides" is necessarily true because having four sides is part of the definition of a square. The proposition simply explicates one of the logically necessary conditions for being a square. Descartes believes that to exist is one of the defining characteristics of God, just as having four sides is one of the defining characteristics of being a square. If Descartes is right, the proposition that God exists must be necessarily true. Furthermore, if existence is one of God's essential attributes, then "God exists" must be incorrigible for anyone. The contrary assumption entails a contradiction. The argument that proves this is exactly like the one we used to prove that "All squares have four sides" is incorrigible for anyone. In "God exists," then, if Descartes is right, we would have an incorrigible proposition that is necessarily true but *existential*. It is supposed to be equivalent to "There exists a being than whom nothing greater can be conceived."

In "I exist" we have an instance of still another category. "I exist" is contingent, incorrigible for me, and existential. Descartes believes that this proposition and its companion, "I think," are of central importance in his system. They are its "Archimedean fulcrum," the point on which everything else in Descartes' philosophical system turns. This, at any rate, is the impression that Descartes himself gives in many places. Specifically, he sometimes gives the impression that "I think, I exist" is the proper starting point for reconstructing the foundations of all the sciences. By 'science', by the way, he does not mean just mathematics and the experimental sciences. He means all systematic knowledge, i.e., all knowledge that consists of beginning at the relevant logical starting points and drawing out their full implications. In some places in the *Meditations,* Descartes gives the impression that these two incontrovertible truths, "I think" and "I exist" (or if you will, their conjunction), exhibit the standard for selecting other incontrovertible truths from which, as premises, we are to deduce (i) that God exists, (ii) that He cannot be a deceiver, (iii) that, therefore, the principle of clarity and distinctness is universally valid, (iv) that there exists a material world, (v) that we can know this through our perceptual experiences, (vi) that the human mind is essentially and exclusively a conscious substance, and (vii) that the mind interacts with a body that is its own.

The Distinctive Features of the Cogito* Propositions

BUT FIRST Descartes has to show that "I think" and "I exist" do have certain quite remarkable properties: that they are incorrigible; that they are known incorrigibly; that they cannot be

---

* As a convenient abbreviation, I shall use the expression 'The *cogito* propositions' to refer to "I think" and "I exist." The Latin for "I think" is *cogito*.

denied, disbelieved, or doubted, without a special kind of absurdity. Descartes has original insights about these propositions, and it may be because he is struggling to say something new that he does not quite succeed in saying it clearly.

"I think, therefore, i am": deduction or intuition?

To begin with, there is some confusion concerning Descartes' formula: "I think, therefore, I am." In the *Discourse on Method,* which was written before the *Meditations,* Descartes says: "I think, therefore I am." *Cogito, ergo sum.* This sounds as if Descartes is offering the following argument:

> If I think, then I exist.
> I think.
> ∴ I exist.

Such an argument is both valid and sound. Its first premise is necessarily true. To know that it is true we need no argument: it is self-evident. Now if a conditional proposition is necessarily true, then its antecedent entails its consequent. Hence, "I think" entails "I exist." The above is also sound. A sound argument is a valid deductive argument whose premises are true. The argument is sound because it comes to this: "I am (now) thinking" entails "I (now) exist," and there are times when "I am (now) thinking" is true. But the conclusion of a sound inference is true. Hence, there are times when "I (now) exist" is true.

That "I think" entails "I exist" is all there is to the contention that one can prove one exists from the fact that one is thinking, and that, therefore, "I think" is "logically prior" to "I exist." "I think" entails "I exist." But "I exist" does not entail "I think." It is true that my asserting the proposition that I exist entails that I think (I am conscious); but that is a different entailment. Some philosophers have said that my existence is "ontologically" prior to my thinking. In simple logical terms this means that my existence is a logically necessary condition of my being conscious. While it is logically necessary, it is not logically sufficient, however, for it is possible that I exist even though I am wholly unconscious. On the other hand, my being conscious is logically sufficient, although not logically necessary, for my existing.

Some of Descartes' contemporaries criticized him by arguing as follows. At the start Descartes doubts everything, including deduction. The two propositions that he does not doubt are "I think" and "I exist." But to prove that he who thinks cannot doubt that he exists, Descartes argues:

> If I think, then I exist.
> I think.
> ∴ I exist.

This is a deduction. If he means what he says, namely, that at the start, before he has proved God's existence, he doubts all deductions, then he cannot *prove* that he who thinks cannot doubt that he exists.

To this Descartes replied as follows:

He who says, 'I think, hence I am, or I exist', does not deduce existence from thought by a syllogism, but, by a simple intuition of the mind, recognizes it as if it were a thing that is known *per se*. This is evident from the fact that if it were syllogistically deduced, the major premise, *that everything that thinks, is, or exists*, would have to be known previously; but yet that has rather been learned from the experience of the individual—that unless he exists, he cannot think. For our mind is so constituted by nature that general propositions are formed out of the knowledge of particulars. (Haldane and Ross, Vol. II, p. 38.[16])

This passage is not entirely clear, but one thing does seem to be clear in it. Descartes seems to be anxious to deny that he is *deducing* his own existence. He seems to be asserting that one *recognizes* one's own existence "by a simple intuition of the mind . . . as if it were known *per se*." These phrases are suggestive and pregnant at the same time that they are obscure. They could mislead us into thinking that "I exist" (and "I think") are self-evident because they are necessarily true propositions. But "I exist" and "I think" are *not* necessarily true propositions. They are contingent (neither necessarily true nor necessarily false). Nevertheless, as we shall see, they have remarkable properties. "I think" and "I exist" are incorrigible for me. Moreover, I can-

[16] I have corrected the translation to accord with the Latin original. See Adam and Tannery, *Oeuvres de Descartes*, Vol. VII, p. 140, 1. 22–23.

not deny, disbelieve, or doubt them, without a special kind of absurdity. None of these conceptual truths would be revealed if we read "I think, therefore I am" as simply a deductive proof of my existence. Taken simply as a deductive proof of my existence, the argument offers not the slightest hint about the significant properties of "I think" and "I exist." It does not show that "I exist" is incorrigible for me. It is not necessary that the conclusion of a valid deductive argument be incorrigible for me, if its premises are. For example,

> I am in pain.
> ∴ Somebody is in pain.

is a valid deductive argument. Its premise is incorrigible for me but its conclusion is not. Hence, even if both "If I think, then I exist" and "I think" were incorrigible for me, the fact that they imply "I exist" would in no way prove that "I exist" is incorrigible for me. All in all, it is missing the point to say that Descartes is trying to prove that he exists. The point Descartes is trying to make is that "I think" and "I exist" are both incorrigible for me, and that neither may be disbelieved, denied, or doubted sensibly. In other words, Descartes is trying to say something about certain philosophically important properties of "I think" and "I exist." He is not just trying to "prove" that he exists, although, in doing what he is doing, he is also "proving" that he exists.

The Distinctive Features of "I Exist"

LET US first concentrate on "I exist." To begin with, recall the conclusion of the first part of the dream argument: that perceptual propositions are corrigible for anyone. And remember that, according to the third part of the dream argument, no one knows incorrigibly a perceptual proposition. Remember, finally, that the conclusion of the third part of the dream argument entails that we have no grounds from perceptual experience alone for deducing that we ourselves are perceiving material objects. Hence, if we follow Descartes' instructions, we must pursue our philosophical investigations without assuming that there are physical objects. For he explicitly exhorts us to assume nothing that we do not know incorrigibly. Hence, at the beginning of the inquiry, we are not to assume that the subject, I, of "I think" or of "I exist" is a physical object.

Very well. I am resolved to do without the assumption that I am a body. Am I then nothing? Not at all. That the evil demon is deceiving me about some proposition or other entails that I exist. It is not possible for the evil demon to deceive me unless I am there to be deceived.

What is more, the proposition that I exist is incorrigible for me. It is impossible for me to believe attentively that I exist and not know that I exist.

This, I think, is what Descartes means to say when he says that I recognize that I exist "by a simple intuition of the mind . . . as if it were a thing that is known *per se*." I would explain that as follows: In order for me to know "by a simple intuition of the mind" that I exist, it is necessary that there be a certain entailment, but an *entailment,* and not an inference. "I think (i.e. I imagine, reason, doubt, believe, am persuaded, am deceived, have sensations, feelings, moods, impressions, or daydreams, etc.)" *entails* "I exist." But in order to intuit the fact that I exist I do not have to infer that I exist from the fact that I think. It is sufficient that I believe attentively that I exist. It is impossible for me to believe attentively that I exist and not to know it. By our definition of attentive belief, if I believe attentively that I exist, then I have some evidence for the proposition "I exist." But if I have any evidence at all for "I exist," then I have conclusive evidence for it. For unless I did exist, I could have no evidence whatever for any proposition. Hence, if I believe attentively that I exist, it follows that I am fully justified, and cannot be mistaken, in believing that I exist. From that, in turn, it follows that I know incorrigibly that I exist. And it is obvious that it is logically possible for me to believe attentively that I exist. Hence, my believing attentively that I exist entails my knowing that I exist. And this is another way of saying that "I exist" is incorrigible for me, from which it follows that I can know it incorrigibly.

But is it really incorrigible for me? What if the evil demon has been deceiving me about my own existence? To assuage whatever misgivings may be evidenced by such expressions of uncertainty, let us think about what the evil demon would have to do in order to deceive me about my own existence.

According to E(Z) (see p. 124), he would have to do one of three things. Either he would have to make me believe that I existed, when I did not exist; or he would have to make me believe that I did not exist, when I existed; or he would have to make me believe that I existed, yet not know that I existed. The first case is ruled out. I cannot believe that I exist while I do not exist. The evil demon cannot lead me to believe that I exist, when I do not exist. It is conceptually impossible for me to be led to believe anything if I do not exist. The power of the evil demon does not extend as far as being able to do conceptually impossible things.

The second way in which the evil demon would have to deceive me about my own existence is for him to lead me to believe, while I do exist, that I do not exist. But there is a kind of absurdity in my believing that I do not exist. *What* I believe is here incompatible with the very fact that I *believe* it. For want of a better label, let us call this kind of absurdity a "pragmatic contradiction," in order to distinguish it from a formal contradiction. (An example of a formal contradiction is the proposition that, although I am over five feet tall, I am not over five feet tall.) We now introduce the concept 'S is pragmatically inconsistent with respect to p', as follows:

> where p is a contingent proposition,
> S *is pragmatically inconsistent with respect to p, if:*
> (1) S believes that p, and "S believes that p" entails that p is false.
> or (2) S asserts that p, and "S asserts that p" entails that p is false.
> or (3) S doubts that p, and "S doubts that p" entails p.

Any one of the conditions (1), (2), or (3) is by itself sufficient for S to be pragmatically inconsistent with respect to p. However, there are, in all probability, other conditions that are sufficiently similar to the ones above to warrant their being added to the list of alternative conditions. For our purposes, however, (1), (2), and (3) are all we need. Descartes, I take it, wants us to see that believing or asserting one's own non-existence, as well as doubting one's own existence, are pragmatically absurd. We shall now explore these points in detail.

We have agreed that "I exist" is incorrigible for me, and in that respect is different from perceptual propositions and from some mathematical propositions. But "I exist" is not the only proposition that is incorrigible for me. There are a great many other propositions that are also incorrigible for me. Now "I exist" differs from many of these other propositions in an interesting way. "I exist" cannot be denied, disbelieved, or doubted without pragmatic inconsistency. The others can be. Compare "I do not exist" with "I do not have a pain." Their denials, "I exist" and "I have a pain," are incorrigible for me. But, even though "I have a pain," like "I exist," is incorrigible for me, I can without absurdity assert that I do not have a pain. I may be lying, but a lie is not a conceptual absurdity. Or else I may truly assert that I do not have a pain.

Now try asserting that you do not exist. In "denying" that you exist, you are presupposing the existence of the very thing whose existence you are "denying." (The word is in double quotes to indicate that this is not a garden-variety case of denying: it involves a conceptual absurdity.) The sense of 'asserts' here and in the second condition that is sufficient for a pragmatic contradiction is partially conveyed by: S asserts that p only if S uses a sentence: i.e., asserting, in the relevant sense, is, among other things, a linguistic act. Now S can, in that sense of 'assert', assert that he does not have a pain, and his making that assertion does not entail that he does have a pain. Here, then, is a proposition, "I have a pain," which is incorrigible for me, yet which I can deny without involving myself in a pragmatic contradiction. But "S asserts that S does not exist" entails "S exists." This entailment is a special case of another entailment: "S asserts that p" entails "S exists," where p is any proposition you please. A nonentity cannot produce sentences in order to make an assertion. If nobody asserted that p, then p was not asserted. Thus, "I exist" is not only incorrigible for me; it is also true that no one can assert "I do not exist" without pragmatic contradiction.

It is equally absurd for me to believe (to think) that I do not exist, while there is nothing absurd in my believing that I do not have a pain. Here, as well as in the first condition that is sufficient for a pragmatic contradiction, *believing* differs from *asserting* in an important respect. A necessary condition for asserting is the use of a sentence. This condition is not necessary for believing. Now "I believe that I am not having a pain" does not entail "I am having a pain." But "I believe that I do not exist" entails "I exist."

I can assert without absurdity that I exist; I can never truly assert that I do not exist. Nor can I think, without absurdity, that I do not exist. Hence, there is no possibility of my proving that I do not exist. Moreover, "I exist" and its denial "I do not exist" are both contingent propositions. They are neither necessarily true nor necessarily false.

The absurdity of *asserting* "I do not exist" is to be distinguished from the absurdity of "I exist and I do not exist." This last proposition is *formally* self-contradictory: the proposition *itself* is necessarily false. It is an interesting question whether one can, without pragmatic contradiction, assert or believe it. To answer the question might require going into complications that are not directly relevant to our present concerns. Whatever the answer to the question, an important difference still exists between "I do not exist" and "I exist and I do not exist." Even if I could not, without pragmatic contradiction, assert "I exist and I do not exist," still, *what* I would be asserting is logically absurd; in the case of "I do not exist," the fact *that* I am asserting it or believing it is what is absurd, not the proposition itself.

Finally, I cannot, without pragmatically contradicting myself, doubt that I exist, although I can doubt that I have a pain—as when I am not sure whether what I feel in my overexercised muscles is merely an unpleasant sensation or a pain. "I doubt that I have a pain" does not entail "I have a pain." But "I doubt that I exist" does entail "I exist." There is absurdity in doubting that which is entailed by the doubting itself. So, when Descartes says that "I exist" or "I think" are "indubitable," that every time I think or assert that I exist, what I think or assert I cannot reasonably doubt, he is right for the reason that to doubt one's own existence is pragmatically self-contradictory.

Thus, the possibility of my believing that I do not exist does not affect the main point, which is that it is impossible for me to believe *falsely* that I exist. That is the most important fact that is called to our attention in Descartes' assertion that no one, not even an all-powerful demon, can deceive me about my own existence. So much for the second way in which I might be deceived by the evil demon.

The third way of being deceived does not affect the main points either. These are that "I exist" is incorrigible for me; that

I cannot *falsely* believe that I exist; and that I cannot *truly* believe that I do not exist. The third way of my being deceived about my own existence would consist of my being led to believe that I exist, when I do not know that I exist. Even if this were possible, the main points would still be true.

It is not possible for me to believe attentively that I exist and not know that I exist. This was proved in the course of the demonstration that "I exist" is incorrigible for me. Hence, the third way of being deceived leaves untouched the logical facts about "I exist" that we have listed so far.

There is one more interesting feature of "I exist." The belief that I exist is *self-certifying*. From a man's believing that he himself exists, it follows logically that he exists. In this respect "I exist" differs from "I am in pain," or from "My pain is just noticeably a throbbing pain." From my believing that I am in pain, it does not follow logically that I am in pain. My being in pain follows logically from my believing *attentively* that I am in pain. Believing attentively that I am in pain requires not only that I believe occurrently that I am in pain, but also that I believe this at a time when I am attending to my sensations and *feeling* a pain.

We can now sum up our findings. "I exist" (and "I think")[17] are *unique* among propositions in that they and they alone are at the same time (1) incorrigible for me, (2) pragmatically incapable of being doubted, denied or disbelieved, and (3) the belief that I exist (or that I think) is self-certifying.

Descartes says enough to get us to see the facts that I have just summarized. But his own way of explaining these important peculiarities of the *cogito* propositions is at times confused. He sometimes thinks that a square's having four sides is "metaphysically doubtful." He wants to find a proposition that is, so to speak, more certain than "A square has four sides." He gives the impression of thinking that "I exist" (or "I think") is just what he is looking for. But his argument for saying that "I exist" is "indubitable" is that, even if there is an evil demon, and he is deceiving me about many things, he cannot deceive me about my own existence because (and this is the crux of Descartes' argument)

---

[17] The argument for coupling "I think" with "I exist" will be given on pp. 145–146.

"The evil demon is deceiving me" entails "I exist." He is assuming an entailment to show that "I exist" is "indubitable." But is there any reason why *this* entailment is metaphysically certain, if "This is a square" entails "This has four sides" is not? There is no such reason. These two entailments stand or fall together. Either both of them are necessarily true or neither one of them is. On the latter alternative, Descartes' argument for the "metaphysical certainty" of "I exist" collapses. Besides, it is obvious that both entailments are necessarily true. Hence, it is perfectly correct to argue that if the evil demon is deceiving me in any way, then I exist. In fact, without apprehending certain necessarily true propositions about what entails what, it would be impossible to bring out into the open the special features of the propositions "I think" and "I exist." Descartes is simply mistaken whenever he proceeds as if he can explain the special status of "I exist" or of "I think" without knowing beforehand that certain other propositions are necessarily true, self-evident, and incorrigible for him, for example that "I am being deceived" entails "I exist."

Section 4

THE SUBJECT OF "I EXIST"

For the time being, we are obeying Descartes' instructions to withhold assent from the proposition that we are, or have, a body. We have agreed that "I exist" is incorrigible for me, and I cannot sensibly disbelieve, deny, or doubt it. We have also agreed that my belief that I exist is self-certifying. The proposition "I think" has these same properties, a fact that tells us something important about the nature of the human mind.

The Distinctive Features of "I Think"

ACCORDING TO Descartes, "thinking" covers an incompletely catalogued multiplicity of mental acts, mental states and mental occurrences. In other words, the proposition, "I think (I am thinking)," is equivalent to the proposition, "I infer or calculate or plan or believe or understand or desire or doubt or affirm or deny or feel pain or feel heat or indulge in a daydream or have an hallucination, etc." This, I think, is what he is saying in the following passage in the Second Meditation: "But what then am I? A thing which thinks. What is a thing which thinks? It is a thing which doubts, understands, [conceives], affirms, denies, wills, refuses, which also imagines and feels." (Haldane and Ross, Vol. I, p. 153.)

The incompletely catalogued disjunction, "I infer or calculate or believe, etc.," is a logically necessary condition of my thinking. Each disjunct is a logically sufficient condition of my thinking. I cannot, for example, infer without thinking, although I can think without inferring. However, I cannot be thinking unless I am either inferring or calculating or believing, etc. So construed, "I think" is identical with "I am conscious." The same entailment relations hold if we replace "I think" with "I am conscious." I cannot, for example, infer without being conscious, although I can be conscious without inferring. However, I cannot be conscious unless I am either inferring or calculating or believing, etc.

"I think," like "I exist," is incorrigible for me; I cannot without pragmatic inconsistency doubt, deny, or disbelieve it; and my belief that I think is self-certifying.

The belief that I am conscious is self-certifying because "I believe that I am conscious" entails that I am conscious. No matter what it is that I believe, the mere fact of my believing it entails that I am conscious.

"I am conscious" is incorrigible for me for fairly obvious reasons. First, it is possible for me to believe attentively that I am conscious. For me to believe this attentively it is sufficient that I believe occurrently that I am conscious at a time when I am attending to my sensations and feeling a pain. Second, it is impossible for me to believe attentively that I am conscious and not to know it. From our definition of attentive belief it follows that if I believe attentively that I am conscious, then I have some evidence for the proposition "I am conscious." But if I have any evidence at all for "I am conscious," then I have conclusive evidence for that proposition. For "I have some evidence that I am conscious" entails that I am conscious. A man who was not conscious would not have any evidence present and revealed to his attentive mind.

We have just shown that "I am thinking" is incorrigible for me and that the belief that I am thinking is self-certifying. I want now to show that "I think" cannot be disbelieved, doubted, or denied without pragmatic inconsistency. To disbelieve p is to believe that p is not the case. "I believe that I am not thinking" entails "I am thinking." Hence, I cannot, without pragmatic inconsistency, disbelieve that I am thinking. Similarly, I cannot, without pragmatic inconsistency, doubt that I think. "I doubt that I think" entails "I think." It is absurd to doubt a proposition that is implied by the doubt itself. Lastly, "I think" cannot be denied by me without pragmatic inconsistency. To deny p is to assert that p is not the case. To deny that I think I must assert that I do not think. But, again, "I assert that I do not think" entails "I think." "I assert that I do not think" is short for "I assert that I do nothing mental, including affirming or asserting." The longer version of "I assert that I do not think" entails "I do something mental," and that entails that I think.

Descartes' Argument That I am Nothing but a Mind

THESE FACTS have some interesting things to say about the nature of myself, whose existence I know incorrigibly. At a time when I am still withholding assent from the proposition that I am or have a body, the proposition that I am thinking is incorrigible for me. Even if it turned out that I had no body, it would still be incorrigible for me that I am thinking. Hence, the following three things are possible at the same time: I exist, I am not a body, I do not have a body. In other words, it is *possible* that I am nothing but a mind existing without a body. I find this conclusion to be wholly justified.

Not until the Sixth Meditation does Descartes offer an argument to prove that (i) the subject of "I exist" is *in fact* nothing but a mind (ii) that can exist without a body. (The text from which the argument is reconstructed is on p. 190 of Vol. I, Haldane and Ross.)

(1) If I know that all things that I conceive clearly and distinctly can be produced by God exactly as I conceive them, and I can clearly and distinctly conceive x apart from y and y apart from x, then I am certain that x and y are distinct (different) from each other and can exist apart from each other.

(2) I know that all things that I conceive clearly and distinctly can be produced by God exactly as I conceive them.

∴ (3) If I clearly and distinctly conceive x apart from y and y apart from x, then I am certain that x and y are different from each other, and can exist apart from each other. (By (1) and (2).)

(4) I find that thinking and thinking only is of the essence of the I of "I think, I exist."

∴ (5) I am only a thinking thing, or a substance whose entire essence is to think. (By (4).)

(6) I have a distinct idea of body, whose essence is to be extended and unthinking.

∴ (7) I have a clear and distinct idea that I and my body are apart from each other. (By (5) and (6).)

∴ (8) I am distinct from my body. (By (3) and (7).)

But (9) If x is distinct from y, then x can exist without y.

∴(10) I can exist without my body. (By (8) and (9).)

Conclusion (5) says that I am *in fact* only a mind. Conclusion (10) says that it is *possible* for me to exist without a body.

I think that (10) has already been proved by the fact that "I think" is incorrigible for me, and that that fact would not change even if it turned out that there were no material objects. Hence, it is possible that I am nothing but a mind existing without a body. But in step (5) of the above argument we are offered the conclusion that not just possibly, but in fact I am nothing but a mind. Is this really proved?

The considerations that show that the I of "I exist" thinks do not show that it does *nothing but* think. If, indeed, there are no bodies, or if I do not have a body, then it follows that thinking is the whole of me, that I am not a body and do not have a body. But there is no argument in Descartes to prove that material objects do not exist. On the contrary, one of Descartes' aims is to prove that we can be certain that they exist.

In the final analysis, then, Descartes offers one and only one reason for believing that I am nothing but a mind: the essence of mind is thought, that of body is extension, and *thought and extension are incompatible*. But that they are incompatible cannot be simply assumed; it must be proved. And there is no proof of it in Descartes. It is not enough to say that I have an idea of body as an extended and unthinking thing. For it is possible that that idea of body does not apply to my body. It may be that my body is extended *and* thinks.

Descartes repeatedly speaks of the I of "I think, I exist" as a *substance*. His notion of *"substance* is just this—that which can exist by itself, without the aid of any other substance." (Reply to Objections IV, Haldane and Ross, Vol. II, p. 101.) This is hardly helpful. Descartes thinks of mind-substance as that which thinks. I am that which thinks. But am I the same thing from moment to moment? Every time that I think that I exist, my existence is for me an incorrigible fact. That has been established. Now consider the following:

(1) At time t I think that I exist.
(2) At time t + 1 I think that I exist.
(3) At time t + 2 I think that I exist.

In each of these the subject, I, is the thinker at the time the thinking is going on. But what warrants the assumption that the word 'I' in (1) refers to the same person as the one referred to in (2) and (3)? Without a warrant for this assumption, I cannot claim to know that I am the same entity from moment to moment. How can I be sure that the self that goes to sleep is the same self that wakes up? Descartes says that even in deep sleep consciousness is not totally obliterated. The implication is that the identity of the self boils down to uninterrupted continuity of consciousness. But the considerations that show that "I exist" is incorrigible for me do not prove that I am an entity that is never altogether unconscious. There is no convincing argument for this in Descartes. The view appears to be an *ad hoc* assumption, devised to guarantee the identity of the self through time.

THE WAX EXAMPLE

THE WAX EXAMPLE toward the end of the Second Meditation is intended to make several points that Descartes thinks are important. The general purpose of the wax example is to dispel what, to common sense, seems to be an anomaly. Descartes has made us see that the contingent propositions, "I think" and "I exist," are incorrigible for me. He now says:

> From this time I begin to know what I am with a little more clearness and distinctness than before; but nevertheless it still seems to me, and I cannot prevent myself from thinking, that corporeal things, whose images are framed by thought, which are tested by the senses, are much more distinctly known than that obscure part of me which does not come under the imagination. Although really it is very strange to say that I know and understand more distinctly these things whose existence seems to me dubious, which are unknown to me and which do not belong to me, than others of the truth of which I am convinced, which are known to me and which pertain to my real nature, in a word, than myself. (Haldane and Ross, Vol. I, pp. 153–154.)

The ego spoken of in "I exist" or "I think" is not another object among such objects as sticks and stones, arms and legs. I cannot perceive it as an object "out there." Nor can I form an image of it. Finally, I cannot experience it in the way in which I experience my aches and pains, or in the way I experience colors, sounds, smells, and tactual qualities. Nevertheless, there are two propositions about myself, "I think" and "I exist," that are contingent yet incorrigible for me. Thus, at a time when I am still withholding assent from such a contingent proposition as "I am now perceiving an apple," I have incorrigible knowledge that I exist and that I am a thinking thing. It seems strange that this should be so. We are naturally inclined to take it for granted that physical objects are known much more readily than anything that we cannot even experience. For we can form images of physical objects; we can (we think) touch them, smell them, or otherwise experience them. None of these things can be done with whatever it is to which the 'I' of 'I exist' refers. But if we reflect, says Descartes, we will find that there is really nothing strange in our having incorrigible knowledge about the nature and existence of an inexperienceable ego, at a time when we are presumably in no position to claim to have knowledge of such palpable things as tables and chairs.

The point that Descartes is making is important. Sometimes he says, or gives the impression of saying, some confusing things about the *cogito* propositions. The important point is that I apprehend the incorrigibility for me of the *cogito* propositions, not through the bodily senses and not through imagination, but through pure reason. Nevertheless, at some points, at the beginning of the Second Meditation, for example, Descartes says things that have to be interpreted with great care. Otherwise, it is easy to think that he is talking nonsense. This is what he says:

> I shall proceed by setting aside all that in which the least doubt could be supposed to exist, just as if I had discovered that it was absolutely false; and I shall ever follow in this road until I have met with something which is certain, or at least, if I can do nothing else, until I have learned for certain that there is nothing in the world that is certain. Archimedes, in order that he might draw the terrestrial globe out of its place, and transport it elsewhere, demanded only that one point should be fixed and immovable; in the same way I shall have the right to conceive high hopes if I am happy enough to discover one thing only which is certain and indubitable . . . (Haldane and Ross, Vol. I, p. 149.)

Is the *Cogito* the Archimedean Fulcrum of Systematic Philosophy?

THE "one thing which is certain and indubitable" turns out to be the *cogito* propositions. Are they *an* Archimedean point or *the* Archimedean point of critical philosophy? Obviously, the *cogito* propositions cannot be *the* Archimedean point of critical philosophy, in the sense of being the logically primary (as distinct from the earliest) certainties from which whatever else I am certain of is to be derived. By reason alone I come to see that the *cogito* propositions are incorrigible for me; that I cannot without pragmatic inconsistency deny, doubt, or disbelieve them; that my belief that they are true is self-certifying. But by reason alone I would come to see nothing, unless I recognized entailments and contradictions. If I am to reason at all, among my "first certainties" there must be some truths of logic. Hence, the *cogito* propositions cannot be *the* logically primary certainties.

It is false to make the even weaker claim that "I think" and "I exist" are the first *contingent* propositions of which I am certain, in the sense that they are incorrigible for me. They are not the only contingent propositions that are incorrigible for me. The contingent proposition "I have a pain" is incorrigible for me. And, although "I have a pain" entails "I am conscious," or as Descartes puts it, "I am thinking," "I have a pain" is a different proposition from "I am conscious." For I can be conscious and not have a pain.

Descartes leads us to see that "I think" and "I exist" are unique among propositions in that at the same time they are (1) incorrigible for me, and (2) pragmatically indubitable, undeniable and incapable of being disbelieved, and (3) the belief that I exist or that I think is self-certifying. If this is in fact true, and we may suppose that it is until someone produces an argument to the contrary, then "I think" and "I exist" indeed enjoy a privileged status as compared with any other contingent proposition. But that does not yet prove that, in the order of philosophical inquiry, these two propositions are either the earliest that we know with certainty, or the logically primary certainties upon which the whole of systematic knowledge must rest. The purely rational inquiry that leads to the apprehension of the distinguishing features of the *cogito* propositions is impossible unless there are logical truths that we know with certainty. For example, we must first know that "S asserts that S does not exist" entails "S exists," in order to see that "I exist" is pragmatically undeniable. It is simply false that in order to know that a certain proposition, p, entails a certain proposition, q, I must first know that "I think" and "I exist" are incorrigible for me.

The view that the *cogito* propositions are *the* Archimedean point of critical philosophy is clearly untenable. Besides, the text does not require us to think that this untenable view is what Descartes meant to hold. The more likely interpretation is that Descartes thought of the *cogito* propositions as *an* Archimedean point of critical philosophy; when it is properly stated, this view is correct.

We have already seen that, as far as we can tell, the *cogito* propositions are unique in exhibiting these three features at the same time: they are incorrigible for me; I cannot doubt, deny, or disbelieve them without pragmatic inconsistency; finally, my belief that I exist (or that I am thinking) is self-certifying. We have, moreover, seen that the proposition "I exist" is *contingent* and *existential*. Whenever I believe occurrently that I exist, I *know incorrigibly that at least one contingent being* (namely I) *exists.* This is an answer to the sceptic, who says that nobody ever knows whether *any contingent being* exists. What is more, we know, through incorrigible knowledge of our own existence, that at least one contingent being exists, and we know this incorrigibly *without having to know that God exists.* (Descartes is not consistent on this point, as I have already pointed out.)

Descartes could have started his philosophy with the ontological argument for God's existence. As we shall see in Part III, this argument purports to deduce the existence of God from His definition. Descartes would hold that the ontological proof gives us clear and distinct intuitive and incorrigible knowledge of God's existence. Descartes could then have deduced his own existence from certain assumptions about God's creativity.

But if Descartes had proved the existence of at least one contingent being this way, and had not made the *cogito* discoveries, he would not have led us to see that, even without God, that is, even without any evidence or guarantees other than the belief in our own existence, we can know incorrigibly that at least one contingent being exists. The sceptic can no longer say that, because we cannot know incorrigibly that God exists and because we cannot know incorrigibly that such contingent entities as tables and chairs exist, we cannot know incorrigibly that at least one contingent entity exists. The *cogito* gives him the lie.

The arguments for God's existence may be questioned. But the fact that I can know incorrigibly that I myself exist, and that hence at least one contingent entity exists, cannot be questioned. This gives us an unchallengeable Archimedean point. The principles of logic, too, are ultimately unchallengeable. But they say nothing about what in fact exists; least of all do they say anything about what contingent entities exist. Logic defines the conditions of existence; it does not provide us with any information as to what exists. Logic tells us that, if a square exists, then it has four sides. It does not say either that there are or that there are not any squares. Thus, the *cogito* propositions are an Archimedean point in a way in which no principle of logic can be.

Thus, one of the main lessons of the wax example is that the *cogito* propositions are examples of propositions that provide incorrigible knowledge of the existence of a contingent mental entity, without the necessity for any assumptions as to the existence of God or material objects. In other words, even if there is no God and no world of material objects, I know incorrigibly that I myself exist and that I am a thinking thing.

The Problem of Other Minds

ANOTHER IMPORTANT point running through the *Meditations* is emphasized in the wax example. Descartes observes that there are first-person-singular, present-tense psychological statements, such as "I am in pain" and "I am experiencing a red patch of color," which he contrasts to second-person and third-person psychological statements, e.g., "You are in pain," "He is in pain," and to propositions about material objects, such as "There is a red apple in front of me." Descartes observes a significant difference among these statements. First-person-singular, present-tense psychological statements are contingent but incorrigible for the person who makes them. Second-person and third-person psychological statements and statements about material objects are also contingent, but they are not incorrigible for the person who makes them. This is a difference with profound implications for the philosophy of mind and the theory of knowledge. Descartes' pioneering work on the nature of the self and of self-knowledge, and the example he sets of basing all claims to knowledge ultimately on first-personal evidence, have had a profound influence.

They have given rise to problems in the philosophy of mind and in the theory of knowledge that are still being debated.

One of the crucial problems in the philosophy of mind is the problem of other minds. In Descartes, the problem of other minds is exactly analogous to the problem of the existence of material objects. The "other minds" problem consists of two questions: Are there other minds besides my own? How do I know that there are, if I know it at all? These questions are exactly parallel to the questions: Are there material objects? How do I know that there are, if I know it at all? According to Descartes, that there are material objects and that there are other minds must be conclusions of *deductive* arguments. This proviso bars Descartes from using the analogical argument for the existence of other minds. That argument purports to prove that, on the available evidence, it is highly probable that each body that behaves like my body is related to a mind like my mind in the way in which my body is related to my mind.

The analogical argument, as an *inductive* argument, is one that a methodological deductivist like Descartes cannot use. Besides, the analogical argument for the existence of other minds presupposes the existence of bodies. And for Descartes there can be no direct deductive link between such premises as "I am experiencing a red patch of color," which are incorrigible for me, and such conclusions as "That red patch is a piece of cloth," which are not incorrigible for me. The reason is that for Descartes a piece of cloth or a piece of wax are material "substances," unobservable "somewhats," to which my visual, tactual, auditory, gustatory, and olfactory experiences, in short, my "sense data," are related *causally*, not logically. This is why the first-person psychological statement "I am experiencing a red patch of color" cannot *entail* the material-object statement "That red patch is a piece of cloth."

Descartes purports to deduce the existence of material objects from the proposition that God exists. God, who is perfectly good, and who has created me with the ineluctable propensity to believe that material objects exist, must have created material objects that correspond to my beliefs. Otherwise He would be a deceiver, which is impossible. But even if, for the sake of the argument, we accept Descartes' God and his material world, he still cannot prove the existence of other minds by analogy. His method prevents him from using inductive proofs. The only answer Descartes can give to the question of the existence of other minds is an answer exactly analogous to his answer to the problem of the existence of the material world: I have an ineluctable belief in the existence of other minds. Hence, every body that is very much like mine in its appearance and behavior must be associated with a mind like mine. Otherwise God would be a deceiver, which is impossible.

However, the argument fails. As we shall see, Descartes' proofs that God exists are unconvincing. Neither the existence of material objects nor that of other minds can be proved by an appeal to God's veracity. Moreover, even if God's existence should be capable of being proved by some argument or other, the deduction of the existence of material objects or of other minds from the veracity of God would not be an inference from premises that are such that I cannot be mistaken in believing them attentively. The inference uses as a premise the proposition that I have an ineluctable propensity to believe in the existence of material objects. But I can be mistaken in believing that proposition attentively. "I believe that I have an ineluctable propensity to believe that material objects exist" does not entail "I know that I have an ineluctable propensity to believe that material objects exist." It is possible that I believe attentively but falsely that I have such an ineluctable propensity. For, in saying that I have an ineluctable propensity, I imply that the propensity will always remain with me. But that is a prediction that can be mistaken. Descartes cannot consistently claim that he has demonstrated the proposition that material objects exist, if in the proof he uses a premise that is not logically indubitable for him.

We begin to sense that Descartes will have to yield somewhere. If he clings to his requirement that philosophical truths must be derived from logically indubitable premises, then he will probably have to give up the requirement that the derivation be one of entailment. In fact, a number of post-Cartesian epistemologists (for example, C. I. Lewis) would be satisfied if they could show that first-person psychological statements, such as "I feel what appears to be a smooth, round, doorknobbish surface," which are incorrigible for me, can provide *inductive* support for the proposition that I am touching a doorknob. If, however, Descartes clings to his requirement that a metaphysical truth, such as the proposition that material objects exist, must be deductively established, then he will probably have to relax the proviso that the premises of the argument must be propositions each of which is logically indubitable for the person who is making the inference.

Sense Experience, Imagination, and Understanding

A FURTHER POINT Descartes makes in the wax example is that the bodily senses and the imagination are not sufficient for understanding the nature of things. Indeed, they are not even necessary. That they are not is evident from such facts as the following. We understand what a chiliagon is: a thousand-sided regular polygon. It is a contingent fact that we cannot tell, merely by looking at a chiliagon, that it is a chiliagon. We cannot, as a matter of contingent fact, merely by looking tell the difference between a chiliagon and a figure that has only nine hundred and ninety-nine sides. As a matter of contingent fact, we are able to tell by looking that a given figure is a triangle. But even if we lacked this ability, it would not follow that we did not understand what a triangle is. It is important to realize that Descartes is making a logical point. He is not saying or implying that, as a matter of contingent fact, human beings do not learn about things by means of observation. He is, rather, saying that "S understands what it is for something to be a thing of a certain kind, K," does not entail "Either S is able to form an image of a K, or S has observed that a thing is a K, or both."

And it is evident that having senses and imagination is not sufficient to have an understanding of, say, what a triangle is. It is possible to tamper with a man's brain in such a way that he can continue to sense colors, smells, textures, and sounds, and to form images, yet be unable to understand what a triangle is. Conceptual knowledge, i.e., knowledge of the logical features of a given concept or proposition, depends neither on the senses nor on the imagination. I have conceptual knowledge of what a chiliagon is. Also, I know conceptually that "I think" and "I exist" are incorrigible for me. If I have conceptual knowledge of what it is to be red, I know that, if a thing is red, then it is colored. Being red entails being colored. Conceptual knowledge requires the exercise of reason.

Problems About Perceptual Knowledge

DESCARTES HOLDS that perceptual knowledge, too, requires the exercise of reason; unlike conceptual knowledge, however, perceptual knowledge also requires as a basis first-person psychological statements, such as "I am experiencing a brownish patch of color." Perceptual knowledge has to do with our perceiving the world around us. Descartes says, about our perceiving the sun, that it looks like a tiny disc some distance away. But our understanding tells us that, if there is such a thing as the sun, it must be many times the size of the earth and at an enormous distance from it. Furthermore, according to Descartes, we never directly perceive physical objects. What we directly perceive are presentations, which need not be representing anything. That I am experiencing a bright disc the size of a small hoop is a presentational report; it is, as such, incorrigible for me. But that I see a star, namely, the sun, is not a presentational report but a perceptual judgment, which is in part an intellectual act, the act of interpreting the presented hoop-sized disc as representing the sun. In judging that I see the sun, I am committed to much more than meets the eye. The sun is a three-dimensional and enormously large object. Moreover, in judging that I see the sun, I am implying that what I see exists independently of my seeing it.

Descartes draws two lessons from all this. One is that everything that is incorrigible for me concerning the wax is exhausted in statements of the sort: I am now aware of a certain smell, I am now aware of a certain texture, etc. Statements of this sort are simply witness to the fact that, whatever else I am, it is incorrigible for me that "I am a thing that thinks"—that I am a conscious being. The other lesson is that the perceptual judgments I make about the wax are not incorrigible for me. Hence, the feeling we all have before we philosophize, that we are very clear and certain about physical objects, is misleading. There is really no anomaly in the philosophical discovery that my own existence as a thinking thing is incorrigible for me, even though I never experience myself as a thing among things. Nor is there an anomaly in the fact that presentational reports, for example that I am experiencing a bright flat shiny disc the size of a small hoop, are incorrigible for me while perceptual judgments are not. All this is encapsulated in Descartes' dictum: My knowledge of myself is prior to, and more certain than, my knowledge of material objects.

Descartes' conception of material objects and his representational theory of perception give rise to serious problems. He conceives of material objects as being in principle unobservable. A material object is, in his view, a *substratum*, an unobservable something that causes us to have experiences of seeing colors, hearing sounds, feeling textures, smelling smells, and feeling heat and cold, pleasant sensations and pain. However, according to the theory, none of the seen colors, heard sounds, felt textures, smelled smells, felt heat and felt cold, felt pleasant or unpleasant sensations are logically connected with the unobservable substratum. In Descartes' view, a material object is not *defined* in terms of seen colors, heard sounds, etc.; nor are those items logically necessary *and* sufficient for there to be a material object, nor are they *either* logically necessary *or* logically sufficient for there to be any material objects. Sometimes all this is reported metaphorically by saying such things as this: that, according to Descartes, "secondary qualities," e.g., heard sounds, seen colors, felt heat, etc., are "in the mind," not "in" in the material object; that only the "primary qualities," e.g., location, duration, the essential property of being extended, are "in" the material object. To say that the essential property of extension is "in" the material object would be to say that "x is a material object = Df. x is an extended object"; whereas to say that the "primary qualities" are "in" the material object would be to say that "x has location, duration, number, etc." entails, and is entailed by, "x is a material object." It should be observed that at least one of the "primary qualities," namely, number, is one whose presence alone does not entail that that which possesses it is a material object. For example, God, who is not a material object, is said to be one.

When we reflect on the nature of perception, we are confronted with the puzzles of illusions, hallucinations, dreams, afterimages, the perception of extinct stars, and the relativity (to the psychological states and physical locations of observers) of the way things appear. In some of these cases, it is possible that no material objects at all are being perceived. For instance, it is possible that a man is sleeping so soundly that not even a fearfully noisy cannonade will wake him. The man is absolutely "dead to the world," which presumably means that for the moment he is completely unconscious of external stimuli. A man in that condition could not be perceiving any material objects. Yet he could be dreaming that a bull was charging him. In others among these cases, it cannot be that a man is perceiving a material object that he believes is there. A hallucinating drunkard is not perceiving snakes on the bedspread, because there are no snakes on the bedspread at the time that he thinks he is seeing them.

Descartes clearly recognizes these facts. He very clearly states that, even if I was dreaming that I was sitting in front of a fire, when I was in fact sound asleep in bed, "still it is at least quite certain that it seems to me that I see light, that I hear noise and that I feel heat. That cannot be false; properly speaking it is what is in me called feeling; and used in this precise sense that is no other thing than thinking." (Haldane and Ross, Vol. I, p. 153.) Even though in a dream I may not be perceiving a material object, I am experiencing something just the same. I can describe my hallucinatory snakes or my dream fireplace. Let us use the term 'sense datum' (plural: 'sense data') to refer to that which I have when I have an experience of red, an experience of a sound, etc. Descartes' view is that, in all experiences, be it a perception of a chair or a dream or a hallucination or an illusion, there are sense data. Having admitted them as entities of some sort, Descartes is then faced with the problem of giving an account of the relation of sense data to material objects. Descartes' account is that the sense data are appearances of a material object, if a material object is being perceived. Take a round coin. Seen from a certain angle, the coin will look slightly elliptical. As I change my position with respect to the coin, the sense data will have different shapes, and hence the different sense data will have geometrically incompatible properties. One would be inclined to conclude from this that no two such sense data can both be part of the same surface. Hence, not all the sense data can be part of the surface. But if not all can be, *which* of them can? We seem to have no way of knowing. For there is no reason why this rather than that sense datum, from among the many with incompatible properties, should be identical with the *real* surface of the coin.

Descartes' theory is not that some sense datum is part of the surface, but rather that every visual sense datum is an *appearance* of the surface. But here we face an exactly analogous problem. Which one of the many appearances of the coin truly represents the coin? From this angle the coin appears to be round; from that angle it appears to be elliptical. Which is it? Descartes cannot say that it is neither. On his view, geometrical properties are among the "primary qualities" of a material object. At any one time the coin has to have *some* definite shape. Descartes provides no criterion for deciding which among the many appearances of an object is a veridical representation of the actual shape of the surface of the object.

And, indeed, he cannot, as Berkeley[18] pointed out. On Descartes' view, we can never observe a material object; we can only be aware of its appearances. But, then, we can never compare a material object with any of its appearances so as to tell which appearance truly represents the object.

Berkeley also argued that the idea of an unperceived material object was self-contradictory, and that there is no evidence whatever for believing that there exist unperceived material objects. He proposed an alternative to Descartes. Certain features of Berkeley's theory are a form of phenomenalism. As it developed later, phenomenalism is the view that statements about material objects are identical with complicated statements about sense data. When Dr. Johnson[19] kicked a stone, thinking that he was thereby refuting Berkeley, he showed that he did not understand Berkeley's position about material objects. What Berkeley denied was the existence of an unperceivable *substratum;* he did not deny that stones and sticks exist. In fact, according to phenomenalism, Dr. Johnson's feeling of lashing out with what he felt to be his foot, his subsequent feeling of impact at what looked to be the point of contact between what looked to be his foot and what looked to be a stone, are just the sorts of experiences you would expect to undergo if there was a stone in front of you. By kicking the stone Dr. Johnson was not proving the existence of a material substratum; Descartes certainly would not think so. He makes it perfectly plain in the wax example that neither sense experience nor imagination grasps what he thinks is perfectly clear to reason: that material objects are extended substrata.

[18] Bishop George Berkeley (1685–1753).
[19] This is Boswell's Johnson.

Neither that proposition nor its contradictory can be proved by anyone's kicking anything.

In "The Refutation of Idealism" (1903), G. E. Moore argues that one of Berkeley's crucial assumptions, namely, that the existence of material objects consists in their being perceived, is false. Without that assumption Berkeley cannot prove that the idea of an unperceived material object is self-contradictory. If Moore is right, then the case in favor of phenomenalism is considerably weakened.

One consequence of phenomenalism is that the proposition "My desk is in my study although no one is now perceiving it" has to be interpreted along these lines: "If anyone were now in my study and he looked in a certain direction, groped in a certain direction, etc., he would have visual, tactual, etc., sense data of such and such description." Moore's fundamental objection to phenomenalism is that it is counter to our Common-Sense (sic.) belief that material objects exist independently of anyone's actually or possibly perceiving them. (See his "A Defence of Common Sense.")

There are other, and perhaps much more serious, objections to phenomenalism. For instance, it has been pointed out that no actual phenomenalistic translation of a material object statement can be given. "That is a stone" seems to say what it says in one breath, as it were. However, according to phenomenalism, that seemingly simple statement is equivalent to an infinite conjunction of phenomenal statements, e.g., if I were to kick it, I would feel an impact on my foot, and if I were to touch it, I would feel a rough surface at my finger-tips, and if I were to heft it, I would feel a pull on my arm muscles, etc. Phenomenalists grant that the translation cannot be completed; but, they say, all that is required of them really is to produce a rule or recipe or formula for how one would go on indefinitely adding to the list of phenomenal statements. They might even cite analogous cases. In arithmetic, for example, we can never complete the process of counting through to the end of the counting numbers, because there is no end to that sequence. But we can give a rule for how one would go on: to get the next number, add one to the last counted number. The trouble with this analogy is that the two sorts of cases differ enormously in other respects. The rule for adding to the list of phenomenal statements is by no means as simple as the rule: add one to the number last counted in the sequence. In the Appendix to his book *Perceiving* (Cornell University Press, 1957), R. M. Chisholm has a powerful argument against phenomenalism. The phenomenalist might hold that the material object statement:

There is a stone in front of me (P)

entails the phenomenal statement:

If such and such sense data should be sensed
(namely, those associated with kicking),
such and such tactual sense data would be sensed (R).

Chisholm argues that (P) does not entail (R). If his argument is decisive, then material object statements cannot be equivalent to complicated conjunctions of phenomenal statements.

But perhaps I have said enough to indicate that post-Cartesian philosophical theories of perception are a series of reactions to the genuine difficulties involved in the Cartesian theory of perception. It should also be said that these other theories are themselves not altogether free of difficulties. They have been, and are being, vigorously debated by some of the ablest recent and contemporary philosophers.

SELECTED BIBLIOGRAPHY

[1] Ayer, A. J. *The Problem of Knowledge*. New York: The Macmillan Co., 1956. Chap. 2, esp. pp. 45–54.

[2] ———. "Professor Malcolm on Dreams," *Journal of Philosophy*, LVII (1960), 517–535.

[3] ———. "Rejoinder to Professor Malcolm," *Journal of Philosophy*, LVIII (1961), 297–299.

[4] Bouwsma, O. K. "Descartes' Skepticism of the Senses," *Mind*, LIV (1945), 313–322.

[5] ———. "Descartes' Evil Genius," *Philosophical Review*, LVIII (1949), 141–151.

[6] Carney, J. D. "Cogito, Ergo Sum and Sum Res Cogitans," *Philosophical Review*, LXXI (1962), 492–496.

[7] Chappell, V. C. "The Concept of Dreaming," *The Philosophical Quarterly*, 13 (1963), 193–213.

[8] Gewirth, A. "Clearness and Distinctness in Descartes," *Philosophy*, 18 (1942), 17–36.

[9] ———. "Experience and the Non-Mathematical in the Cartesian Method," *Journal of the History of Ideas*, 2 (1941), 185 ff.

[10] Hintikka, J. "Cogito, Ergo Sum: Inference or Performance?" *Philosophical Review*, LXXI (1962), 3–32.

[11] ———. "Cogito, Ergo Sum as an Inference and as Performance," *Philosophical Review*, LXXII (1963), 487–496.

[12] Lucas, P. G. "Descartes and the Wax—Two Rejoinders to Mr. Smart," *Philosophical Quarterly*, I (1950), 348–352.

[13] Malcolm, N. "Dreaming and Scepticism," *Philosophical Review*, LXV (1956), 14–37.

[14] ———. *Dreaming*. New York: Humanities Press, 1959.

[15] ———. "Professor Ayer on *Dreaming*," *Journal of Philosophy*, LVIII (1961), 294–297.

[16] ———. "Descartes' Proof that His Essence is Thinking," *Philosophical Review*, LXXIV (1965), 315–338.

[17] Miller, L. G. "Descartes, Mathematics and God," *Philosophical Review*, LXVI (1957), 451–465.

[18] Pears, D. F. "Professor Norman Malcolm: Dreaming," *Mind*, LXX (1961), 145–163.

[19] Peirce, C. S., "Questions Concerning Certain Faculties Claimed for Man," *Journal of Speculative Philosophy*, 2 (1868), 103–114.

[20] ———. "Some Consequences of Four Incapacities," *Journal of Speculative Philosophy*, 2 (1868), 140–157.

Both [19] and [20] are reprinted in P. P. Wiener, ed., *Values in a World of Chance*. Garden City: Doubleday & Co., 1958.

[21] Ryle, G. *The Concept of Mind*. New York: Barnes & Noble, 1949. Chap. I.

[22] Smart, J. J. C. "Descartes and the Wax," *Philosophical Quarterly*, I (1950), 50–57.

[23] Stout, A. K. "The Basis of Knowledge in Descartes," *Mind*, XXXVIII (1929), 330–342, 458–472.

[24] Weinberg, J. R. "Cogito, Ergo Sum: Some Reflections on Mr. Hintikka's Article," *Philosophical Review*, LXXI (1962), 483–491.

[25] Wright, J. N. "Descartes and the Wax—Two Rejoinders to Mr. Smart," *Philosophical Quarterly*, I (1950), 352–355.

[26] Yost, R. M. "Professor Malcolm on Dreaming and Scepticism," *Philosophical Quarterly*, IX (1959), 142–151, 231–243.

[6] and [24] are responses to [10]; [11] is a rejoinder to [6] and [24]. [2], [3], [7], and [18] are critical of [14]. [26] is critical of [13], but it is pertinent to [14] as well. [15] is a response to [2], and [3] is a response to [15]. Many acute objections to Descartes' *Meditations* that were made by some of Descartes' illustrious contemporaries, together with Descartes' replies, may be found under the heading [27] *Objections Urged by Certain Men of Learning Against the Preceding Meditations with the Author's Replies*, in *Philosophic Works of Descartes*, (Haldane and Ross, Vol. II).

PART III

Descartes and the Problem of God, Meditations on First Philosophy, III-VI

WHY PROVE
THAT GOD EXISTS?

IF THE EXISTENCE of God could be proved, finding a proof would surely be a major accomplishment. It would answer a question that millions of ordinary human beings and scores of great thinkers have asked. Among the great thinkers who have asked the question, the philosophers have by and large been interested in the answer for technical philosophical reasons, in addition to the more common motives of curiosity, religion, and morality. Plato's *demiurgos* is primarily a creative power that Plato introduces in order to explain life, movement, and order in the universe as he conceives it. Aristotle's fifty-odd prime movers are "first principles" of his cosmology rather than objects of religious adoration. Among modern philosophers who antedate the secular age in which we are now living and for most of whom God was a living presence, Descartes is by no means alone in making technical use of the proposition that God exists. He is, however, remarkable among the great moderns for the way in which he makes his metaphysics and theory of knowledge so entirely dependent upon that one proposition, that God exists. For Descartes, therefore, the question: "Why prove that God exists?" is a central *philosophical* question. His entire philosophical system depends on it in a way that I shall now explain, before we examine Descartes' and some other philosophers' attempted proofs of God's existence.

Descartes has created for himself three major technical problems, and he believes that they can all be solved if, and only if, it can be proved that God exists. The three problems are: the justification of memory, the problem of justifying perceptual beliefs, the problems posed by the evil demon postulate.

God and the Problem of Memory
in Perceptual Judgments

THE PROBLEM of memory crops up in connection with perceptual judgments, as well as in connection with deduction. Descartes' representational theory of perception assumes that every perceptual judgment (that is, a belief that a certain perceptual proposition is true) is the product of an intellectual act, or an interpretation put upon a presentational datum. My perception of the sun is a case in point. The presentational datum, that item in my field of awareness whose presence and properties are incorrigible for me, is a flat shiny disc of a diameter of approximately so many inches. When I judge that that is the sun, upon being presented with the sun-datum, I am saying something quite different from: I am now aware of a shiny flat disc of such and such approximate diameter. I am talking about the sun, which, if it exists at all, is a fiery ball many times bigger than the earth and millions of miles away.

An analogy is the men in cloaks in the Second Meditation. I look down from my window and see cloaks and hats moving about on the sidewalk. I judge that the moving things are people whom I do not see. They are wholly hidden from my eyes by the hats and cloaks they wear. How then do I come to judge this way? Presumably, Descartes' view is that I have in the past seen people in hats and cloaks; and when I see the cloaks and hats but not the men, I interpret what I *see* on the basis of what I remember. The case of the sun is analogous to the case of the men in cloaks in the following way: my seeing the cloaks and hats corresponds to my being aware of the sun-datum; my interpreting the sun-datum to be a representation of the sun corresponds to my judging that the hats and cloaks are covering men. The analogy is, however, imperfect. The hats, the cloaks, and the people covered by them, being physical objects, could be seen in the same way if they could be seen at all. But we never see the sun in the same way that we perceive the sun-datum. In fact, on Descartes' view, in a certain sense of 'see', we never *see* hats, coats, people and the sun. We are never directly aware of physical objects. What we are directly aware of is the contents of our own consciousness.

So memory does not function in perceptual judgments in quite the same way that common sense might presume it to function in the case of the hats and cloaks and people. But it does function in another way. Suppose that I am aware of an apple-datum, say of a characteristic smell. I *recall* that whenever I have perceived that smell, I have perceived, simultaneously or soon afterwards, a characteristic shape, color, size and texture. We might call them "apple-properties." Of these we are directly aware. So I *interpret* the smell as representing an apple; I judge that an apple is present in my vicinity. Memory plays a dual role in this theory. The theory supposes that I remember that a number of perceptual data have been experienced by me in a group. The sun-group includes the following perceptual data: a flat disc, which is luminous, and roughly of such and such diameter. The apple-group includes a certain characteristic smell, a certain texture, color, apparent size, apparent shape. The theory further supposes that whenever I experience a characteristic apple smell, I normally expect certain other experiences to occur because I remember that they normally did occur under those circumstances in my past. The other role that memory plays in perceptual experience concerns the men-in-cloaks type of case. According to the theory, when I judge that the hats and cloaks are covering men, I am directly aware of perceptual data that are members of hat-groups and cloak-groups. I am not directly aware of perceptual data that are members of groups representing human bodies. But on the basis of previous experience with hat-data and cloak-data, I normally believe that if I were now to remove these hats and pull open these cloaks, I would experience perceptual data that are members of groups representing human bodies. This, too, is an act of interpretation and an anticipation of further experience, and it too depends on memory.

This double dependence of perceptual judgments on memory makes every perceptual judgment doubtful. The argument for this is not in Descartes, but it is one that he would surely accept. Assume that (1) right now I seem to remember that on at least one occasion I had a mistaken memory. This assumption could also be put as follows: I have right now an impression that on at least one occasion I had a mistaken memory. The point is that the assumption is not meant to entail that right now what I seem to remember really happened. The assumption states a proposition that is incorrigible for me. Now the following conditional is necessarily true, and demonstrably so: (2) For any time, t, if I seem to remember at t that on at least one occasion I had a mistaken memory, then there is at least one occasion on which I have had or am having a mistaken memory. Here is an argument for (2): My present impression that on at least one occasion I had a mistaken memory is either veridical or it is mistaken. If it is veridical, then there is at least one occasion, namely, in the past, when I have (had) a mistaken memory. If my present impression is mistaken, then there is at least one time, namely, right now, when I have a mistaken memory. Hence, (2) is necessarily true. From (1) and (2) we deduce: (3) There is at least one time when I have a mistaken memory. The argument shows that memory impressions *can* be a source of incorrigible knowledge. I know that (3) is true because I have deduced it from (1), a proposition that is incorrigible for me and (2), a necessarily true proposition. But it is a principle of logic that if (p and q) entails r, and q is necessarily true, then p alone entails r. Hence, (1) alone entails (3), And because (1) is incorrigible for me, I know (3) incorrigibly, even though (3) is not incorrigible for me. But even though I know that there is at least one time when I have a mistaken memory, I do not know that my *present* impression that such and such happened in the past is veridical nor do I know that it is mistaken. I have so far no basis for claiming to know how to tell whether, on any particular occasion of my seeming to remember something, my memory is veridical or not. Hence, I must trust none of my memories. This policy is dictated by the dictum Descartes has laid down in the very first Meditation: do not believe any proposition to be true insofar as you have no way of being sure that it is true. Until I find some way of vindicating memory, therefore, I must not believe any of my perceptual judgments. Their truth presupposes the truth of what memory tells me.

God and the Problem of Memory in Deduction

THE PROBLEM of memory crops up again in connection with deduction. According to Descartes, everything we know is known either immediately or mediately. The crucial distinction is this: that which we know immediately we know without having to prove it, while that which we know mediately we know only by demonstrative inference. Some demonstrative inferences are so simple and short that we have immediate knowledge of their validity. For example, from:

He kicked a ball,

we can infer:

He kicked something.

We can see, in a single instant, as it were, that the premise implies the conclusion. There is no reliance on memory here. But the most interesting demonstrative arguments require many steps. Even if we assume that each step can be seen to be valid, to go through several steps takes time. When we have reached the conclusion, what assures us then that each preceding step was validly taken? We remember that it was. Hence, given that until further notice memory is not to be trusted, we cannot claim to know anything by means of complicated demonstrative inferences. Yet, so much of what we know depends on complicated demonstrative inferences that we have not provided an adequate logical reconstruction of knowledge until we justify our reliance on memory.[1]

The problem just posed is one that Descartes must face. He does not mention it as such in the *Meditations*, but toward the end of the Fifth Meditation he does mention a closely related issue. In these passages Descartes is clearly enunciating the view that all *mediately* achieved conclusions that we recollect, at times

[1] Some of the most pertinent discussion outside the *Meditations* concerning the rôle of memory in mediate knowledge are in *Rules for the Direction of the Mind*, esp. Rules III, VII, XI, and in *The Principles of Philosophy*, Part I, Principle XIII. In Principle XIII, Descartes premises the solution of the problem of memory upon the existence of God.

when we no longer remember the premises from which we derived them, are conclusions that we do not know. We have only vague and vacillating opinions about them as long as we are uncertain of God's existence.

> Thus, for example, when I consider the nature of a (rectilinear) triangle, I who have some little knowledge of the principles of geometry recognize quite clearly that the three angles are equal to two right angles, and it is not possible for me not to believe this so long as I apply my mind to its demonstration; but so soon as I abstain from attending to the proof, although I still recollect having clearly comprehended it, it may easily occur that I come to doubt its truth, if I am ignorant of there being a God. . . . But after I have recognized that there is a God . . . although I no longer pay attention to the reasons for which I have judged this to be true, provided that I recollect having clearly and distinctly perceived it, no contrary reason can be brought forward which could ever cause me to doubt of its truth; and thus I have a true and certain knowledge of it. (Haldane and Ross, Vol. I, p. 184.)

The difference between this and the previous case is subtle. In the earlier case, it was a question of remembering that all the steps of the inference that we had just completed were validly taken. In the latter case, it is a matter of remembering that a certain conclusion that we remember having proved, but whose proof we have either forgotten or are at the moment not thinking of, *was* in fact proved.

Descartes offers an argument that purports to prove that God's veracity guarantees the truth of some of our memory impressions. Toward the end of Section I in Part II, that argument was examined and found to be inconclusive. In this Part, we shall find that the arguments for God's existence are inconclusive.

The situation, however, is not as hopeless without God as Descartes would think. Suppose that there is no God. If at any time I have doubts about whether or not some time ago I really ran through a demonstrative proof of a certain proposition, it is always possible for me to reconstruct the proof. If I cannot reconstruct it, or find somebody else's proof that I can check, then I may continue to wonder if, after all, the proposition is a demonstrated truth. If I am able to reconstruct the proof or check somebody else's proof, then doubts should be allayed, as far as this particular issue is concerned. The question of my being a theist or an atheist has no bearing on it.

God and the Existence of Material Objects

WE HAVE already seen that, insofar as memory is involved in perceptual judgments, they are not to be trusted unless memory is to be trusted. But there is a second problem involving perceptual judgments. According to Descartes' theory of perception, every perceptual judgment that I make involves my believing that a certain physical object exists or that a certain physical object has this or that property. These "opinions [are] in some measure doubtful . . . and at the same time highly probable, so that there is much more reason to believe in them than to deny them." (Haldane and Ross, Vol. I, p. 148.) This is said toward the end of the First Meditation. At the beginning of the Third Meditation Descartes says:

> But there was yet another thing which I affirmed, and which, owing to the habit which I had formed of believing it, I thought I perceived very clearly, although in truth I did not perceive it at all, to wit, that there were objects outside of me from which these ideas proceeded, and to which they were entirely similar. And it was in this that I erred, or, if perchance my judgment was correct, this was not due to any knowledge arising from my perception. (Haldane and Ross, Vol. I, p. 158.)

For example, when I believe that that is an apple, I believe that there, where I see it, there is an object that has a life of its own independently of my consciousness. All I have in the way of evidence are propositions, each of which is a report of what I am now experiencing, viz., I now perceive a certain smell while at what seems to be the same time I seem to be touching what seems to be a smooth, cool, red, shiny, apple-shaped object. Descartes insists that all such reports of immediate experience are incorrigible for whoever is making the report or is having the experience. But it seems obvious that no matter how many statements of that sort we conjoin, their conjunction will not imply deductively that here is an apple. In short, in anything that is incorrigible for me, there is no warrant for deducing that this or that is a physical object.

This is just a repetition of one lesson of the wax example: what is incorrigible for me tells me a good deal about myself as a conscious entity and nothing at all about the existence of a material world. For all I know, I may be dreaming, or an evil demon may be making me believe in the independent existence of bodies when in fact there are none such. But if God exists, He (being all good, and hence not a deceiver) would not have made me believe in the separate existence of physical objects and yet not made physical objects that correspond to my corrigible beliefs. And he would not have given me to understand the difference between dreaming and waking, and yet not made it possible for me to tell, when I am awake, that I am awake. How am I to know that right now, for instance, it is not in a dream but in waking life that I am judging that object to be a piece of cheese?

Toward the end of Section 1 in Part II, I examined Descartes' attempt to solve this problem by an appeal to God's veracity. That solution, too, was found to be unsatisfactory. For, even if God's existence can be proved, Descartes relies on a *coherence* criterion for distinguishing dreaming from waking, and no coherence criterion of the sort proposed can provide for logically indubitable judgments. Besides we will find that even God's existence is not proved. As a consequence, Descartes' attempts to solve philosophical problems by the appeal to God are unconvincing.

God and the Problem of the Validity of Reasoning Deductively

FINALLY, the evil demon hypothesis creates special difficulties for Descartes. You will recall that, according to certain passages in the *Meditations,* perfectly straightforward examples of necessarily true propositions, such as that a square has four sides, are "metaphysically" doubtful. For in these passages Descartes says that no matter how "clear and distinct" the idea of a square is, so long as it is possible that an evil demon has me in his power, he may be making me think falsely in spite of the fact that what I think is "clear and distinct."

According to this line of reasoning, even the simplest demonstrative inferences are doubtful. Take for example:

He kicked a ball.

∴ He kicked something.

It is clear that this inference is valid, which comes down to saying the same thing as that the conditional statement:

If he kicked a ball, then he kicked something,

is necessarily true. Every valid demonstrative inference has a corresponding conditional that is necessarily true. But sometimes Descartes entertains "metaphysical" doubts about such necessarily true propositions as that all squares have four sides. Hence, he must at such times have "metaphysical" doubts about all necessarily true propositions and, hence, about even the simplest deductive inferences. This means that he must at such times have "metaphysical" doubts about all inferences, the complicated as well as the simple ones. These doubts would disappear and all "clear and distinct" ideas would once and for all be freed of all doubt, if God's existence were proved. If God exists, then we are not at the mercy of an evil spirit. This line of attack generates a circle. (See Section 7, below.)

However, the passages in which Descartes says that God is needed in order to guarantee even our most evident intuitions are an unfortunate aberration. The fairest and most generous interpretation of Descartes is that God is needed to guarantee the truth of *some*, not *all*, of our clear and distinct perceptions. Specifically, Descartes thinks that God is needed to guarantee the truth of (1) all our clear and distinct perceptual judgments, (2) all our clear and distinct perceptions of our own states of wakefulness, (3) all clear and distinct memory impressions, and (4) all clear and distinct perceptions of mathematical propositions that are such that it is possible to believe attentively that they are true, although they are false, or to believe attentively that they are false, although they are true.

For Descartes, then, to prove the existence of God, is crucial, for *technical* philosophical reasons. I shall contend that Descartes' arguments for the existence of God fail to prove that God exists. (See Section 4 and 5, below.) In fact, no argument so far invented has proved that conclusion. Inasmuch as Descartes fails to prove that God exists, his program of logically reconstructing knowledge fails. But even if he had been able to prove that God exists,

God would not have helped him *technically* as much as Descartes seems to believe He would. Descartes needs God so that he can deduce the principle of clarity and distinctness, i.e., the principle that all clear and distinct perceptions are true. I have already argued (Section 1, Part II) that the derivation of the principle of clarity and distinctness is incomplete. There I also pointed out that Descartes proposes a coherence criterion for distinguishing clear and distinct perceptual propositions from their opposites and also for distinguishing the occasions when I clearly and distinctly perceive that I am awake from the occasions when I do not perceive this clearly and distinctly. The coherence criterion provides for *inductive* confirmation, not for the kind of certainty that rules out the possibility of mistaken belief. As a result, even if the principle of clarity and distinctness had been proved, we would not be able to apply it on the occasions when we wanted to know, with the kind of certainty that rules out the possibility of mistaken belief, whether we ourselves were awake or whether we ourselves were clearly and distinctly perceiving a perceptual fact.

Section 2

ARE SENTENCES CONTAINING THE WORD 'GOD' OR SOME SYNONYM MEANINGFUL?

IT IS COMMONLY taken for granted that one can sensibly think and talk about God. Consequently, it may sound odd to ask: Does talk about God make sense? To be sure, many philosophers and religious seers have said that the limitless nature of God cannot be fully comprehended by the limited human mind. But they have not meant to imply that no one can understand anything at all about God. Some philosophers believe that man can understand enough to know that God must be omnipotent, omniscient, perfectly good, creator, lawgiver, judge and lord of the universe.

There are philosophers who have argued that God, so conceived, is an impossible being. Yet in saying this they are assuming that the idea of God is intelligible. Take an analogy. It is a demonstrable truth that an even integer that is odd is impossible. The proof requires understanding that necessarily an even integer is an integer divisible by two without remainder, that necessarily an odd integer is an integer not divisible by two without remainder, and that therefore an odd even integer would be an integer that is and is not divisible by two without remainder. It follows immediately that necessarily no odd integer is even, i.e., that it is logically impossible for an integer to be both odd and even, i.e., an even odd integer is a logical impossibility. This proof requires, and depends on nothing but understanding what it is to be an even integer, what it is to be an odd integer, what it is to be an even odd integer, and thinking clearly. It is because we understand that an even odd integer is an integer divisible by two without remainder and not divisible by two without remainder that we know such a thing is logically impossible. Similarly, anyone who offers an argument to prove that God, conceived as omnipotent, omniscient, perfectly good, creator, lawgiver, and judge, is a logical impossibility implies that he understands that at least two of these supposedly divine attributes are incompatible, i.e., that it is impossible for one thing to have both of them, or that at least one of them is a self-contradictory property, i.e., that it is logically impossible for anything to have that property.

Still other philosophers have argued not that God is a logical impossibility but that he in fact does not exist. They, too, are committed to the proposition that we understand what God is. They believe that there is factual evidence that there is no God, just as there is factual evidence that there are no mermaids, unicorns, centaurs, and similar mythical creatures. The proposition that there are no mermaids is contingent as well as corrigible. Hence, we cannot know it to be true only by understanding what a mermaid is and by thinking clearly, nor can we know it just by believing it. We know that there are no mermaids because all the evidence we have, from observation and scientific theory, supports the hypothesis that mermaids do not exist. However, it is widely believed today that scientific evidence cannot either establish or refute the claim that God exists.

The Verifiability Criterion of Meaningfulness

THERE IS a school of thought, Logical Positivism, that flourished from about 1924 to 1950. Although positivism is no longer vigorous or fashionable, it made a strong and, in some ways, salutary impact on philosophy. Logical positivists have still another point of view concerning talk about God. They do not believe that the nature of God is understood, even imperfectly; they do not believe that God is a logical impossibility; nor do they believe that factual evidence shows that God does not exist. They believe that people who think and talk about God are literally thinking and talking nonsense. Their theory is that thinking and talking about God have emotional causes and emotional effects, and that an emotional tone pervades such thought and talk, but that there is no "intellectual content" or "cognitive meaning" present in any of it.

To get some idea of the positivistic theory about such a word as 'God', imagine a tribe in which parents say "Och!" whenever they are feeding a child, or bathing him or putting him in a warm, clean bed and, in general, whenever they are doing pleasant and comforting things for him; they encourage him to say "Och!" when such good things are being done for him, but it is clear that "Och!" does not mean *bath, warm bed, food, good thing, thank you,* or anything of the sort. It is a noise regularly uttered in pleasant circumstances, so that in later life, when one hears the sound "Och!" one feels good automatically, one expects good things, even when one's circumstances are such as to make it unreasonable to expect any good thing happening to one in the immediate future. On the logical positivist view, the word 'God' and the word 'Och!' are essentially alike. Thinking and talking about God simply evoke certain feelings; they make no sense, in the radical sense of having no "intellectual" or "cognitive" content.

That sentences about God are devoid of "cognitive" meaning is a consequence of logical positivism's theory of what makes a sentence "cognitively" meaningful. Let us now take a close look at that theory to see exactly what it is and whether it is true. The theory is contained in the following rough formula: a sentence is cognitively meaningful if, and only if, it is either analytic or logically false or capable of being shown to be true or false by sense experience. The positivists use the word 'verifiable' as short for 'capable of being shown to be true or false by sense experience'. According to this theory, those and only those sentences are "cognitively" meaningful that are either analytic, logically false, or verifiable. Commands ("Stand up!"), entreaties ("Please stand up!"), resolutions ("Let us stand up"), evaluations ("Killing is wrong; honesty is a good thing"), poetry, religious discourse ("God is the Father of us all"), and extra-religious metaphysical utterances ("There are unexemplified properties") are all devoid of "cognitive" content: they lack cognitive meaning. Given that, by 'cognitively meaningful', positivists mean *capable of being true or false,* what they say is true of commands, entreaties, resolutions, questions, and the like. Such locutions have no truth value. But that this is also true of evaluations, religious discourse and general metaphysical discourse is by no means obvious. On the contrary, it is generally taken for granted that these classes of propositions are true or false, although sometimes it is difficult if not impossible to determine the truth-value of a particular proposition belonging to one of those classes. I shall argue that the positivists have not succeeded in producing any convincing reasons why common sense is wrong in this matter.

ANALYTICITY AND RELATED CONCEPTS

In order to understand and evaluate the positivist theory of "cognitive" meaning, we must understand the positivist conception of analyticity. What follows is a somewhat simplified positivist theory of analyticity and its related concepts. Let us begin by introducing 'W occurs essentially in S', where W is a word and S is a sentence:

Df. (1): W occurs essentially in S = Df. (1) W occurs in S (2) by replacing every occurrence of W in S with a word W', it is possible to produce a sentence S', and (3) S and S' have opposite truth-values.

Thus, the sentence, 'All snakes are mammals' taken in its custom-ary sense is false.[2] In this sentence, the words 'snakes' and 'mammals' occur *essentially*. By replacing 'snakes' with 'cows' we get a sentence 'All cows are mammals', which, in its customary sense, is true. And, again, by replacing 'mammals' with 'reptiles', we get the sentence 'All snakes are reptiles', which is true.

Next we introduce a list of *logical words*. There is no definition of 'logical word'. We can only enumerate instances of logical words, and the enumeration is somewhat arbitrary. Some logicians may include in the list of logical words certain words that other logicians would want to exclude. The logical positivists were in agreement with the logic of Russell and Whitehead's *Principia Mathematica*. The list of logical words in the tradition of that book consists theoretically of three words: 'all', 'neither-nor', and 'is a member of'. These three words are sufficient for defining every word that logicians in this tradition would regard as a logical word. The logical words of English include 'not', 'any', 'and', 'although', 'even if', 'if-then', 'if, and only if', 'while', 'but', 'is'. This last can mean either *exists* or *is included in* (as in "The class of cats is included in the class of animals") or *is a member of* (as in "Two is a member of the class of even integers") or *is identical with* (as in "Cicero is Tully"). Because the definition of analyticity is in terms of logical words, the concept of analyticity is relative to our choice of logical words.

We now define:

Df. (2): S is *logically true* = Df. (1) S is true regardless of the number of objects in the universe and (2) only logical words occur essentially in S.

We need this restriction about the number of objects in the universe. The sentence 'There is exactly one object' is equivalent to a sentence in which only logical words occur essentially. The equivalent sentence is: 'There exists an x such that for anything y, y is identical with x'. If what the sentence says is true, it is not necessarily true, hence it cannot be logically true; and if what it says is false, it is not logically false. We rule out such

[2] Let the reader keep in mind that I am trying to explain the essentials of the positivist theory of analyticity. I would not, myself, speak of *sentences* as being true or false, analytic or self-contradictory. I believe that these are properties of propositions, not of sentences.

sentences by the first condition in the *definiens* of Df. (2). Notice that 'x', 'y', 'z', etc. must be included in the list of logical words. They are "pronominal variables" or "variables of quantification." They are convenient ways of keeping cross-references straight. They do the job of words like 'the former' and 'the latter'. For instance, 'If something is larger than something else, the latter is smaller than the former' can be neatly said as follows: 'For any x and any y, if x is larger than y, then y is smaller than x.'

Thus, the sentence, 'All cows are mammals' is true, but not logically true. 'Cows' and 'mammals' are not logical words, and yet they occur essentially in the sentence. Again, the sentence 'All snakes are mammals' is false, but not logically false. The extra-logical words 'snakes' and 'mammals' occur in it essentially. Now consider the sentence:

If all *men* are *mortal* and *Socrates* is *a man*, then *Socrates* is *mortal*.

The italicized words are extra-logical, and none of them occurs essentially in S. The words in that sentence that are not italicized are logical words, and no word other than a logical word occurs essentially in the sentence. No matter what word is made to replace any of the italicized words, provided that the replacement takes place for every occurrence of the word and provided that the result of this uniform replacement is a sentence, the resulting sentence is true. But if we replace, say, 'If—then' with 'it is not the case that', we get the false sentence, 'It is not the case that: all men are mortal, and Socrates is a man, and Socrates is mortal'. The colon indicates that the denial 'It is not the case that' applies to the conjunction of the three sentences following the colon. The falsity of the sentence may be easier to see if we write it in an equivalent form: 'If all men are mortal and Socrates is a man, then it is not the case that Socrates is mortal'. Take another sentence:

(1) *If* Jones *is* ill, *then* Jones *is* ill.

This, too, is a logical truth. The logical words are italicized. The sentence (1) is true, and for every uniform replacement of its extra-logical words by which we get a sentence, we get a true sentence. But if we replace the logical word 'if-then' by 'or', we get the sentence:

(2) Jones is ill or Jones is ill,

which is redundant for:

(3) Jones is ill.

That is, (2) and (3) are equivalent, and obviously (3) may be false. This shows that in (1) only the logical words occur essentially.

Df. (3): S is *logically false* = Df. (1) S is false regardless of the number of objects in the universe and (2) only logical words occur essentially in S.

Thus, the sentence, 'Something *is* blue *and nothing is* blue', is logically false. The italicized words are the only logical words in the sentence. They all occur essentially, while the only extra-logical word in the sentence, the word 'blue', occurs inessentially. 'Something is blue and nothing is blue' is synonymous with 'Something is blue and it is not the case that something is blue'; it is plain that this sentence is false, regardless of the number of objects in the universe, and remains false, no matter what word we put in place of 'blue', provided that the replacement yields a (grammatical) sentence. ('Something is or and nothing is or' is not a (grammatical) sentence.)

We now define 'S is analytic':

Df. (4): S is *analytic* = Df. Either S is logically true or, together with a definition, it yields a logically true sentence.

Thus, the sentence:

(4) All fathers are male parents,

although not itself a logical truth, is analytic. We have the definition: x is a father = Df. x is a male parent. Now let S' be a sentence that is obtained by replacing in S a word or phrase with its *definiens*, if it has one; the resulting sentence, S', will have the same truth-value as S.[3] Accordingly, (4) yields:

[3] A word of caution. Consider the following examples:
  (1) The sentence he uttered contained the word 'father', but not the expression 'male parent'.
  (2) He uttered the sentence, 'Jones is a father'.
In (1) and (2) certain words and expressions occur within single quotes. The single quotes are a convention for forming *names* of words and expressions. If I want to talk *about* the word, 'cat', I put single quotes around it, as I

(5) All male parents are male parents,

which is a logical truth. Hence, (4) is analytic. Here is a further definition:

Df. (5): S is *synthetic* = Df. S is not analytic, not logically false, and not reducible, by means of a definition, to a sentence that is logically false.

According to the positivist theory of meaning, as we have noted, one class of cognitively meaningful sentences, the non-factual ones, consists of sentences that are either analytic or logically false or reducible to logical falsehoods by means of definitions. The positivists believed that their way of defining an analytic sentence gave precise sense to the traditional notion that an analytic proposition is one that is true in every possible universe. But, the positivists reasoned, if a sentence is true in "every possible universe," it can provide no information about any particular universe. That is, it cannot tell us, for example, what particular states of affairs or laws characterize our actual universe, as compared with some other conceivable one. Likewise, the logically false sentences, as well as the ones that are reducible to logical falsehoods by means of suitable definitions, cannot give us information about any particular universe because they are false for every possible world. It is for this reason that the positivists said that analytic sentences, logically false sentences, and sentences reducible to logical falsehoods are not factual. Such sentences, they said, are empty of factual information. All of logic and mathematics was said to be analytic.

The second class of cognitively meaningful sentences, the synthetic ones, are the ones that are verifiable. The theory of factual meaningfulness, the verifiability criterion, is supposed to show

---

have just done. Now let S′ be a sentence that is obtained by replacing in S the *name* of a word or phrase with the *name* of its *definiens*. Thus, from (1) we would get (3): The sentence he uttered contained the word, 'male parent' but not the expression 'male parent'. (3) is self-contradictory, hence, necessarily false, whereas (1) is contingent and might very well be true. This shows that replacing *names* of words or expressions with names of their *definientia* is not a way of preserving truth-value. This is not an exception to the rule that replacing a *word* or an *expression* with its *definiens* is truth-value preserving. If we want our deductions to be valid, we must guard against replacing *names* of expressions with *names* of the *definientia* of those expressions.

that all synthetic[4] sentences about God are unverifiable, hence cognitively meaningless. Being cognitively meaningless, synthetic sentences about God are devoid of content, and they are not true or false. The same thing is true of other "metaphysical" sentences, e.g., 'The absolute is the real', 'The finite and limited presupposes that which is unlimited'. The positivists thus divided the class of sentences that were "devoid of content" into two subclasses. One of these included the sentences of logic and mathematics and their denials. While these were devoid of content they were meaningful, and true or false. The synthetic and unverifiable sentences, on the other hand, were devoid of content and meaningless, and hence useless. The sentences of logic and mathematics, while also being devoid of content, were very useful indeed. It is true that they provided no information about any particular world, yet they were thought to be indispensable intellectual tools that made it possible for people to extract, by means of inference, all sorts of information contained in factual premises. For example, if I know that a certain object weighs one pound and is ten times as heavy as another object, I can deduce that the other object is one tenth of a pound. I do not have to weigh the other object to find out its actual weight.

Let us now turn to the positivist theory of the cognitive meaningfulness of synthetic sentences. In order to assess the positivist claims about synthetic sentences in general and synthetic sentences about God in particular, we must see exactly what the verifiability criterion of cognitive meaning is. There is no single criterion: there is a series of unsuccessful attempts to formulate a criterion that would be immune from attack.[5]

[4] The theory does not exclude an analytic sentence such as 'All Gods are Gods' from the class of the cognitively meaningful. The theory has no way of deciding that the sentence in question is not analytic. If it is a sentence at all, it is analytic. Now in a natural language such as English, the above is certainly a sentence; and in other natural languages such as French and German, there are sentences synonymous with it. If positivism purports to be providing a theory of "cognitive" meaning for natural languages, then it must allow that some sentences about God, namely, the analytic ones, are "cognitively" meaningful. It can try to prove only that synthetic sentences about God are devoid of "cognitive" meaning.

[5] See C. G. Hempel, "Problems and Changes in the Empiricist Criterion of Meaning," *Revue internationale de Philosophie*, 4, 11 (1950); reprinted in *Semantics and the Philosophy of Language*, L. Linsky, ed. (Urbana: University of Illinois Press, 1952).

The Principle of Conclusive Verifiability

ONE OF THE earliest formulations (circa 1925) may be put as follows: a synthetic sentence is cognitively meaningful if, and only if, it is conclusively verifiable. Let us call this "the principle of conclusive verifiability." Following Professor Hempel's suggestion, let us mean by 'an observable property' a property or a relation of physical objects whose presence or absence can, in suitable circumstances, be ascertained by "direct" observation. It is supposed that such properties as being green, soft, liquid or longer than are observable properties, while being radioactive, having a tendency to paranoia or being a hydrocarbon are unobservable. By 'observation predicate' we are to mean a term that designates an observable property. Thus, 'green', 'soft', 'liquid', are examples of observation predicates, 'radioactive' and 'hydrocarbon' are not. By 'observation sentence' we are to understand a sentence of the form 'x is ϕ' where 'x' is a name for, or a definite description of, a particular physical object, and ϕ is an observation predicate. Given our earlier notion of a perceptual proposition, a more straightforward way of introducing observation sentences is simply to say that they are sentences that are normally used to assert perceptual propositions. But this way of introducing observation sentences presupposes that propositions are entities distinct from sentences and not definable in terms of them. Logical positivism does not recognize such entities. Hence, it must introduce observation sentences without presupposing propositions in the above sense.

This way of defining an observation sentence is characteristic of physicalistic verificationism. There is also phenomenalistic verificationism. The issue between physicalists and phenomenalists is epistemological. Physicalists think that physicalistic observation sentences are adequate rock-bottom evidence for verifying (or for corroborating) all genuinely empirical hypotheses. Phenomenalists believe that physicalistic sentences are not rock-bottom because they are corrigible. Surely, says the phenomenalist, I can be mistaken in believing that the (physical) object two feet in front of me is a red ball. But I cannot be mistaken in thinking that I seem to see a red ball at what looks like a distance of two feet from me. The phenomenalist does not want his observation sentences to be such that each of them entails that there exists a physical object. He wants them to be incorrigible reports of what a person is experiencing. For example, a phenomenalist would not speak of afterimages when talking of what he believes to be the rock-bottom level of empirical report. For an afterimage is, by definition, "a usu. visual sensation occurring after the external stimulus causing it has ceased to operate." (*Webster's Seventh New Collegiate Dictionary*.) To describe a present experience as the experience of an afterimage is, therefore, to refer to causes that are not now operative, hence not now experienced. One can be mistaken in believing that an external stimulus that was operating at an earlier time but not now operating, caused a certain visual experience. But one cannot be mistaken in reporting that one is now experiencing bluish, roundish color patches, in concentric circles, which move, gradually diminish in size, and finally disappear into thin air. This is a phenomenalistic description of *what* we are experiencing now, a description that does not entail the existence of causes distinct from the contents of the present experience. The phenomenalist and the physicalist both want incorrigible sentences to serve as the basic verifiers of all higher-level claims to empirical knowledge. They simply differ as to what the incorrigible base is. The point of these extended remarks about physicalism and phenomenalism is this: all the forthcoming criticisms that show that none of the verifiability criteria so far proposed is an adequate criterion of being a meaningful synthetic sentence apply with equal force to both physicalistic and phenomenalistic verificationism.

We can now state the principle of conclusive verifiability as follows: a synthetic sentence is cognitively meaningful if, and only if, it is entailed[6] by a finite and logically consistent set of observation sentences. The proviso that the finite set of observation sentences be consistent is needed to bar any synthetic sentence whatever from being cognitively meaningful. A logically inconsistent set of sentences entails *any* sentence whatever. (This is the logical positivist statement of a principle of logic that, in its correct version, would be not about sentences but about

---

[6] Again, the terminology is that of positivism. I do not subscribe to it because I do not believe that entailment is a relation between sentences. I believe that it is a relation between propositions.

propositions). This principle is an immediate consequence of our definition of entailment. We have defined:

p entails q = Df. It is not possible that p is true and q is false.

If p is logically inconsistent, it cannot possibly be true, in which case the *definiens* is satisfied. For if p cannot be true, then the case of p true and q not true does not arise. Hence, for any sentence p, and any sentence, q, if p is logically inconsistent, then p entails q.

The principle of conclusive verifiability is defective for reasons that are well-known. First, it makes all synthetic sentences in universal form, e.g., 'All men are mortal', cognitively meaningless. For no finite set of observation sentences entails a universal sentence. According to the principle of conclusive verifiability, large segments of science, including all its fundamental laws, would be cognitively meaningless. Apart from its being counterintuitive, however, such a result cannot be tolerated by positivists. For them the factual sciences, particularly physics, are the paradigms of knowledge. They cannot either happily or consistently proclaim a theory of cognitive meaning that implies that physics is not knowledge. Second, assume that a finite set of observation sentences entails a synthetic sentence S. Hence S is cognitively meaningful by the principle of conclusive verifiability. But the sentence 'S or N', where 'N' is any sentence you please, is entailed by 'S'. Hence the finite set of observation sentences entails the sentence 'S or N'. But 'S or N' could be the sentence 'This is green or God is the Father of us all', and by the principle of conclusive verifiability such a sentence would be cognitively meaningful. Positivists cannot tolerate this result because part of their aim is to rule out as devoid of "cognitive" meaning just such sentences as 'God is the Father of us all' singly or in any sort of combination with other sentences. Third, let 'P' be an observation predicate. Then the sentence 'There is something that is P' is completely verifiable. It is entailed by at least one observation sentence, e.g., 'The book in your hand is P'. But the denial of 'There is something that is P' is the sentence 'Whatever you may select, it is not P'. The latter is a universal sentence, and we have already seen that universal sentences are *not* completely verifiable. Moreover, the universal sentence in question is neither analytic nor logically false. Hence, it is cognitively meaningless,

by the principle of complete verifiability. But this result is para-
doxical. Since the sentence, 'There is something that is P', is
cognitively meaningful by the principle, it is capable of being
either true or false. If it is true, its contradictory must be false;
if it is false, its contradictory must be true. But its contradictory
'Whatever you may select, it is not P', is by the principle not
cognitively meaningful; hence, it can be neither true nor false.
This shows that the principle of complete verifiability is inconsistent with the principle of non-contradiction and with the
assumption that 'There is something which is ϕ' is the contradictory of 'Nothing is ϕ' ('Whatever you select, it is not ϕ'). The only
reasonable conclusion to draw from all this is that the principle
of complete verifiability is hopelessly deficient.

The Principle of Complete Falsifiability

EXACTLY similar difficulties beset another attempt to formulate
the verifiability criterion. This criterion—let us call it 'the principle of complete falsifiability'—says that a synthetic sentence is
cognitively meaningful if, and only if, it can be conclusively
refuted by a finite set of observations. In other words, a synthetic
sentence is cognitively meaningful if, and only if, its denial is
synthetic and is entailed by a finite set of observation sentences.
This criterion says that a synthetic sentence is cognitively meaningful if, and only if, its denial can be conclusively shown to be
true. The first difficulty with this criterion is that it rules out all
sentences of the form 'There is something that is P'. The denial
of that sentence is: 'Nothing is P'. But 'Nothing is P' cannot be
conclusively shown to be true by any finite set of observations.
The principle also rules out sentences such as this one: 'Whatever
you may select, there is something such that the latter is larger
than the former'. The denial of that sentence is: 'There is something such that, whatever you may select, it is not the case that
the latter is larger than the former'. This last sentence cannot be
conclusively shown to be true by any finite and consistent set of
observation sentences. Hence, according to the principle of complete falsifiability, its denial cannot be cognitively meaningful.
Second, assume that the sentence 'S' is completely falsifiable,

while the sentence 'N' is not. For example, let 'S' be 'This thing is red' and 'N' be 'God is the Father of us all'. Now the sentence 'S and N' is completely falsifiable. For if a finite and consistent set of observation sentences entails the denial of 'S', it also entails the denial of 'S and N'. In this way, the sentence, 'God is the Father of us all', which is clearly meant to be excluded, turns out to be a component of a meaningful sentence. Third, if 'P' is an observation predicate, then the sentence, 'Everything is P', is cognitively meaningful because its denial, 'There is at least one thing that is not P', can be conclusively shown to be true simply because it is logically possible to find a physical object that is observed to lack P. But the sentence 'There is at least one thing that is not P', cannot itself be cognitively meaningful because its contradictory, 'All things are P', is not deducible from any finite and consistent set of observation sentences. But this gives rise to precisely the same paradox that we found in the third difficulty involved in the principle of complete verifiability. The principle of complete falsifiability is inconsistent with the principle of non-contradiction, and with the assumption that 'Something is ϕ' and 'Nothing is ϕ' are contradictories. Once again, the only reasonable conclusion to draw is that the principle of complete falsifiability is hopelessly defective.

Ayer's Verifiability Criterion

THESE RESULTS indicate that any verifiability criterion will lead to difficulty, if it construes the logical relation between observation sentences and sentences that are not observation sentences but nevertheless verifiable as being one of entailment from the former to the latter. The verifiability criteria we have so far discussed were typical of the early days of the Vienna Circle (from about 1924 to 1935). In 1936 the English philosopher A. J. Ayer, who is now a Professor of Philosophy at Oxford, published *Language, Truth and Logic*. This little book became a classic of logical positivism. In it Ayer tries to pull together the various strands and doctrines of logical positivism and to make it into a comprehensive and consistent empiricism. As one would expect, Ayer devotes much effort toward stating the verifiability criterion in a form that will be immune from criticism. But he fails. Ayer's first formulation is in the first edition of *Language, Truth and Logic*. In the Introduction to the second edition (1946), Ayer criticizes his first formulation and offers another.

Ayer's first formulation is this. A (synthetic) sentence is cognitively meaningful if, and only if, together with certain other sentences it entails an observation sentence that these other sentences alone do not entail. Note that Ayer's criterion no longer requires of any verifiable sentence that it be either an observation sentence or a sentence entailed by a finite and consistent set of observation sentences. Even so, Ayer's first formulation fails. Ayer himself points out, in the Introduction to the second edition (p. 13), that this criterion allows any "indicative sentence" to qualify as "cognitively" meaningful. Consider the following: If God is our Father, then snow is white. But God is our Father. Therefore, snow is white. The conclusion of this valid deductive argument would be an observation sentence for Ayer. It follows from 'God is our Father' when that is taken together with, 'If God is our Father, then snow is white', but it does not follow from the latter sentence alone. Hence, by Ayer's first criterion, 'God is our Father' is cognitively meaningful, although it is neither analytic nor self-contradictory. But this is precisely the sort of result the verifiability criterion is intended to rule out.

Ayer's second criterion, again stated in our terminology, is as follows: A (synthetic) sentence (which purports to be factual)[7] is cognitively meaningful if, and only if, it is either directly or indirectly verifiable. A sentence is *directly verifiable* if, and only if, (a) it is an observation sentence, or (b) in conjunction with one or more observation sentences, it entails at least one observation sentence that is not deducible from these other premises alone. A sentence is *indirectly verifiable* if, and only if, (a) in conjunction with certain other premises it entails one or more directly verifiable sentences that are not deducible from these other premises alone, and (b) these other premises do not include any statement that is not either analytic or directly verifiable or capable of being independently established as indirectly verifiable.

Carl Hempel has shown[8] that this criterion, like the criterion

---

[7] This provision excludes synthetic imperative sentences, e.g., "Come!" and all other synthetic sentences that have no truth-value.

[8] *Op. cit.*, p. 50.

of complete falsifiability, qualifies as cognitively meaningful any conjunction, 'S and N', where 'S' satisfies Ayer's second criterion and 'N' is a sentence intended to be disqualified, e.g., 'God is our Father'. If 'S and O' together entail 'O_1', then 'S and N and O' together entail 'O_1', ('N' being any sentence whatever). Hence, 'This is white and God is our Father' qualifies as a cognitively meaningful sentence, contrary to what is intended. Alonzo Church has another criticism, which is even more devastating.[9] Let 'p', 'q', and 'r' be observation sentences, none of which entails any of the others, and let 'S' be any sentence whatever. Church shows that, by Ayer's second criterion, either 'S' is *indirectly verifiable*, or the negation of 'S', namely, '~S', is *directly verifiable*. In other words, Church proves that by Ayer's criterion *any* sentence, hence, any synthetic sentence, is cognitively meaningful. In order to follow Church's argument in detail we need to know the propositional calculus, the basic level of formal logic. Those who are unfamiliar with this area of logic may rest assured that Church's argument is correct. Let us use a dot, '.', to represent the word 'and', and a wedge, 'v', to represent the word 'or'. The tilde, '~', stands for 'It is not the case that'. Now:

$$\text{'p.}[(\sim p.q) \text{ v } (\sim S.r)]\text{' implies 'r'.}$$

Hence, by Ayer's criterion, '$(\sim p.q)$ v $(\sim S.r)$' is *directly* verifiable. Together with an observation sentence, 'p', it entails an observation sentence 'r,' which 'p' alone does not entail. Now either '$(\sim p.q)$ v $(\sim S.r)$' entails 'q' or it does not entail 'q'. If it entails 'q', then '~S.r' entails 'q'. This means that, if '$(\sim p.q)$ v $(\sim S.r)$' entails 'q', then '~S' is *directly* verifiable. For under those circumstances, '~S' together with the observation sentence 'r' entails the observation sentence 'q', which is not entailed by 'r' alone. If '$(\sim p.q)$ v $(\sim S.r)$' does not entail 'q', then:

$$\text{'(S.}[(\sim p.q) \text{ v } (\sim S.r)])\text{' entails 'q'}$$

in which case 'S' is *indirectly* verifiable. Together with the directly verifiable sentence '$(\sim p.q)$ v $(\sim S.r)$' it entails the observation sentence 'q', which is not entailed by '$(\sim p.q)$ v $(\sim S.r)$' alone. Hence, given that there are at least three observation sentences

[9] See his review of *Language, Truth and Logic*, 2nd ed., in *The Journal of Symbolic Logic*, 14 (1949), 52–53.

none of which entails any of the others, for any sentence 'S', either 'S' is indirectly verifiable or '~S' is directly verifiable. Thus, Ayer's second criterion is altogether too liberal. It bars no sentence, hence no synthetic sentence whatever, from being cognitively meaningful.[10]

There have been attempts to restate Ayer's second criterion satisfactorily, but perhaps enough has been said to incline the reader to suspect that attempts to formulate a satisfactory verifiability criterion are, like attempts to prove that God exists, unlikely to succeed. This is the prevailing opinion among philosophers. But suppose that the verifiability criterion could be formulated in such a way as not to allow every purportedly factual synthetic sentence to be verifiable. Assume, in particular, that the criterion ruled out 'God exists' or 'The real is the rational'. Would that prove that these sentences are devoid of factual content, that they are "cognitively" meaningless? The answer to that question depends upon what is said in favor of accepting the verifiability criterion.

Assessment of Verificationist Theories of Meaning

No ONE HAS asserted that the verifiability criterion is recorded in any standard dictionary as giving the meaning of 'meaningful synthetic sentence'. The word 'synthetic', as used by philosophers, is not a word in everyday use. One would normally expect to see it defined only in a dictionary of philosophical terms. Hence, one would not expect to find a definition of 'meaningful synthetic sentence' in any of the standard dictionaries.

Some positivists have said that the verifiability criterion is a philosophical explication. It is supposed to make explicit a standard that every intelligent adult in fact uses, without necessarily being aware of it, in order to decide whether a synthetic sentence is meaningful. As a factual claim this is false. Many intelligent

---

[10] An attempt to save Ayer's criterion from Church's criticism is P. Niddich's "A Defence of Ayer's Verifiability Principle Against Church's Criticism," *Mind*, LXX (1961), 88–89. The futility of this attempt and the cogency of Church's type of criticism is demonstrated by Israel Scheffler, *The Anatomy of Inquiry* (New York: Knopf, 1964), p. 154.

adults believe that 'God exists' is not a tautology and is not veri-fiable, yet they think that it is a meaningful sentence. In everyday life some people believe that God exists; others believe that God does not exist; still others believe that either God exists or He does not exist, but that human beings do not know whether or not God exists. Perhaps people who talk this way are confused; perhaps they are being inconsistent without knowing it; perhaps they are wrong in taking it for granted that 'God exists' and its denial are meaningful sentences. But all this has to be shown, and until it has been shown, the claim that the verifiability criterion is a real explicative definition is totally groundless.

If the verifiability criterion is not a real definition to be found in a standard dictionary, and if it is not an explicative real defini-tion that formulates what any intelligent adult, upon reflection, would recognize as being a correct statement of a standard that he uses implicitly, perhaps it is a proposal. Now some proposals are not worthy of serious consideration. We have had occasion to observe that it would be absurd for anyone to argue as follows: "It is, after all, false that all fathers are male parents. For I propose that by 'father' we mean a *female parent;* from which it follows that 'all fathers are male parents' is false." The fact is that, *as normally used,* the sentence 'All fathers are male parents' expresses a necessarily true proposition. That fact cannot be disproved by stipulating a definition of 'father' different from its customary meaning. Now it may seem just as absurd to propose that a synthetic sentence is meaningful if, and only if, it is verifiable. But the analogy is unfair. In English there is a stand-ard use of the word 'father', and it is a fact that in that use 'father' means *male parent.* But there is no standard use in Eng-lish of the phrase 'meaningful synthetic sentence'. There is a standard use of 'meaningful sentence', but that is not the same thing. The technical phrase 'meaningful synthetic sentence' cor-responds to the vague notion of a "meaningful sentence about matters of fact." The purpose of the verifiability criterion may be to replace the vague notion with a precise, or relatively more precise, concept. This in itself would be neither silly nor objec-tionable. The objection to the verifiability criterion is not that it is more precise than anything we have in our uncritical thinking, but that it is simply unfairly restrictive.

The verificationist thinks that there is an important difference between such statements as "Water is H_2O" and "God is merciful." He thinks that the former is "saying something" while the latter is not. The anti-verificationist also thinks that there is a difference between the two statements, but that the difference is not what the verificationist thinks it is. The anti-verificationist thinks that both statements are "saying something"; the significant difference between them is that the former is saying something that can be, and is, established by procedures and reasonings characteristic of the natural sciences, whereas the latter is saying something that in principle cannot be settled by such reasonings and procedures. But that difference is not the difference between having factual content and lacking factual content, unless it is assumed that all and only those statements whose truth or falsehood can be established by reasonings and procedures that are characteristic of the natural sciences have factual content. That assumption, however, is unproved and implausible. And without it the move from "unverifiable" to "lacking in factual content" is unwarranted. A theist can produce sentences synonymous with 'God exists'. One such sentence is 'A supremely perfect being exists'. Another sentence about God, although not synonymous with 'God exists', is 'There exists a person who is omniscient, omnipotent, and perfectly good'. The theist can propose (as we shall see in the next section) definitions of the terms that occur in the second sentence. To the anti-verificationist (and that includes a large number of people), these words and sentences seem to make sense. To be sure, not all of them have been satisfactorily defined. For example, there are serious problems, as we shall see, in the concept of omnipotence. Many an anti-verificationist believes that these deficiencies can be remedied. Until it is proved to him that he is confused or inconsistent in thinking so, the anti-verificationist is in a safe position. Even if a satisfactory verifiability criterion existed, it could at most be proposed as an explicative definition of 'meaningful synthetic sentence normally used to make scientific statements'. It could not, without further argument, provide evidence for the proposition that, if we were clear-headed and preferred precision over vagueness, we would identify the property of being a meaningful synthetic sentence with the property of being verifiable.

Section 3

IS GOD A POSSIBLE BEING?

THE PROPOSITION that no empirical evidence can prove or disprove the assertion that God exists is highly controversial. I am among those who believe that the proposition is true. Given that assumption, if the logical positivist verifiability criterion had turned out to be a satisfactory explication of the "cognitive" meaningfulness of "factual" propositions, one immediate consequence would have been that talk about God makes no sense, hence the question of God's possibility cannot even arise as a question. Now the fact that the verifiability criterion is unsatisfactory does not answer the question of whether or not God is a possible being. The failure of the verifiability criterion does not imply that God is a possible being. There may be other reasons for believing that God is not a possible being.

In 1676 Leibniz constructed an *a priori* argument to prove once and for all that God is a possible being.[11] Let A and B be "simple" qualities, and let there be a proposition such as:

A and B are incompatible.

Leibniz asserts that this proposition cannot be proved unless we can define A or B or both. But, being simple properties, A and B are indefinable. Therefore, this proposition cannot be proved. "But it could be proved . . . if it were true, for it is not true *per se;* but all necessarily true propositions are either demonstrable, or known *per se.* Therefore, this proposition is not neces-

[11] The argument is in his *New Essays Concerning Human Understanding* and is reprinted in Russell's *A Critical Exposition of the Philosophy of Leibniz,* 2nd ed. (London: Allen & Unwin, 1949), p. 287.

sarily true." Leibniz concludes that all simple properties are compatible, hence God is a possible being because God is conceived as a being having all perfections, and a perfection is any "simple quality which is positive and absolute."

Leibniz' argument is formally valid, but it is inconclusive. It depends upon two dubious, and certainly highly controversial, assumptions. One is that there are "absolute and simple" properties. The other is that all necessary truths are "analytic." It is impossible to explain simply and briefly what Leibniz meant by 'absolute and simple' and by 'analytic', and why his two assumptions are controversial. The issues involved are among the most fundamental and far-reaching in philosophy. Suffice it to say that, inasmuch as Leibniz' argument depends upon two extremely contentious assumptions, it is inconclusive.

Omnipotence, Omniscience, and Perfect Goodness

However, that does not mean that God is not a possible being. We have to make a fresh start. Three of the salient properties of God are omnipotence, omniscience, and perfect goodness. Some philosophers have argued that it is logically impossible for God to be omnipotent, omniscient, and perfectly good, and also for evil to exist. If God is omnipotent and omniscient, He could not have allowed evil to exist if He is all good. If He is all-good and all-knowing, then, since He has allowed evil to exist, He cannot be omnipotent. But evil does exist. Hence, the argument concludes, God is impossible. This, too, is a highly controversial issue. However, I am persuaded by a recent discussion that the problem of evil poses no insuperable obstacle to the proposition that God is a possible being.[12]

The next possible source of difficulty may be in the concepts of omniscience, omnipotence, and perfect goodness taken severally. The following definitions seem to capture what theists include in the notions of omniscience, omnipotence, and perfect goodness.

[12] The discussion is Alvin Plantinga's "The Free Will Defense," in *Philosophy in America,* Max Black, ed. (London: Allen & Unwin, 1965).

1. x is omnipotent = Df. There is something x is capable of doing, and for any action A, if the proposition "x does A" is not self-contradictory, then x is capable of doing A.[13]

We will allow proper names and definite descriptions to be substitutions for 'x'. Because we are allowing definite descriptions as substitutions, we need the clause that there is something that x is capable of doing. Otherwise a being who was capable of doing nothing would be omnipotent, which is absurd. Let x be the being that is capable of doing nothing. Now the proposition of the form "x does A" is: the being that is capable of doing nothing does A. But, for any action A, the proposition of the form: the being that is capable of doing nothing does A, is self-contradictory. For it entails that the being that is capable of doing nothing is capable of doing something. Hence, the antecedent of the conditional clause of the *definiens* is false; hence, the conditional clause is true (because a conditional with false antecedent is true). Thus, if 'x is omnipotent' were defined simply as *for any action, A, if the proposition, "x does A," is not self-contradictory, then x is capable of doing A*, and if definite descriptions were allowed to be substitutions for 'x', then if x was not capable of doing anything, then under the description, "the being that is capable of doing nothing," x would be omnipotent.

2. x is omniscient = Df. For any proposition, p, if p is true, then x knows that p.[14]

---

[13] Descartes seems to have something like this definition in mind when, at the beginning of the Sixth Meditation, he says: ". . . and I have never deemed that anything was impossible for Him, unless I found a contradiction in attempting to conceive it clearly." (Haldane and Ross, Vol. 1, p. 185.)

[14] This definition is criticized by John Lachs in his "Professor Prior on Omniscience," *Philosophy*, XXXVIII (1963), 361–364. Lachs' argument is this:

(1) If x cannot experience some psychological state, S, then x cannot fully understand propositions in which the term 'S' or some synonym occurs.

(2) If x cannot fully understand a proposition, p, then x cannot in any important sense be said to know p.

∴ (3) If x cannot experience some psychological state, S, then x cannot in any important sense be said to know any proposition in which the term 'S' or any of its synonyms occurs.

3. x is perfectly good = Df. (1) For any action, A, if it is wrong for x to do A, x does not do A, and if x ought to do A, then x does A; (2) for any attitude, disposition and feeling, if x ought to have it, then x has it, and if x ought not to have it, then x does not have it; and (3) x performs acts of non-obligatory well-doing.

I include clause (2) because an agent who simply fulfills his obligations and refrains from wrongdoing is not as good a person as one who also has the attitudes, dispositions, and feelings that a person ought to have. I include clause (3) because a thoroughly good person will do favors and kindnesses above and beyond the call of duty. God is thought to be infinitely merciful, loving, and compassionate. Any definition of 'x is perfectly good' that applies to God must make the performance of supererogatory acts a necessary condition for being perfectly good.

We would do better not to assume that the concepts of omnipotence, omniscience, and perfect goodness are altogether free of difficulties. Take, for example, the concept of omnipotence. According to the above definition of omnipotence, God is capable of creating the first man now. This follows from the definition, because the proposition that God creates the first man now is not self-contradictory. But it is a fact that men have already been "created." Hence, God is not capable of creating the first man now, which shows that the above definition of omnipotence is in need of refinement. There is no easy way of showing how it can be refined satisfactorily. And there is no easy way of showing that it cannot be. Until the problem is solved, whatever depends upon the definition of omnipotence is at least as problematic as the definition itself.

---

   (4)   But an omniscient being, i.e., a being which knows every true proposition, could not experience doubt.

∴ (5)   An omniscient being cannot in any important sense be said to know any proposition in which the term 'doubt' or any of its synonyms occurs.

∴ (6)   There is no omniscient being.

This argument is inconclusive because premises (1) and (2) are false, or, at least, highly questionable.

Supreme Perfection and Degrees of Perfection

THE NEXT possible source of difficulty may lie in the fact that theists conceive of God as being supremely perfect. The notion of supreme perfection entails the notion of one thing being more perfect than another. No matter how we define 'x is supremely perfect', it is true that "x is supremely perfect" entails "for any y (the same as x or different from x), it is not the case that y is more perfect than x" (i.e., nothing is more perfect than x). Now suppose that the idea of degrees of perfection turns out to be either incomprehensible or inconsistent. Theists would not thereby be forced to concede that the idea of supreme perfection is also incomprehensible or inconsistent. For if the theist can make some consistent sense of the idea of supreme perfection, he has the option of denying that supreme perfection entails degrees of perfection. This would indeed be a desperate and, to my mind, purely arbitrary salvaging operation. However, the theist need not be reduced to such desperate measures. It is possible to define degrees of perfection. I shall offer one such definition later on. But it will be a problematic definition because the *definiens* contains the concept of omnipotence.

I think we can grant that supreme perfection does entail degrees of perfection. We can also admit that, consequently, if the idea of one thing being more perfect than another is inconsistent or incomprehensible, so is the idea of supreme perfection. If these ideas are inconsistent or incomprehensible, then Descartes' causal and ontological arguments merit no serious consideration. Descartes' causal argument makes use of the notion of one thing being more perfect than another. The argument has such premises as this. If x is the cause of y (y may be identical with x or different from x), then y cannot have more reality than x. The ontological argument makes use of the notion of supreme perfection. Inasmuch as supreme perfection entails the idea of one thing being more perfect than another, the ontological argument, no less than the causal argument, assumes that the idea of one thing being more perfect than another is consistent and intelligible.

Now the question is: are the notions of supreme perfection and of one thing being more perfect than another consistent and comprehensible? We can examine this question in some detail through a critical exposition of C. D. Broad's views on it. In "Arguments for God's Existence," reprinted in *Religion, Philosophy and Psychical Research* (New York: Harcourt, Brace, 1953), Broad argues that neither notion is consistent. That they are neither clear nor precise may be granted forthwith. But that they are not even consistent is not so plain.

Broad first attacks the notion of one thing being more perfect than another; he believes, correctly, that if that notion is discredited, then so is the notion of supreme perfection. For we have seen that, if the notion of one thing being more perfect than another is inconsistent, then the notion of supreme perfection is also inconsistent. He then goes on to argue that even independently of the notion of one thing being more perfect than another, the notion of supreme perfection itself is inconsistent. I shall first examine Broad's criticisms of the notion of supreme perfection and then take up his criticism of the notion of one thing being more perfect than another. I am reversing Broad's order of exposition because, if some of the things I have to say relative to the problem of supreme perfection are said first, then what I have to say relative to the problem of one thing being more perfect than another will be easier to understand. We can do this without in the least weakening Broad's case against the two notions.

Against the notion of supreme perfection itself Broad argues as follows: Traditionally, 'x is supremely perfect' has been used to mean either of two things:

(a) It is not possible that there exists a being more perfect than x,

or

(b) x has all positive powers and qualities to the highest degree.

Now either all positive qualities are compatible or they are not. If they are not all compatible, then nothing can have all positive qualities; hence (b) specifies an impossible entity. On the other hand, (a) leads to trouble also. For suppose that there are just three qualities, Q_1, Q_2, and Q_3, any two of which are compatible but not all three. There are many examples of properties that fulfill these compatibility conditions. For instance, let

$Q_1 = $ x is tall or x is poor
$Q_2 = $ x is short
$Q_3 = $ x is rich

Any two of these can characterize one thing, but all three cannot characterize the same thing. If Q_1, Q_2, and Q_3 were all the properties there are, it would be possible to have three supreme beings. In other words, if not all positive properties are compatible, and we define 'x is supremely perfect' to mean *it is not possible that there exists a being greater than x,* then we could have more than one supremely perfect being. Nothing then would answer to the description, "*the* most perfect being." Moreover, it would be impossible to deduce God's uniqueness from His supreme perfection, as Descartes does during the course of the development of his ontological argument.

Now suppose that all positive qualities are compatible. Then nothing could satisfy condition (a) if it did not satisfy (b). For imagine a thing that has only two positive qualities, while it is possible to have three positive qualities. Since we have assumed that all positive qualities are compatible, the thing that has two out of three qualities would not be supremely perfect. But nothing can satisfy condition (b), because of the requirement in (b) that the qualities possessed by a supreme being be possessed to the highest degree. This will be impossible to fulfill unless there is an intrinsic upper limit to every positive quality that admits of degrees. But the fact is that, while some qualities that admit of degrees do have an intrinsic upper limit, others do not. Here are examples of ones that do admit of an intrinsic upper limit. One proper fraction may be greater than another, as 1/2 is greater than 1/4. But it is not possible for any fraction to exceed the ratio 1/1. Again, it is not possible for a negative integer to be greater than −1. In contrast to these cases, positive integers, for instance, while admitting of degrees, do not admit of an intrinsic upper limit. There is no such thing as the greatest positive integer. Broad gives three other examples of qualities that admit of degrees but have no intrinsic upper limit: temperature, length, and pain. Note that Broad's argument does not assume either that all positive qualities are compatible or that they are not. Nor does he define the notion of "positive quality."

Let us now see if Descartes can be defended against Broad. If omnipotence can be satisfactorily defined, then Descartes can be defended by making use of a distinction that occurs in the *Meditations*, one that Descartes adopted from his medieval predecessors. The distinction I have in mind is between God's possessing some properties *formally* and others *eminently*. 'x is *formally* Q' simply means that x is Q. Descartes does not define what it is, in the context of his thought, to have a property *eminently*. The following definition is, I think, an accurate explication of what he intends.

> x is Q eminently = Df. x is not Q, but x is capable of producing something that is Q.

If the definition of omnipotence on p. 197, above, was satisfactory, we could prove that for any entity x and for any property, P, if x is omnipotent and it is logically possible for x to bring it about that something is P, then x is P either formally or eminently.

Assume: (1) x is omnipotent.

∴ (2) If it is possible that x brings it about that something is P, then x is capable of bringing it about that something is P. (From (1) and Df. of 'x is omnipotent')

∴ (3) If [(it is possible that x brings it about that something is P) and x is not P], then [(x is capable of bringing it about that something is P) and x is not P]. (From (2))

But (4) If [(x is capable of bringing it about that something is P) and x is not P], then x is P eminently. (From Df. of 'x is P eminently')

∴ (5) If [(it is possible that x brings it about that something is P) and x is not P], then x is P eminently. (From (3) and (4))

But (6) If [(it is possible that x brings it about that something is P) and x is P], then x is P formally. (Tautology)

∴ (7) If it is possible that x brings it about that something is P, then x is P either formally or eminently. (From (5) and (6))

Thus, if the definition of omnipotence on p. 197 above was a good one, we would have proved that: an omnipotent being has any property whatever either formally or eminently, provided that it is logically possible for him to bring it about that something has that property. Now the vast majority of theists define 'x is supremely perfect' in such a way that supreme perfection entails omnipotence. Therefore, it would be necessarily true that if a being, x, is a supremely perfect being, then for any property, P, if it is logically possible for x to bring it about that something is P, then x is P formally or eminently. This would mean that in virtue of his omnipotence, the supremely perfect being possesses formally or eminently every property that is such that it is logically possible for him to bring it about that something has that property. Thus, if the property of being omnipotent as defined on p. 197 was consistent and intelligible, we would have a consistent and intelligible conception of a supremely perfect being, whose supreme perfection *entails* that he possesses, formally or eminently, not only all *positive* attributes (whatever 'positive attribute' may mean) but *any* attribute whatever, provided that it is logically possible for him to bring it about that something has that attribute.

We would then have explained the idea of a supremely perfect being as a being who "has all positive powers and qualities" in terms of our definition of omnipotence. But we know that that definition is in need of refinement. We should, therefore, entertain the above idea of a supremely perfect being as problematic. We cannot be sure that it is consistent until we have a satisfactory definition of omnipotence. We can, however, say this: A supremely perfect being is one who has, formally or eminently, any attribute that is such that he can bring it about that something has that attribute. Which attributes a supremely perfect being possesses formally or eminently will depend on what his omnipotence makes him capable of doing. And that will depend on what omnipotence is. If omnipotence turns out to be an inconsistent or incoherent notion, then our way of trying to explain how a supremely perfect being would be a being that "has all positive powers and qualities" would have to be given up. For our explanation makes use of the concept of omnipotence.

There remains the problem of God's uniqueness. Broad says that if not all positive properties are compatible, then *supreme perfection* cannot be identical *with being a being than which nothing more perfect* is possible, lest it be possible that there is more than one supreme being. We would then have no right to speak of God as the supremely perfect being. Broad's observation is true of supreme perfection, as we have just interpreted it. I have given no argument—indeed, I am not able to give an argument—that there can be only one supreme being. The definition of omnipotence and the result that an omnipotent being has, formally or eminently, any property whatsoever that is such that it is logically possible for him to bring it about that there is something that has that property, do not by themselves entail either that it is possible that there is more than one supreme being or that there can be no more than one supreme being.

Monotheistic philosophers have in the main not built uniqueness into the definition of supreme perfection. They have, instead, tried to deduce the uniqueness of God from certain of His attributes. Perhaps this is an unworkable program. In that case, it is always open to the monotheist to make the uniqueness of God an article of faith. It is also open to the monotheist to build uniqueness into the definition of God. This is the alternative Descartes chooses. For, in the Third Meditation, he writes: "By the name God I understand a substance that is infinite [eternal, immutable], independent, all-knowing, all-powerful, and by which I myself and everything else, if anything else does exist, have been created." (Haldane and Ross, Vol. I, p. 165.) The last clause says that everything other than God has one single creator, namely, God. This is a controversial clause. Many philosophers since Plato have believed for powerful reasons that there is an infinite number of eternal (uncreated) objects, viz., properties, classes, propositions, perhaps numbers. These philosophers would modify the last clause to read somewhat as follows: "by which I myself and everything else that is not eternal, have been created." But now God's uniqueness is not guaranteed by definition. For it is possible that there are eternal objects that are supremely perfect and yet distinct from God. God may be only one of a number of supreme beings.

We have next to deal with Broad's contention that, even if all positive attributes are compatible, still supreme perfection is an impossible property. Here the crux of the matter is the allegation that among qualities that admit of degrees some have no intrinsic upper limit.

Now the cases from arithmetic are not hard to dispose of in

Cartesian terms. God's omnipotence does not include the ability to do the logically impossible. Hence, God cannot even eminently be a proper fraction exceeding the ratio 1/1, nor can God even eminently be the greatest positive integer.

That leaves us the examples from outside arithmetic. Can God have length eminently to the highest degree?[15] Broad implies that nothing can have length to the highest degree, because length has no intrinsic upper limit. But to say that length has no intrinsic upper limit is to say that a line may be infinitely long. We think we understand what that means. Descartes can say that God *eminently* is long to the highest degree by which he means that God can make a line that is perfectly long, namely, infinitely long, although He himself is not an infinitely long line. Indeed, if we think that He has created the world, we must grant that in fact He has created an infinite number of infinitely long lines. Start anywhere on the surface of the globe and trace a line. There is no theoretical limit to it. Theoretically, you could go on and on, never leaving the surface of the globe and never coming to an end. You can do this starting from any point on the globe and there are an infinite number of them. But suppose that all this was, in the final analysis, unintelligible. We can always argue in terms of exclusive and exhaustive alternatives. Either the proposition "God makes an infinitely long line" is self-contradictory or it is not. If it is self-contradictory, then God's inability to be even eminently infinitely long in no way detracts from His perfection. If the proposition is not self-contradictory, then God is eminently infinitely long.

Can God have temperature to a perfect degree? To say that God is eminently perfectly hot and eminently perfectly cold is to say that He is capable of producing an infinitely hot object and an infinitely cold object without Himself being hot or cold. If there is no logical impossibility in God's doing these things, then God is eminently hot to a perfect degree and eminently cold to a perfect degree. If these things are logically impossible for God to do, then He is not eminently perfectly hot or perfectly cold. But this does not mean that He is not supremely perfect. All it means is that a supremely perfect being cannot have certain properties

---

[15] There can be no question of God's *formally* having length, because God is immaterial and hence He cannot have length. The same thing is true of His being hot or cold, blue or green.

eminently if it is logically impossible for him to bring it about that there are things that have those properties. And that takes nothing away from His supreme perfection. Exactly similar remarks can be made about God's eminently having pain to the highest degree.

Let us now examine Broad's argument against the notion of one thing being more perfect than another. He begins by suggesting that theologians and philosophers who use phrases of the form 'A is more perfect than B' mean by it something like the following:

A is more perfect than B = Df.

either   (i) A has all the positive powers and qualities that B has, plus some that B lacks.

(This is the condition of A's *extensive* superiority over B.)

or

(ii) A is either extensively equal or extensively superior to B; some of the positive qualities and powers that are common to A and B are present in A with a higher degree of intensity than they are in B, and none of them is present in B with a higher degree of intensity than they are in A.

(This is the condition of A's *intensive* superiority over B).

Broad shows that these two conditions do not provide, even in principle, a way of arranging everything in a single scale of perfection. Consider these cases.

(a) A has some powers and qualities that B lacks and B has some that A lacks. For example: fish can breathe in water, but dogs cannot; dogs can produce puppies, but fish cannot. This means that fish are neither extensively superior or inferior or equal to dogs. But then fish and dogs are not intensively inferior or superior or equal, either, because the criterion of intensive superiority requires the existence of extensive superiority.

(b) A may be extensively superior to B, but not so intensively. Imagine that A has three properties Q_1, Q_2, and Q_3, while B has only Q_1 and Q_2. This makes A extensively superior to B. But let us suppose that Q_1 is present in B with a higher degree of intensity than in A. Then, A would not satisfy the criterion of intensive superiority, and hence would not be intensively superior to B. And because B is not extensively superior to A, it could not be intensively superior to it, either. It is easy to see that, under these conditions, A and B cannot be placed in a single scale of perfection.

(c) Suppose that A and B are extensively equal, but that some of A's qualities are greater in intensity than B's, and some of B's are greater in intensity than A's. For example, assuming that the minds of any two human beings are extensively equal, how would we compare with respect to intensive superiority a mathematical genius of very slight musical ability with a musical genius of very slight mathematical ability?

Broad is perfectly right in saying that the conditions of extensive and intensive superiority are not sufficient for arranging everything in a single scale of perfection. But this in itself does not prove that it is impossible for one thing to be more perfect than another. For the idea that one thing is more perfect than another does not entail that everything fits into a single scale of perfection. What we are after is not a criterion that will enable us to fit everything exactly into a single scale of perfection. We are after a definition of 'x is more perfect than y' that will be intelligible and consistent, even though it may be vague and somewhat unclear. Such a definition is perhaps the following:

x is more perfect than y = Df. x resembles the supreme being more closely than y resembles him.

The relation of x being more perfect than y is transitive (i.e., if x is more perfect than y and y is more perfect than z, then x is more perfect than z), irreflexive (i.e., nothing is more perfect than itself), and hence asymmetrical (i.e., if x is more perfect than y, then y is not more perfect than x). But the fact that the relation is transitive does not imply that everything fits into a single scale of perfection, from the least perfect to the most perfect. For it may be that there is one single thing that is more perfect than anything other than itself, while the other things are exactly equal in

perfection. The relation *weighs more than* is also transitive, irreflexive, and hence asymmetrical, but that fact does not imply
that everything fits into a single scale of ascending weights. It is
logically possible for one single thing to weigh more than everything other than itself, while the other things are exactly equal in
weight. Of course, if the other things happened not to be exactly
equal in weight, we could find out which things were heavier
than others. This is because we have fairly exact means of determining relative weights. We have no comparable means, however, of determining relative perfections. That is another way of
saying that the concept of relative weights is fairly exact,
whereas the concept of relative perfection is rather imprecise.
But there is an enormous difference between words and phrases
that are considerably vague and unclear, and those that are either
unintelligible or intelligible, yet name impossible entities or specify impossible states of affairs.

The phrase 'x is more perfect than y', as we have defined it,
may be intelligible and consistent. Whether it is or not depends
upon our eventually producing a satisfactory definition of omnipotence. If we cannot produce such a definition, we cannot be
sure that the notion of supreme perfection is intelligible or consistent. If we show that there is no possible way of refining the
definition of omnipotence, then we will have shown that it is
impossible to explain supreme perfection in the manner suggested
above. However, even if eventually someone should suggest a
satisfactory revision of our definition of omnipotence, the notion
of relative perfection is likely to remain vague and unclear. That
implies that a degree of imprecision and unclarity will characterize any argument, such as Descartes' causal and ontological arguments, that uses premises formulated in terms of the idea that
one thing is more perfect than another. So far as we can tell, then,
this idea and the theistic idea of God associated with it are not
impossible to define. Consequently, as far as Descartes' causal
argument and Descartes' and St. Anselm's ontological arguments
are concerned, we cannot dismiss them for having unintelligible
or necessarily false premises or conclusions. At the present stage
of our philosophical knowledge, they have to be criticized on
other grounds.

DESCARTES' MAIN CAUSAL ARGUMENT FOR GOD'S EXISTENCE

THIS ARGUMENT is constructed from passages in the Third Meditation. It deduces God's existence from the presence in my mind of the idea of God:

(1) Everything that comes into existence must have a cause. (This, Descartes claims, is known "by the natural light," it is "intuitive," "self-evident")

(2) The cause of a thing must have at least as much reality as its effect. (Also true "by the natural light")

∴ (3) Something cannot come from nothing, and the more perfect cannot come from the less perfect. (By (1) and (2))

(4) I have the idea of a being with infinite formal reality (a supremely perfect being). (This is incorrigible for me)

∴ (5) Something must be the cause of my idea of a being with infinite formal reality. (By (3) and (4))

(6) But this something cannot be another idea, for "even though it might happen that one idea gives birth to another idea, that could not continue indefinitely: but we must finally reach a first idea, the cause of which" has formally all the reality that is contained objectively in the idea.

(7) The objective reality of the idea of a thing = Df. the formal reality that is possessed by that thing, or would be possessed by it if it existed.

(8) Hence, the cause of the idea of a being with infinite formal reality must have infinite formal reality.

(9) Hence, a being with infinite formal reality, namely, God, exists.

We cannot begin to understand this argument if we have no idea of what is meant by 'objective reality' and 'formal reality'. Perhaps an analogy will give us some idea of what these notions mean. Imagine two photographs that are made of identical paper, have identical dimensions, etc. As photographs, they are exactly on a par; they have the same "formal" reality. But observe that one of them is a picture of a lion, the other of an elephant. The two things that are exactly alike *as photographs* differ in respect to their *pictorial content*. Now Descartes uses the word 'idea' ambiguously to stand, among other things, for thoughts, mental images, and states of consciousness (mental states). Let us assume that, in the context of talk about the objective reality of an idea, an idea is a mental state, and that every mental state has a content. Belief, for example, is a mental state, and belief is always belief that something or other is the case. The content of the belief is what is believed. Similarly, a daydream is a mental state, but my daydream may be of a dish of ice cream, yours of an apple pie. Or I may form a mental image of a lion while you form a mental image of an elephant. Now my seeing a lion "in my mind's eye" and your seeing an elephant are, as mental states, on a par. Each has the formal reality that is characteristic of mental states, or more particularly, they have the formal reality characteristic of *being aware in imagination,* which is a specific mental state. But the content of my idea is a lion-image; the content of yours is an elephant-image. This difference in content makes for the difference in the objective realities of the specific mental states. The objective reality of my mental state is the reality of a lion; the objective reality of your mental state is the reality of an elephant. If we assume that in some unspecified way an elephant has more formal reality than a lion, then the lion-idea would have less objective reality than the elephant-idea.

There is more than one questionable assumption in Descartes' causal argument. To begin with, there is one in step (6). In that step Descartes seeks to conclude that an idea cannot have an indefinitely long chain of ideas as its cause. This is derived from the assumption that the ultimate cause of an idea must be something other than an idea; in Descartes' own words, "there must be a first idea." But no reason is given why this must be so. Descartes grants that it is possible for one idea to be caused by another. He cannot use as a reason, therefore, the proposition that ideas have no causal efficacy. But without proof of the assertion that ultimately the cause of an idea must be a non-idea, Descartes has no reason to conclude that an idea cannot have as its cause an indefinitely long chain of ideas. This is a significant gap in the argument. We have no proof that my idea of God cannot be caused by nothing but a chain of ideas. That means that we have no proof that the cause of my idea of God must ultimately be a thing that is itself not an idea. But that in turn means that we have no grounds for going on to deduce God's existence.

Descartes would have a case if he was able to prove that the idea of God must have something other than an idea as its cause. He might have argued thus. The cause of the idea of God is either an idea or something other than an idea. If it is an idea, then it must have as much objective reality as the idea of God has, otherwise the principle would not be true that the cause must have at least as much reality as its effect. But there is only one idea whose objective reality is as great as that of the idea of God, namely, the idea of God itself. This is so because the idea of God is the idea of a supreme being, which is greater than any being except itself. Hence, no idea other than the idea of God could have caused the idea of God. Hence, either the idea of God is self-caused or it is caused by something other than an idea. In order to complete the proof that the idea of God is caused by something other than an idea, Descartes would have to prove that the idea of God could not be self-caused. Speaking of himself, Descartes says: "But [were I independent of every other and] were I myself the author of my being, I should doubt nothing and I should desire nothing, and finally no perfection would be lacking to me; for I should have bestowed on myself every perfection of which I possessed any idea and should thus be God." (Haldane and Ross, Vol. I, p. 168.) He seems to be assuming that if a thing had caused itself, it would have made itself perfect. But my idea of God is an imperfect idea of a perfect being. ". . . in God there is an infinitude of things which I cannot comprehend, nor possibly even reach in any way by thought; for it is the nature of the infinite that my nature, which is finite and limited, should not comprehend it." (Haldane and Ross, Vol. I, p. 166.) Hence, my idea of God cannot have caused itself. Therefore (6a) it must be caused by something other than an idea. This conclusion gives Descartes one of the things he needs to have in step (6) of the causal argument, in order to complete the causal argument.

The other thing he needs in step (6) is (6b), the proposition that the cause of an idea must have formally all the reality that the idea has objectively. (6b) is a consequence of (6a), (3), and (7). Since the cause of the idea of God must be something other than an idea, it can have no objective reality; only ideas have objective reality. The cause of the idea of God must have formal reality, as any entity must. It may also have eminent reality. What we have here is a distinction between two kinds of formal reality. One kind of formal reality is the opposite of objective reality. The other kind of formal reality is the opposite of eminent reality. All entities have formal reality in the first sense, but only ideas have objective reality as well. Now if the formal reality of the cause of the idea of God was less than the objective reality of the idea of God, there would be a violation of the principle that the cause must have at least as great a degree of reality as its effect. Hence, the cause of the idea of God has infinite formal reality. These steps do not depend upon our being able to place things into a single hierarchy of perfection. All we need is the contrast between supreme perfection and imperfection.

Step (8) in the causal argument (viz., the "proposition"[16] that the cause of the idea of a being with infinite formal reality must itself have infinite formal reality) is a deductive consequence of step (7) and (6b), namely, that the cause of an idea must have formally all the reality that the idea has objectively. The details of this deduction are as follows:

(6b) If [(x is the idea of y) and (w' is the objective reality of x) and (z is the cause of x) and (w is the formal reality of z)], then w is equal in greatness to, or greater than, w'.

(7) w' = Df. w" (the formal reality of y)

(7.1) If [(x is the idea of y) and (w' is the objective reality of x) and (z is the cause of x) and (w is the formal reality

16 I put the word in double quotation marks to indicate that I am not committed to (8) being a proposition. I am not sure what (8) is really saying.

of z)], then w is equal in greatness to, or greater than w″. (By (6) and (7))

(7.2) If [(I have the idea of God) and (infinite reality objectively belongs to the idea of God) and (something, z, is the cause of my idea of God) and (w is the formal reality of the cause of my idea of God)], then w is equal in greatness to, or greater than, the formal reality of God. (An instance of 7.1)

(7.3) But I do have the idea of God, and infinite reality objectively belongs to my idea of God, and something, z (other than an idea), is the cause of my idea of God, and w is the formal reality of the cause of my idea of God.

∴ (8) w is equal in greatness to, or greater than, the formal reality of God.

∴ (9) A being possessing the formal reality of God, namely, God, exists.

The deduction is valid, but (8) seems to be false. It says, in English, although not in plain English, that nothing less real than God can cause the idea of God. Descartes subscribes to the general principle that nothing less real than an x can cause the idea of an x. I do not see how, arguing as he does, Descartes can deny that a can of beans is "less real" than the demons and horrible monsters in a nightmare. But if I eat a can of beans just before going to sleep at midnight, I might have just such a nightmare. I do not offer this as a decisive counter-example to the general principle. But it *seems* to be a counter-example to what the general principle *seems* to be saying. It is up to Descartes to make the issue more precise, and nothing in his writings gives us the slightest clue as to how he might have gone about doing that. If (8) is false, as it seems to be, at least one of its premises must be false, i.e., either (6b) or (7) or both are false. I suppose (6b) is the culprit. The can of beans seems to give it the lie. Does this seem plausible?

If my nightmare is the idea of monsters, and w′ is the degree of objective reality possessed by my nightmare, and a can of beans is the cause of my nightmare, and w is the degree of formal reality possessed by the can of beans, then w is equal in greatness to, or greater than, w′.

Mind you, $w' =$ Df. the degree of formal reality that the monsters of my dream would possess if they existed.

Hence, the degree of formal reality possessed by the can of beans is equal to, or greater than, the degree of formal reality of the monsters. This is contrary to the assumption that we can, I think, justly attribute to Descartes, that a can of beans is "less real" than monsters and other terrifying creatures. It seems implausible that a can of beans should have a "degree of formal reality," whatever that means, that is equal to, or greater than, the degree of formal reality possessed by the terrifying creatures of my nightmare.

Another problem is this. How can Descartes be sure, "metaphysically certain," that an evil demon is not fooling him into thinking that the causal principles he uses are trustworthy? If he needs proof of God's existence in order to allay any lingering metaphysical doubts about such principles, these doubts must carry over to the conclusion that God exists. Besides, as it is formulated by me, Descartes' causal argument is a deduction that requires nine steps. How can he trust deduction *before* he has proved God's existence, if God's existence is a necessary condition of the "metaphysical" trustworthiness of deduction? These problems are among the ones that are involved in the Cartesian Circle (see Section 7, below).

Moreover, one might challenge the assertion that the causal principles that are assumed in the argument are self-evident. There is no contradiction in the supposition that some things simply pop into existence, like a magic rabbit. The alleged self-evidence of the assumption is therefore not supportable by the reason that the denial of the assumption is formally self-contradictory.

That leaves two possibilities. Perhaps the causal principles are self-evident not because their denials are formally self-contradictory but because the principles are necessarily true in the way in which "Orange resembles red more closely than does green" is necessarily true. Or, perhaps the causal principles are self-evident because they are clear and distinct in the same way as the *cogito* propositions are clear and distinct. I want now to show that the causal principles are not self-evident in either of these two ways.

First let me explain why necessarily true propositions, such as the one about red, orange, and green, are not like those necessarily true propositions whose denials are formally self-contradictory. Compare the proposition about orange, red, and green with another whose denial is formally self-contradictory. Take "If red is a color, then red is a color." Its denial is: red is a color, but it is not the case that red is a color. This proposition cannot be true and we can tell that it cannot be true just by understanding the terms 'is', but', 'is not', 'if . . . , then'. In Part III, Section 2, these were included among "logical words." 'Red' and 'color' are not included in the list. We do not have to have experienced instances of red in order to know that "If red is a color, then red is a color" cannot be false. We do not have to know that "Red is a color" is true. We do not even have to know what it is saying. All we have to know are two things: that "Red is a color" is a proposition, and what the logical words mean. If we know these two things, then we know that "If red is a color, then red is a color" cannot be false, which comes to the same thing as saying that its denial cannot be true.

Now we cannot tell that "Orange resembles red more closely than does green" is necessarily true just by knowing that this is a proposition and by knowing what the words included in the list of "logical words" mean. We have to have an acquaintance with orange, red, and green in order to tell that orange resembles red more closely than green does, and that this is necessarily so. It is so simply because of what orange, red, and green are. We have a primitive capacity to notice similarities and differences. We also have a primitive capacity to recognize degrees of similarity and difference. We must exercise this latter capacity in order to know that orange resembles red more closely than does green. We do not have to exercise it in order to know that "Red is a color, but it is not the case that red is a color" is formally self-contradictory.

Thus, there is a difference between propositions that are self-evident because their denials are formally self-contradictory and propositions that are self-evident for other reasons. I have already said that the denials of the causal principles do not seem to be formally self-contradictory. It seems to be equally true, however, that they are not self-evident in the way in which the proposition about orange, red, and green is. Among the current speculations about the nature of the physical universe, there is one that is propounded by the astrophysicist, Fred Hoyle. According to Hoyle, hydrogen is continually being generated spontaneously. If the causal principle "Everything that comes into existence has a cause" were necessarily true, Hoyle's theory would be necessarily false. It would be envisaging an impossibility. But to my knowledge this is not one of the criticisms that are being made of it by Hoyle's scientific peers.

That still leaves the possibility that the causal principles are self-evident because they are clear and distinct in the way in which the *cogito* propositions are. But it is by no means evident that this is so. The *cogito* propositions are clear and distinct in precisely discernible ways: they are incorrigible for us; they cannot be denied, doubted, or disbelieved without pragmatic contradiction; and the belief that one is thinking and that one exists are self-certifying beliefs. They entail that which is believed. But the causal principles exhibit none of these features. The belief that something cannot come from nothing, for example, is not self-certifying. The mere fact of my believing this does not entail that it is true.

The premises in question are certainly not pragmatically indubitable, undeniable, or incapable of being disbelieved. One would not contradict oneself pragmatically by doubting, denying, or disbelieving them. Besides, these pragmatic features can be true only of contingent propositions. The causal principle, if true, would be necessarily true.

Moreover, the causal principles are not incorrigible for me. Take, for example, the principle: A cause must have at least as much reality as its effect. This is incorrigible for me if, and only if, my believing it attentively entails my knowing it, and it's possible for me to believe it attentively. But what would count as my believing it attentively? Perhaps believing that causal principle attentively requires attending to the nature of cause and effect and to the relation of one thing having more reality than another. But to explain believing the causal principle attentively in these terms requires a detailed analysis of the concepts of cause and effect, and of one thing having more reality than another. This Descartes does not provide. On the contrary, he appears to think that the causal principles themselves provide an insight into the nature of cause and effect. This is to put the cart before the horse. Descartes and his contemporaries may have thought that these principles did provide an explanation of the nature of cause and effect. But they do not strike us that way.

The causal principle, "Everything that comes into existence must have a cause," is assumed in every important causal argument for God's existence. The fact that it is not incontrovertibly self-evident makes every causal argument for God's existence, including Descartes', inconclusive, if not implausible.

Section 5

DESCARTES' ONTOLOGICAL ARGUMENT FOR GOD'S EXISTENCE

No ONTOLOGICAL argument for the existence of God can be either conclusively refuted or conclusively established at present, because every known and conceivable ontological argument involves profoundly controversial and unsettled questions in logic. These questions are so intricate and so technical that, in an introductory presentation, it is not possible even to explain the problems they pose, let alone to provide definitive solutions for them and thereby to settle the status of the ontological argument once and for all. We can begin to appreciate the complexities if we run through a number of different versions of the ontological argument. In this section we shall take a look at Descartes' ontological argument. In Section 6 we shall go through four more ontological arguments, all of them ascribed to St. Anselm (1033–1109), who was the originator of ontological arguments for God's existence.

The main outline of Descartes' ontological argument occurs early in the Fifth Meditation (Haldane and Ross, Vol. I, pp. 180–181):

(1) If I find in my mind the idea of something, then all that I clearly and distinctly recognize as characterizing this thing does in reality characterize it.

(2) I find in my mind the idea of God, i.e., of a supremely perfect being.

∴ (3) All that I clearly and distinctly recognize as characterizing God does in reality characterize him.

(4) I clearly and distinctly recognize that actual and eternal existence characterizes God.

∴ (5) Actual and eternal existence characterizes God, i.e., God actually and eternally exists.

This is a valid argument. Therefore, the conclusion is true, if all the premises are true. The premises are (1), (2), and (4). Now premises (1) and (2) are superfluous; (4) alone entails that God actually and eternally exists. This is so because, according to Descartes, "I clearly and distinctly recognize that p" entails "I know that p." But "I know that p" entails p. Hence, (4) is all we need to conclude that God exists. The crux of the ontological argument, one would expect, is a proof of (4).

Descartes seems to be arguing for (4) as follows:[17]

(a) I clearly and distinctly recognize that all supremely perfect beings actually and eternally exist.

(b) I clearly and distinctly recognize that God is a supremely perfect being.

[17] "[The existence of God] is not at first manifest, since it would seem to present some appearance of being a sophism. For being accustomed in all other things to make a distinction between existence and essence, I easily persuade myself that the existence can be separated from the essence of God, and that we can thus conceive God as not actually existing. But, nevertheless, when I think of it with more attention, I clearly see that existence can no more be separated from the essence of God than can its having its three angles equal to two right angles be separated from the essence of a [rectilinear] triangle, or the idea of a mountain from the idea of a valley; and so there is not any less repugnance to our conceiving a God (that is, a Being supremely perfect) to whom existence is lacking (that is to say, to whom a certain perfection is lacking), than to conceive of a mountain which has no valley." (Haldane and Ross, Vol. I, p. 181.)

∴ (4) I clearly and distinctly recognize that God actually and eternally exists, i.e., that actual and external existence characterizes God.

This argument is invalid as it stands. It would be pointless to try to formulate additional assumptions that would be both necessarily true and sufficient to make the argument valid. For the ontological argument is supposed to proceed from premises that are not contingent to a conclusion that is not contingent. Because of the autobiographical element in them, (a), (b), and (4) are all contingent propositions. Now obviously Descartes is not writing the story of his life in the *Meditations*. He means to be making logical points; indeed, the point of asserting (a) and (b) is logical. Together with the Cartesian assumption that, if I clearly and distinctly recognize that p, then I know that p, (a) entails that A1: All supremely perfect beings exist, and (b) entails that A2: God is a supremely perfect being. This gives us the premises of a demonstrative argument (A).

A1: All supremely perfect beings exist (actually and eternally).
A2: God is a supremely perfect being.
∴ A3: God exists (actually and eternally).

Descartes' reason for asserting A1 is that the denial of A1 is self-contradictory. For a supremely perfect being is a being who has all positive perfections, of which eternal and actual existence is one. Because (A) is a valid deduction and Descartes believes the premises to be true, he would say that (4) is true. For he says in the context of the ontological argument in the Fifth Meditation:

For example, when I imagine a triangle, although there may nowhere in the world be such a figure outside my thought, or ever have been, there is nevertheless in this figure a certain determinate nature, form, or essence, which is immutable and eternal, which I have not invented, and which in no wise depends on my mind, as appears from the fact that diverse properties of that triangle can be demonstrated, viz., that its three angles are equal to two right angles, that the greatest side is subtended by the greatest angle, and the like,which now, whether I wish it or do not wish it, I recognize very clearly as pertaining to it, although I never thought of the matter at all when I imagined a triangle for the first time, and which therefore, cannot be said to have been invented by me. (Haldane and Ross, Vol. I, p. 180.)

But if the reason why (4) is true is that there is a demonstrative argument (and Descartes knows that there is) whose conclusion is that actual and eternal existence characterizes God, then Descartes would not be first proving (4) and then deducing that actual and eternal existence characterizes God. On the contrary, he would first be proving that actual and eternal existence characterizes God and then be making the claim that he clearly and distinctly recognizes that actual and eternal existence characterizes God. But if that is the case, then Descartes' ontological argument is really (A) and not the one that he says it is. Premise (4) then also turns out to be superfluous. I shall, therefore, go on the assumption that the crux of Descartes' ontological argument, indeed Descartes' ontological argument itself, is argument (A). I shall now try to show that (A) is an inconclusive argument.

First, those philosophers who have argued that existence is not a property would object to argument (A) because the reason Descartes gives for saying that its first premise is necessarily true assumes that eternal and actual *existence* is a perfection, hence a property. It is easy enough to introduce 'exists' as a predicate by defining:

$$x \text{ exists} = Df. \ x = x.$$

According to this definition, existence is a tautological, a necessarily universal property. For, $x = x$ is tautologically true for any value of x; everything is self-identical. But this way of defining the predicate 'exists' will in no way help the ontological argument.[18] What the ontological argument needs is 'exists' as a non-tautological, non-universal predicate. In other words, the ontological argument needs a logic in which existence is a property that does not necessarily belong to every consistently thinkable entity. For the ontological argument is intended to show that God is the only consistently thinkable entity whose actual and eternal existence follows deductively from His definition as a being than which none greater or more perfect is possible. In Russellian logic, existence is not a property at all. The idea of existence is sym-

[18] See, for instance, G. Nakhnikian and W. C. Salmon, "'Exists' as a Predicate," *Philosophical Review*, LXVI, 4 (1957), 535–542.

bolized by the existential quantifier, '(∃ x)', which does not function as a predicate. The ontological argument requires a non-Russellian logic in some respects, and to date no logic of the sort required has been devised in sufficient detail. But even if the question of whether existence is a property of the required sort were somehow settled to everyone's satisfaction, other problems remain.

Take premise A1 of Descartes' ontological argument. A1 may be understood in two ways:

A1.1: There are supremely perfect beings and every one of them eternally and actually exists.

A1.2: If anything is a supremely perfect being, then it eternally and actually exists.

The difference is that A1.2 does not assert or imply that there are supremely perfect beings.

A1.1 will not do as a premise. It asserts the conclusion itself. If we know that it is true, we do not need the ontological, or any other, argument to prove that God exists. Conversely, if we need the ontological argument or any other argument to prove that God exists, then we do not know that A1.1 is true, and hence we cannot prove anything on its testimony.

A1.2 will not, by itself, imply that God exists. To arrive at that conclusion, it is enough to conjoin A1.2 and A2, which says that God is a supremely perfect being. But then how are we to read A2? It has three possible interpretations:

A2.1: All Gods are supremely perfect.

A2.2: God ('God' being a proper name) is supremely perfect.

A2.3: God is supremely perfect ('God' being an abbreviation for some particular definite description, viz., 'the being than whom no greater is possible').

A2.1 raises the same problems as A1. It may be interpreted in one of two ways:

A2.1(i): There are Gods and every one of them is supremely perfect.

A2.1(ii): If anything is God, then it is supremely perfect.

A2.1(i) will not do as a premise because it assumes that there are supremely perfect beings, and this is the very thing that argument (A) is supposed to prove. If we know that A2.1(i) is true, then we need no argument to prove it; conversely, if we do need an argument to prove it, then we do not know it. But then we can prove nothing on its testimony. A2.1(ii) will not do the job either. It, together with A1.2, will work as follows:

> A2.1(ii): If anything is God, then it is supremely perfect.
> A1.2: If anything is supremely perfect, then it actually and eternally exists.
> ∴ (C): If anything is God, then it actually and eternally exists.

This is a valid argument, but (C) is not what we want. (C) does not assert that God actually and eternally exists.

In A2.2, 'God' is a proper name. Now grammatically speaking, 'Washington' and 'Pegasus' are both proper names. But Russell distinguishes between grammatically proper names and logically proper names. By a logically proper name he means a name that actually denotes, i.e., a name such that the entity it names exists. Thus, 'Pegasus' is not a logically proper name, because there is no such thing as Pegasus, past, present or future. Pegasus is a mythological horse. 'Washington', the name of the city, on the other hand, is a logically proper name. The point of this distinction, as far as our present interests are concerned, is that Russell's logic does not allow us to deduce "Santa Claus is fat" from "Everything is fat" alone. When "Everything is fat" is taken together with "Santa Claus exists," the combination entails that "Santa Claus is fat."

Now is 'God' merely a grammatically proper name, or is it a logically proper name? If in using the name 'God' we are assuming that it names an existent, then when we introduce a premise in the ontological argument that contains the name 'God', we are assuming the conclusion of the ontological argument by asserting that premise. This is a blatantly circular procedure. If, on the other hand, the name 'God' is the name of a nonentity, then according to Russellian logic, argument (A) is invalid. For argument (A) would go as follows:

> A1: All supremely perfect beings exist.
> ∴ (2): If God is a supremely perfect being, then God exists.
>   (Instance of A1)

A2: God is a supremely perfect being.
∴ A3: God exists.
> (From (2) and A2)

In the first place, Russellian logic does not allow the move from A1 to (2). That move is permitted only if 'God' is a logically proper name. In the second place A3 is not deducible from (2) and A2 alone. Russell's logic requires an additional assumption to the effect that God exists, i.e., that 'God' is a logically proper name. Hence, in terms of Russelian logic, argument (A) is invalid, if 'God' is not a logically proper name.

Now if we are not bound by Russell's restrictions, then we have the following argument. Either 'God' is a logically proper name or it is not. If it is, then God exists and that is the end of the matter. If, on the other hand, 'God' is not a logically proper name, then from the assumption that 'God' is not a logically proper name *and* A1 *and* A2, we deduce A3, that God exists. But A1 and A2 are assumed to be necessarily true. So, " 'God' is not a logically proper name" (= "God does not exist") alone entails that God exists. But for any proposition p, if not p entails p, then p. Therefore God exists. One way this argument can be defeated is by proving that A1 and A2 together entail a contradiction. Another way is to prove that A1 is false or meaningless because 'exists' occurs in it as a predicate. There is no easy or obvious way to do either of these things.

In view of the argument above, one might say: "So much the worse for Russellian logic; Descartes must have had a different logic in mind." Fair enough. Only it is now up to the defender of Descartes to produce the system of logic that Descartes is presumed to be assuming. At the present stage of logical theory, there seems to be no reason for ruling out such a feat. But, until it is accomplished, under the assumption that 'God' is not a logically proper name, argument (A) is invalid.

In A2.3 'God' is short for 'the being than whom no greater is possible'. Accordingly, A2.3 could be written as:

A2.3 The being than whom no greater is possible is supremely perfect.

Now there are two theories about statements like A2.3. According to the contemporary English philosopher, P. F. Strawson, A2.3 "presupposes" the existence of the being than whom no

greater is possible. This sense of "presuppose" is that A2.3 is not
an assertion if the being than whom no greater is possible does
not exist. That means that the existence of that being has to be
known before we undertake to assert premise A2 of argument
(A), viz., that God is a supremely perfect being. But then, if the
premise can be asserted, it cannot be used to prove the existence
of God to anyone who is not already convinced that God exists.
Conversely, if there is someone who is not already convinced
that God exists, he will not admit that "God is a supremely perfect being" is a premise because he will regard it as neither true
nor false. In other words, argument (A) will either be an exercise
in futility or it will not be an argument at all. I do not mean to
imply that all arguments must have conclusions and premises that
are either true or false. There are arguments some of whose premises or whose conclusion do not admit of truth or falsehood;
for example:

> Come only if it is a sunny day.
> It is not a sunny day.
> ∴ Don't come.

Here the first premise is a conditional demand, the conclusion a
flat demand. Demands (*what* one is demanding when one makes
a demand) are neither true nor false. Granted all this, it is still
the case that argument (A) is understood to be made up entirely
of propositional steps. On Strawson's view, if God (the being than
whom no greater is possible) did not exist, then the second line of
the argument (A) would not be a proposition (something admitting of truth or falsehood), and, hence, it would not be a
premise of the intended sort. Hence, (A) would not be an
argument.

The earlier analysis of such statements as A2.3 is Russell's
theory of definite descriptions. According to it, the proposition
A2.3 (The being than whom no greater is possible is supremely
perfect) is the conjunction of the following three propositions:

> (i) There exists an object than which no greater is possible.
> (ii) At most one object is one than which no greater is possible.
> (iii) That object is supremely perfect.

If (i) is part of what A2.3 asserts, then if we know that A2.3 is
true, we do not need an argument to prove that the being than

whom no greater is possible exists or that it exists "actually and eternally." But that there exists an object than which no greater is possible is precisely what Descartes sets out to prove. Therefore, he would be begging the question in a blatant way if one of his premises was that conclusion itself.

Therefore, regardless of whether we prefer Russell or Strawson on definite descriptions, argument (A) fails to prove that God (actually and eternally) exists, if 'God' is short for some such expression as 'the being than whom no greater is possible'.

But this is not the end of the matter. For it may be that both Strawson and Russell are wrong about definite descriptions. Perhaps a more suitable logic can be constructed in which talk about the so-and-so commits us neither to presupposing nor to asserting the existence of the so-and-so in question.

To sum up, argument (A) seems to be the only argument that we can reasonably take to be Descartes' ontological argument. But (A) is inconclusive. At the present stage of our philosophical knowledge, we are under no rational compulsion to accept its conclusion as having been proved to be true.

Section 6

ST. ANSELM'S FOUR ONTOLOGICAL ARGUMENTS FOR GOD'S EXISTENCE

THE READER may be convinced of the inconclusiveness of Descartes' ontological argument, yet he may not be convinced that another ontological argument would not accomplish what this did not. There is, as far as I know, no way of proving that it is in principle impossible to construct a convincing ontological argument for God's existence. However, if we run through a number of seemingly powerful ontological arguments and take note of their failings, we may come to suspect that no ontological argument is likely to succeed. To this end, and also because it is rewarding to study them critically, I shall examine four ontological arguments that are strongly suggested, if not explicitly found, in St. Anselm. The first three were given to me in their present form by William Rowe. The fourth formulation is attributed to R. M. Chisholm.

St. Anselm's First Ontological Argument

(1) It is possible that God exists.

(2) It is not possible that there exists a being greater than God.

(3) For any property ϕ, if nothing is ϕ although it is possible that something is ϕ, then it is possible that: there exists something that is ϕ, and there exists something that is greater than the thing that is ϕ.

∴ (4) God exists.

The second premise is one way of saying that God is supremely perfect. The third premise formulates the idea that an actually existing being is greater than one that is only possible.

The argument is valid but premise (3) is false. Let ϕ = being an entity equal in greatness to every other entity.[19] Now, it is true that:

(a) It is not the case that there is an entity equal in greatness to every other entity, although it is possible that there is an entity equal in greatness to every other entity.

But it is false that:

(b) It is possible that there exists an entity equal in greatness to every other entity, while there exists an entity greater than it.

[19] This example was suggested by Hector-Neri Castaneda.

Now an 'if—then—' statement is false when it has a true antecedent and a false consequent. Hence, (3) is false. Hence, although the argument is valid, it fails to prove that the conclusion is true.

A way out of this difficulty may be to reject the general principle (3) and to work with a premise that is about God only. The argument is now as follows:

(1) It is possible that God exists.

(2) It is not possible that there exists a being greater than God.

(3) If God does not exist but it is possible that God exists, then it is possible both that God exists and that a being greater than God exists.

∴ (4) God exists.

The argument is formally valid. Hence, if all the premises are true, the conclusion is proved true. But not all the premises are beyond doubt. I am prepared to grant that (1) and (2) are necessarily true. But because (2) is necessarily true, the consequent of (3) is necessarily false. Hence, if (3) is necessarily true, then its antecedent is necessarily false. But the antecedent of (3) is not necessarily false. Hence, (3) is not necessarily true. Hence the argument does not prove that necessarily God exists. The only controversial claim I have made is that the antecedent of (3) is not necessarily false. On the face of it, it seems perfectly consistent to think that, although it is possible that God exists, in fact God does not exist. If the defender of the ontological argument believes otherwise, the burden is on him to prove that the belief in question, which seems to be perfectly consistent, is really necessarily false. The ontological argument that we are now examining proves no such thing.

There is one more move open to the defender of this ontological argument. He may admit that perhaps (3) is not necessarily true, yet insist that (3) is contingently true. Now, still assuming that the consequent of (3) is necessarily false, (3) is contingently true only if its antecedent is contingently false. But anyone who has admitted that it is possible that God exists and who is thinking clearly will admit that the antecedent of (3) is false only if he admits that "God does not exist" is false. Now anyone who doubts that God exists will have no reason to change his mind about God's existence on the basis of anything he has been told so far. Hence, he will have been given no reason for believing that "God does not exist" is false. He will have been told dogmatically that (3) is true, but he will be under no rational compulsion to believe what he is told. Hence, although everyone would grant that, if (1) and (2) are necessarily true and (3) is contingently true, then it is true that God exists, no one, not even those who believe that (3) is true, has any reason for insisting that the conclusion has been proved true. For, on the basis of anything said so far, no one has any grounds for believing that (3) is true.

Let us try one more emendation. This time we will make use of St. Anselm's distinction between *existing in the understanding* and *existing outside the understanding*.

The argument is as follows:

(1) It is possible that outside the understanding God exists.

(2) It is not possible that outside the understanding God exists and also that outside the understanding there exists a thing greater than God.

(3) If in the understanding there exists a thing that is God, and outside the understanding no God exists, while it is possible that outside the understanding God exists, then it is possible that outside the understanding God exists and also that outside the understanding there exists a thing greater than God.

(4) In the understanding God exists.

∴ (5) Outside the understanding God exists.

The argument is valid, but it suffers from exactly the same defect as the immediately preceding version. This time, granted that (1) and (2) are necessarily true, the consequent of (3) is necessarily false. Hence, if (3) is necessarily true, then its antecedent is necessarily false. But the antecedent of (3) is not necessarily false, and hence (3) is not necessarily true. The claim that the antecedent of (3) is not necessarily false seems to be obviously true. The present version of the ontological argument provides no reason whatever for thinking otherwise. Hence, the argument does not establish the truth of its conclusion. That this is so we know without having to decide what is meant by 'existing in the understanding' and 'existing outside the understanding'. All we need is the supposition that these expressions can be interpreted in such

a way as to make every step of the argument a proposition, something that can be true or false.

Nothing will be gained by asserting that (3) is contingently
true. We have already gone through the sort of argument that
shows the futility of making this last assertion.

St. Anselm's Second Ontological Argument

(1) It is possible that there exists a being whose non-
existence is impossible.

(2) If it is possible that x does not exist, and it is possible
that there exists a being whose non-existence is impossible, then it is possible that there exists a being
greater than x.

(3) It is not possible that there exists a being greater than
God.

∴ (4) It is not possible that God does not exist or it is not
possible that there exists a being whose non-existence is
impossible. (By (2) and (3))

∴ (5) It is not possible that God does not exist. (By (1) and (4))

The trouble with the argument lies in the first two premises. By
'a being whose non-existence is impossible', we are presumably to
understand *a necessarily existing* being. But what sort of property
is necessary existence? In ordinary contexts we use 'necessary'
adjectivally in such examples as:

He has the necessary courage to face the danger.
He has the necessary intelligence to pass the test.
He has the necessary self-control to resist her sexual blandish-
ments.

In these and similar cases, "necessary" has the force of "sufficient,"
"enough of what it takes" to complete some task, to realize a
goal. Necessary courage and just plain courage are not two
different properties. There is no such property as necessary
courage. Similarly, even if existence were a property, there is no
such property as *necessary* existence.[20] Hence, the first two prem-

[20] Cf. Paul Henlé, "Uses of the Ontological Argument," *Philosophical
Review*, LXX (1961), 102–109.

ises of the second ontological argument are false. This is easy to see when we observe that "x is P" is short for "x has the property P." But "x has the property P" entails that P is a property. Therefore, if P is not a property, then every proposition of the form "x is P" is false. In so far as necessary existence is not a property, "x necessarily exists," "it is possible that x necessarily exists," "it is necessary that x necessarily exists" are all false. Even worse, they are meaningless. 'He has the necessary courage' is a meaningful sentence because we know what 'necessary courage' means. But we really do not know what 'necessary existence' means if it is supposed that necessary existence is a property; hence the sentences 'God necessarily exists,' 'It is possible that God has necessary existence', and 'It is necessary that God have necessary existence', could be said to be unintelligible.

'God has necessary existence' could mean that it is necessarily true that God exists. Now premise (1) would be saying the following:

(a) It is possible that it is necessary that something exists.

But "it is possible that it is necessary that something exists" entails "It is necessary that something exists." Hence, we cannot know (a) to be true unless we know that it is necessary that something exists. But we know that it is necessary that something exists. For instance, it is necessarily true that properties exist. The proposition:

Whatever is red is red

is logically true, hence, it is necessarily true, and it entails the proposition:

There is a property such that whatever has it is red.

This proposition itself is necessarily true because it is deducible from a necessarily true proposition. Hence, it is necessarily true that properties (e.g., the property of being red) exist. Thus, if (1) is identical with the proposition that it is possible that it is necessary that something exists, then (1) is true.

But (2) is implausible. It says in effect that a thing whose existence is necessary may be greater than anything that does not exist. Imagine a thing that has all the perfections of God but lacks existence. Is it obvious that the property of being red may be greater than it? Far from it. In fact, if we recall our earlier definition:

x is more perfect than y = Df. x resembles a supremely perfect being more than y resembles it,

then if non-existent things can sensibly be said to possess any properties at all, a non-existent God would resemble an existent God more closely than the color red would resemble Him. Hence, a non-existent God would, if anything, be more perfect than the color red, which exists necessarily.

St. Anselm's Third Ontological Argument

(1) If it is possible that x exists but in fact x does not exist, then it is possible that x comes into existence.

(2) It is possible that God exists.

(3) It is not possible that God comes into existence.

∴ (4) Either it is not possible that God exists, or God exists. (By (1) and (3))

∴ (5) God exists. (By (2) and (4))

Although the argument is valid, its first premise is false. Let x be the eternal monster of Loch Ness. Now it is true that:

(α) It is possible that there exists the eternal monster of Loch Ness, although it is false that such a monster exists.

While it is false that:

(β) It is possible that the eternal monster of Loch Ness comes into existence.

It is false that it is possible for the eternal monster of Loch Ness to come into existence because an eternal being is, by definition, a being that cannot come into existence and cannot go out of existence. Because (α) is true and (β) is false, premise (1) is false. A conditional with a true antecedent and a false consequent is false. The argument does not prove its conclusion to be true because one of the premises is false.

St. Anselm's Fourth Ontological Argument

(1) If a being than whom no greater can be conceived does not exist, then a being than whom no greater can be conceived is not a being than whom no greater can be conceived (for a greater can be conceived, namely, one that exists).

(2) The consequent of (1) is self-contradictory.

∴ (3) A being than whom no greater can be conceived exists.

The argument is vitiated by the fact that either (2) is false, in which case the conclusion is not proved to be true; or the conclusion is the trivial tautology, "Either God exists or God does not exist," which needs no proof and is not what the ontological argument is meant to prove, anyway.

The second premise, (2), is false, that is, the consequent of (1) is not self-contradictory, if we adopt its modern interpretation. The consequent of (1) says:

(i) A being than whom no greater can be conceived is not a being than whom no greater can be conceived,

and this would be normally understood as saying that:

(ii) All beings than whom no greater can be conceived are not beings than whom no greater can be conceived.

I mentioned earlier that statements like (ii) may be read in two ways (see Part III, Section 5). Modern logicians would read it as:

(iii) If anything is a being than whom no greater can be conceived, then it is not a being than whom no greater can be conceived.

But (iii) is not self-contradictory. It is equivalent to the proposition:

(iv) There are no beings than whom no greater can be conceived.

(iv) may be false, but it is not self-contradictory. Hence, if we adopt the modern interpretation of (ii), premise (2) is false.

But another interpretation is possible. Traditional logicians, following Aristotle, read (ii) as:

(v) There are beings than whom no greater can be conceived and every one of them is not a being than whom no greater can be conceived.

Now (v) is self-contradictory, which we can see easily enough.

(vi) Every being than whom no greater can be conceived is not a being than whom no greater can be conceived.

is equivalent to:

(vii) It is not the case that there are beings than whom no greater can be conceived.

Hence, (v) is the conjunction of (vii) with the denial of (vii), and such a conjunction is self-contradictory. To assure the truth of (2) we must assume that St. Anselm is interpreting (ii) in the traditional way.

And now we are committed to interpreting every statement in the argument of the form:

All A's are B's

in the traditional way. Accordingly, the antecedent of (1) is equivalent to:

(viii) There exist beings than whom no greater can be conceived and none of them exists.

But this is a flagrant self-contradiction. To be sure, the fact that the antecedent of (1), namely, (viii), is self-contradictory makes (1) true without further ado. For, a conditional statement whose antecedent is false is true. But this is to secure the truth of (1) at the price of vitiating the argument. For, now the conclusion of the argument is the trivial tautology:

(ix) Either a being than whom no greater can be conceived exists, or it is not the case that a being than whom no greater can be conceived exists.

Propositions like (ix) are too obvious to need proving, and, anyway, the aim of the ontological argument is to prove a quite different proposition.

The antecedent of (1) is supposed to be what the atheist asserts. The ontological argument is offered as proof of the falsity of what the atheist asserts. But if what the atheist asserts is a blatant self-contradiction, it would be strange that philosophers should have invented arguments trying to disprove it. In fact, the atheist's assertion is not self-contradictory, although it may be false, and may even be necessarily false. Not all necessarily false propositions are self-contradictory. By so interpreting the premises of the present version of the ontological argument as to make them true, we trivialize the whole argument and force it to miss its mark.

Section 7

THE "CARTESIAN CIRCLE"

DESCARTES' friend, the Reverend Father Mersenne, circulated the *Meditations* in manuscript among a few theologians and philosophers, including Hobbes, Arnauld, and Gassendi. Their criticisms together with Descartes' point by point replies were collected under the heading, *Objections Urged by Certain Men of Learning Against the Preceding Meditations; with the Author's Replies*. This was appended to the first edition of the *Meditations* (1641).

The term 'Cartesian Circle' is the name given to an alleged circularity in Descartes' system. One of the first to make the charge is Arnauld in the Fourth set of Objections:

The only remaining scruple I have is an uncertainty as to how a circular reasoning is to be avoided in saying: the only secure reason we have for believing that what we clearly and distinctly perceive is true, is the fact that God exists. But we can be sure that God exists, only because we clearly and distinctly perceive it; therefore prior to being certain that God exists, we should be certain that whatever we clearly and evidently perceive is true. (Haldane and Ross, Vol. II, p. 92.)

According to Arnauld, the circle seems to be this:

(1) God exists.
∴ (2) Whatever I perceive clearly and distinctly is true.
But (3) I perceive clearly and distinctly that God exists.
∴ (1) God exists.

I believe that a circle of this sort does exist in Descartes' system, but it exists if, and only if, we assume what I earlier identified as the aberrant view. This is the view that even the most clearly and distinctly intuited propositions, including the *cogito* propositions, are known with metaphysical certainty to be true only by those who know that God exists, and that He cannot be a deceiver. In the *Meditations,* this aberrant view occurs clearly in one place. In the Third Meditation, Descartes says: "for as long as I am ignorant of this [namely that God exists and that He is not a deceiver], I do not see that I can ever be certain of anything else." (Haldane and Ross, Vol. I, p. 159. I have corrected the translation.) In the context of this utterance, it appears that even the *cogito* propositions are not exempt. An omnipotent God may, if He wants to, "cause me to err even in those matters that I regard myself as intuiting . . . in the most evident manner." (Haldane and Ross, Vol. I, p. 158. I have corrected the translation.)

Independently of the aberrant view, Descartes is committed to the proposition that he must prove the principle of clarity and distinctness. He is further committed to the proposition that the principle can be proved only by being deduced from the proposition that God, who is not a deceiver, exists. Thus, in the Synopsis of the *Meditations,* he writes: ". . . it is requisite that we know (Lat.: *scire;* Fr.: *savoir*) that all the things which we conceive clearly and distinctly are true in the very way in which we conceive them; and this could not be proved previously to the Fourth Meditation." (Haldane and Ross, Vol. I, p. 140.)

I have corrected the translation by replacing "may be assured" with "know" in the sense of *scire* or *savoir.* This is important.

Descartes uses *scire* (or *savoir*) as a technical term for knowledge of theorems, i.e., of demonstrated conclusions. In the passage quoted from the synopsis, Descartes is saying that we must know as a theorem the principle of clarity and distinctness. And, in saying that he cannot prove this principle prior to the Fourth Meditation, he is implying that the proof proceeds from the premise that God exists. For the existence of God is not "proved" until the Third Meditation. Besides, as we saw in Part II, Section 1, in the Fourth Meditation there is an argument that purports to deduce the principle of clarity and distinctness from God's existence and veracity. Thus, independently of the aberrant view, Descartes is inalienably wedded to the move from (1) God exists to (2) whatever I perceive clearly and distinctly is true.

But we get into a circle if we add the aberrant view to this move. For what is Descartes now saying? He is saying that he must know that (1) God exists, in order to prove that (2), the principle of clarity and distinctness is true. But in order to know that (1) is true, he has to deduce it from premises that he knows to be true. Yet, according to the aberrant view, no matter how clearly and distinctly he perceives the premises for God's existence, he does not know they are true unless he knows that the principle of clarity and distinctness is true. But in order to know that the principle of clarity and distinctness is true, he must know that God exists. We are thus in a vicious circle. We must prove that God exists, but in order to prove that God exists, we must assume that God exists.

Although Arnauld does not say enough for us to be certain of this, the circularity I have just described may have been the one he meant to single out.

In his reply to Arnauld, Descartes tacitly disowns the aberrant view:

> . . . to prove that I have not argued in a circle in saying, *that the only secure reason we have for believing that what we clearly and distinctly perceive is true, is the fact that God exists; but that clearly we can be sure that God exists only because we perceive it,* I may cite the explanation that I have already given at sufficient length in my reply to the second set of Objections, numbers 3 and 4. There I distinguished those matters that in actual truth we clearly perceive from those we remember to have formerly perceived. For first we

are sure that God exists because we have attended to the proofs that established this fact; but afterwards it is enough for us to remember that we have perceived something clearly, in order to be sure that it is true; but this would not suffice, unless we knew that God existed and that he did not deceive us. (Haldane and Ross, Vol. II, pp. 114–115.)

In this reply, Descartes refers to his replies to the Second set of Objections, numbers 3 and 4. The point under 4 has to do with God's veracity; that point is not immediately relevant. But the answer to 3 is relevant. This is what Descartes says: ". . . when I said that we could know (*scire*) nothing with certainty unless we were first aware that God existed, I announced in express terms that I referred only to the science apprehending such conclusions as can recur in memory without attending further to the proofs which led me to make them." (Haldane and Ross, Vol. II, p. 38.) Here Descartes must be referring to the passages toward the end of the Fifth Meditation (Haldane and Ross, Vol. I, p. 183–184) where indeed he makes it clear that he is talking about conclusions that recur in memory. But this ignores the passages early in the Third Meditation where Descartes exempts nothing, not even the *cogito* propositions, from needing God's guarantee. By ignoring these passages, Descartes is tacitly disowning the aberrant doctrine expressed in them. Indeed, as he now makes it clear, he distinguishes perception or apprehension (Lat.: *notitia;* Fr.: *connaissance*) of first principles from knowledge (Lat.: *scientia;* Fr.: *science*) derived by deduction. ". . . apprehension (*notitia*) of first principles is not usually called knowledge (*scientia*) by dialecticians . . ." (Haldane and Ross, Vol. II, p. 38.)

Descartes goes on in this passage to say that the *cogito* propositions are apprehended intuitively. These propositions are "first principles." Our cognition of their truth is immediate, nondemonstrative. By disowning the aberrant view according to which nothing, not even the *cogito* propositions, are known to be true without God's guarantee, Descartes can avoid the kind of circularity that Arnauld may have been attributing to him.

Descartes must disown the aberrant view not only to avoid circularity in his own system, but also to avoid utter absurdity. According to the aberrant view, as long as Descartes is ignorant that God exists, he "doubts" all mathematical propositions. But to doubt all mathematical propositions is to doubt deduction itself.

This last remark needs explaining. There are two problems involved in deduction, only one of which is relevant in the present context. One problem has to do with the fact that, in a long deduction, I have to *remember* at the last step that every previous step was intuitively certain. Related to this, for Descartes, is the problem that sometimes I *remember* having proved a theorem whose premises or whose proof I do not remember at all. Descartes gives the impression that in his view these problems call for an argument that proves that clear and distinct memory impressions are true. In other words, these are fundamentally problems about the reliability of memory. That problem is not the one I am thinking of when I say that to doubt all mathematical propositions is to doubt deduction itself.

The fact about deduction that is relevant to this issue is that for every valid deductive inference there is a corresponding conditional that is necessarily true. For instance, "The first President of the United States was a good man" deductively implies "At least one President of the United States was a good man." This is equivalent to saying: It is necessarily true that if the first President of the United States was a good man, then at least one President of the United States was a good man. In the aberrant passages Descartes says that mathematical propositions, such as the proposition that $2 + 2 = 4$ or that a square has four sides, are "doubtful." But take "A square has four sides." That is short for "If a thing is a square, then it has four sides." But that conditional is necessarily true. It is the conditional corresponding to the valid deduction schema, "x is a square; therefore, x has four sides." Anyone who "doubts" that a square has four sides *ipso facto* "doubts" that "x is a square" entails "x has four sides." Hence, anyone who "doubts" all mathematical propositions must also "doubt" the validity of deductions.

This generates a vicious circle in Descartes' system somewhat different from the one we have already described. The vicious circle arises as follows: Descartes want to say that because he has deduced God's existence from certain premises, he is "metaphysically" certain that God exists. But how can he be "metaphysically" certain that his deductions are valid when, without God

and God's goodness, not even necessarily true conditionals are
"metaphysically" certain? In other words, Descartes uses deduction to prove that he knows with "metaphysical" certainty that
God exists. But he wants to prove that he knows with "metaphysical" certainty that God exists, in order to prove, among
other things, that he knows with "metaphysical" certainty that
valid deductive inferences are "metaphysically" certain. This is
viciously circular.

Moreover, the aberrant view is intrinsically absurd. It leads
to intellectual hara-kiri. Descartes' "metaphysical" doubts about
mathematical propositions are part and parcel of the aberrant
view. The fundamental trouble Descartes creates for himself by
his "metaphysical" doubt of mathematical propositions is that,
once he professes this doubt, he can make no distinction between
valid and invalid inference. For to doubt all mathematical propositions is to doubt all necessarily true conditionals. But a man
who doubts all necessarily true conditionals must, if he follows
Descartes' injunction, treat them all as if they were false, i.e. he
must withhold assent from all necessarily true conditionals. Such
a man cannot make a distinction between valid and invalid inference, and anyone who cannot make that distinction cannot be said
to be reasoning. Descartes' "metaphysical" doubt about mathematical propositions is, therefore, radically self-stultifying. One
cannot philosophize without reasoning, and one cannot reason
without taking for granted certain logical principles.

Descartes concedes that this is so in many places in his writing.
For that reason, and also because the view is intrinsically absurd,
I regard as aberrant those passages in which he says or implies
that one who is ignorant of God cannot trust even his most evident intuitions.

I have been arguing that the Cartesian Circle is generated *if*
the aberrant view is assumed to be an integral part of Descartes'
doctrine. I shall now explain why I believe that a circle arises
only if the aberrant view is assumed. Descartes wants to prove
that God exists so that he can prove the principle of clarity and
distinctness. Now suppose that we do not assume the aberrant
view. That is, suppose that, whether or not God exists, some
clearly and distinctly perceived propositions are known to be true.
Then it is open to Descartes to say that the premises from which
he deduces God's existence and veracity are clear and distinct

propositions, which do not need God's guarantee. God's guarantee is required, Descartes might say, to show that the following are true: all clearly and distinctly perceived perceptual propositions, all clear and distinct memory impressions, all clear and distinct perceptions of our own states of wakefuness, and all clearly and distinctly perceived mathematical propositions that are such that it is possible to believe them attentively when they are false or to believe attentively that they are false when they are true.

In Part II, Section 1, I explained why we should not be satisfied with Descartes' attempts to prove the truth of all clear and distinct perceptual propositions, all clear and distinct memory impressions, and all clear and distinct perceptions of our own states of wakefulness. The proof of God's existence, the proof of the principle of clarity and distinctness, and the attempt to explain the clarity and distinctness of memory impressions and perceptual propositions in terms of a coherence criterion are the fundamental stumbling blocks. However, these are less than cogent not because of circularity, but for other reasons. The system that I have attributed to Descartes is not circular. It is simply incomplete, and perhaps uncompletable; but it is certainly not inescapably circular. It becomes circular if, and only if, we add to it the aberrant view that *no* clear and distinct intuition is known to be true, except by those who know that God exists.

If I am right about this, then inasmuch as Descartes ultimately disowns the aberrant view, his system does not generate the Cartesian Circle in either one of the two forms that I have discussed.

SELECTED BIBLIOGRAPHY

[1] Alston, W. P. *Philosophy of Language*. Englewood Cliffs: Prentice-Hall, 1964. Chap. 4 contains an illuminating discussion of the verifiability criterion.

[2] Doney, W. "The Cartesian Circle," *Journal of the History of Ideas*, XVI (1955), 324–338.

[3] Frankfurt, H. G. "Memory and the Cartesian Circle," *Philosophical Review*, LXXI (1962), 504–511.

[4] ———. "Descartes' Validation of Reason," *American Philosophical Quarterly*, 2 (1965), 149–156.

[5] Gewirth, A. "The Cartesian Circle," *Philosophical Review*, L, (1941), 389–390.

[6] Kneale, W. C. "Is Existence a Predicate?" *Aristotelian Society, Supplementary Volume* 15 (1936); reprinted in H. Feigl and W. Sellars, eds., *Readings in Philosophical Analysis*. New York: Appleton-Century-Crofts, 1949.

[7] Nakhnikian, G., and W. C. Salmon. "'Exists' as a Predicate," *Philosophical Review*, LXVI (1957), 535–542.

[8] Plantinga, A. (ed.). *The Ontological Argument*. Garden City: Doubleday & Co., 1965. This volume includes an introduction by Richard Taylor and selections ranging from St. Anselm to our own contemporaries.

[9] Scheffler, I. *The Anatomy of Inquiry*. New York: Alfred A. Knopf, 1963. Part II of this book is a fine critical survey of criteria of meaningfulness. Sections I–V of Part II survey the logical positivist verifiability criteria.

BIBLIOGRAPHY

[1] ...

[2] ...

[3] ...

[4] ...

[5] ...

[6] ...

[7] ...

[8] ...

[9] ...

PART IV

William James on Meaning, Truth, and Religious Belief

JAMES' THEORY
OF MEANING

LOGICAL positivism's theory of "cognitive" meaningfulness, which we discussed in Part III, Section 2, is a species of empiricism of the most uncompromising sort. Its proponents intended it to be used to bludgeon religion and metaphysics. William James[1] distinguishes two types of philosophers, the "tender-minded" and the "tough-minded." The "tender-minded" are "rationalistic, intellectualistic, idealistic, optimistic, religious, free-willist, monistic, dogmatical." The "tough-minded" are "empiricist, sensationalistic, materialistic, pessimistic, unreligious, fatalistic, pluralistic, sceptical." Even if not all these terms are meaningful to the reader, the difference James has in mind is clear enough. The logical positivists clearly belong in the class of the "tough-minded." James makes the claim that his pragmatism is a species of empiricism. But it is definitely "tender-minded." Indeed, it is so "tender-minded" that most empiricists, and certainly the logical positivists, would regard it as counter-empirical. James asserted that his pragmatism mediates between the "tough-minded" and the "tender-minded," presumably by preserving the best and rejecting the worst in both philosophic tendencies. Pragmatism "can satisfy both kinds of demand. It can remain religious like the rationalisms, but at the same time, like the empiricisms, it can preserve the richest intimacy with facts." If James had meant to say that a thoroughly "tough-minded" scientific attitude is not logically incompatible with being religious, he would have said what is correct but unexciting.

1 William James (1842-1910), American philosopher and psychologist, is brother of the writer, Henry James. William James is one of the classic American pragmatists, together with John Dewey and Charles S. Peirce.

Nothing in science, nothing in its methods or results, has the slightest tendency either to prove or to disprove any of the assumptions and beliefs of sophisticated religious people. The nineteenth-century quarrel between science and religion was not a quarrel between science and religion. It was a quarrel between those who tended to read the Bible as if it contained scientific propositions and those who argued, with perfect logic, that so taken, the Bible is a mass of equivocations and downright falsehoods. From this, one need not conclude that the Bible is worthless. James, however, set out to establish something much less obvious than that there is no real logical conflict between religion and scientific facts. He meant to say that there are vitally important truths that go beyond anything science has to tell us, and that if we are "tender-minded" we stand a good chance of knowing those vital truths, whereas if we are "tough-minded" we stand no chance at all of knowing them. That is a central theme of "The Will to Believe." This is an exciting claim, morally as well as philosophically. It is exciting philosophically because, if it is true, it would be a contribution to the theory of knowledge. Morally, it would enrich our lives to know that there are ways of knowing just those vital truths that would make us not only informed but also wise concerning first and last things. Thus pragmatism would emerge as a return to philosophy in the classic and etymological sense: namely, the love, the passionate pursuit, of wisdom.

Lest I induce unrealizable hopes in the reader, let me anticipate a conclusion that we shall be forced to accept in the end. James' exciting theme rests upon a cluster of confusions. Perhaps there is a way of keeping the best and leaving out the worst of both the "tender-minded" and the "tough-minded" philosophic attitudes; but we shall not find it in James.

We are ultimately interested here in exploring the exciting themes in "The Will to Believe." But two essential preliminaries are interesting to explore in their own right. These are James' theory of meaning and his theory of truth. His theory of truth is original; his theory of meaning is not. James maintains that he is espousing Charles S. Peirce's theory of meaning. This gives rise to two questions: What is Peirce's theory of meaning? Did James adopt it without modification? It is impossible to answer these questions in a precise way. Peirce has to be interpreted on the basis, for the most part, of voluminous notes, together with the relatively few complete essays that he left. And the interpreters do not agree, while James himself does nothing to contribute to our understanding of Peirce's doctrines on meaning. If we had a more exact notion of what Peirce's theory of meaning is, we might be in a better position to say whether James adopted it wholesale. The fact that James says he did proves nothing: he may not have understood what Peirce was really saying. There is some evidence for believing that Peirce thought that James failed to understand him.[2] Let us, therefore, pursue what follows with all these reservations in mind.

Peirce's Theory of Meaning

IN 1898 JAMES delivered a lecture at the University of California, in Berkeley. The title he gave it is "Philosophical Conceptions and Practical Results."[3] In that lecture he first enunciated his allegiance to Peirce; in 1907, in lectures published under the title *Pragmatism, A New Name for Some Old Ways of Thinking,* he reaffirmed his debt to Peirce. In both instances, James referred to Peirce's paper "How to Make Our Ideas Clear" in the *Popular Science Monthly,* January, 1878. To understand James' pragmatic theory of meaning, we must, therefore, look first into Peirce.

In the 1878 paper, Peirce enunciates the pragmatic theory of meaning as follows: "Consider what effects, that might conceivably have practical bearing, we conceive the object of our conception to have. Then, our conception of these effects is the whole of our conception of the object." Commenting on this in Lecture II of *Pragmatism,* James says:

> Mr. Peirce, after pointing out that our beliefs are really rules for action, said that, to develop a thought's meaning, we need only de-

[2] See Arthur W. Burks' introduction to the Peirce selections in *Classic American Philosophers,* Max H. Fisch et al., eds. (New York: Appleton-Century-Crofts, 1951), pp. 41–53.

[3] *The University Chronicle* (Berkeley, California), September, 1898. Reprinted in *Collected Essays and Reviews* (New York: Longmans, Green and Co., 1920). Also reprinted, with minor omissions, in *Readings in Twentieth-Century Philosophy,* W. P. Alston and G. Nakhnikian, eds. (New York: The Free Press of Glencoe, 1963).

termine what conduct it is fitted to produce: that conduct is for us its sole significance. And the tangible fact at the root of all our thought-distinctions, however subtle, is that there is no one of them so fine as to consist in anything but a possible difference of practice. To attain perfect clearness in our thoughts of an object, then, we need only consider what conceivable effects of a practical kind the object may involve—what sensations we are to expect from it, and what reactions we must prepare. Our conception of these effects, whether immediate or remote, is then for us the whole of our conception of the object, so far as that conception has positive significance at all.

James speaks of "sensations we are to expect" and "reactions we must prepare." The first suggests affinities to positivist verificationism. The second sounds as if something else besides expected sensations might enter into the definition of the meaning of a "thought." Is there such a dichotomy in Peirce?

Peirce students are not of one mind concerning Peirce's theory of meaning. Some find him to be a crude verificationist; others think that Peirce's pragmatism is very different from verificationism. There are many passages in Peirce that justify ascribing to him a verificationist position. Consider the following:

> In order to ascertain the meaning of an intellectual conception one should consider what practical consequences might conceivably result by necessity from the truth of that conception; and the sum of these consequences will constitute the entire meaning of the conception. (5.9)[4]

> Now this sort of consideration, namely, that certain lines of conduct will entail certain kinds of inevitable experiences is what is called a 'practical consideration'. (5.9)

> If one can define accurately all the conceivable experimental phenomena which the affirmation or denial of a concept could imply, one will have therein a complete definition of the concept, and *there is absolutely nothing more in it.* . . . (5.412).

> The total meaning of the predication of an intellectual concept is contained in an affirmation that, under all conceivable circumstances

[4] The references are to Peirce's *Collected Papers of Charles Sanders Peirce*, Vols. I–VI, Charles Hartshorne and Paul Weiss, eds.; Vol. VII and VIII, Arthur W. Burks, ed. (Cambridge, Mass.: Harvard University Press, 1958.) The standard way of referring to the *Collected Papers* is to specify volume and paragraph numbers. Thus, (5.9) means volume 5, paragraph 9.

of a given kind . . . the subject of the predication would behave in a certain way—that is, it would be true under given experimental circumstances. . . . (5.467).

. . . any hypothesis, therefore, may be admissible, in the absence of any special reasons to the contrary, provided it be capable of experimental verification, and only insofar as it is capable of such verification. . . . (5.197)

It is such quotations as these that lend support to those interpreters of Peirce who take him to be a somewhat crude precursor of verificationism. The parting of the ways comes at the point of deciding what Peirce meant to include under "practical consequences." To understand Peirce's theory of meaning at all, we must begin with his theory of belief. The theory of meaning is a logical outgrowth from the theory of belief.

According to Peirce, a belief is a conscious, deliberate habit of action. To be disposed to act, consciously and deliberately, is not just a criterion of holding a certain belief. It is identical with having that belief. In Part II, Section 1 we distinguished occurrent belief from dispositional belief. Peirce presumably means to define both kinds of belief in terms of deliberate habits of action. But such a definition is extremely implausible, at least for occurrent beliefs. For example, suppose you believe occurrently, i.e., you now think that from Detroit the shortest route to Breezewood, Pa., is via the Ohio and Pennsylvania Turnpikes. According to Peirce, that is equivalent to conditional propositions of the following sort: If you want to go from Detroit to Breezewood by car, using the shortest way, you will take the Ohio and Pennsylvania Turnpikes. If you want to take the longer route, you will avoid either the Ohio Turnpike or the Pennsylvania Turnpike or both. But to this definition of belief there is a serious objection. If I believe that from Detroit the shortest route by car to Breezewood is by way of the Ohio and Pennsylvania Turnpikes, then whenever I want to go by car and using the shortest route from Detroit to Breezewood, I shall take what I believe to be the Ohio and Pennsylvania Turnpikes. My simply taking those roads, however, is not enough to show that I believe them to be the shortest way of getting where I want to go by car. Nor is my taking the New York Thruway sufficient reason for judging that I really do not believe that the Ohio and Pennsylvania Turnpikes are the shortest route. For I may have gone on the New York Thruway thinking that it was the Ohio Turnpike. Thus, believing, which Peirce is supposed to define in terms of conscious and deliberate habits of action, recurs in the proposed *definiens*. This makes Peirce's definition viciously circular. Hence, Peirce has not given us an explanation of the nature of occurrent belief in purely behavioristic or purely dispositional terms. I doubt that such an explanation is possible.

It is, at any rate, from this conception of belief that Peirce derives his pragmatic conception of meaning. If a belief is a conscious and deliberate habit of action, then the content of a belief consists of such habits and nothing more, and any two beliefs with identical practical consequences do not differ in their meaning. But what are we to understand by 'practical consequences'? What does Peirce mean to include in them? If Peirce restricts practical consequences to what sensations we can expect, then he is a precursor of verificationism. If he allows other factors than expected and experienced sensations to count as practical consequences, then he holds to a theory different from verificationism. What might these other factors be? We must make a distinction between (a) the logical consequences of a proposition and (b) the logical and (c) the psychological consequences of believing it. Thus, one of the logical consequences of "Today is Saturday" is that tomorrow is Sunday. One of the logical consequences of "S believes that today is Saturday" is that S exists. One of the psychological consequences of "S believes that today is Saturday" may be that S is in a state of joyous anticipation of tomorrow's sermon. In any particular case, the psychological consequences of someone's believing a proposition depend upon additional information about the believer and upon some psychological generalizations.

Now consider the proposition: God answers my prayers. Does it have practical consequences? "Yes," someone might say, "because that proposition implies that my prayers are answered, and this is a consequence that I have found to be true every time I have prayed." To this, the logical positivists and Peirce would say that, if indeed "My prayers are answered" is found to be true, and if the only empirically testable consequences of the proposition that God answers my prayers are that every time I pray, I get what I pray for, then all we have shown is that the proposition that God answers my prayers and the proposition that my prayers are answered are not two different propositions. We are supposing that the only verifiable consequences of the first proposition are identical with the evidence that verifies the second. Hence, by the pragmatic criterion, we have here not two hypotheses, but one. The proposition that God answers my prayers has no "surplus" meaning. But the speaker may object to this as follows: "The proposition that God answers my prayers has for *me* practical consequences that the proposition that my prayers are answered does not have. For one thing, the proposition that God answers my prayers implies that God exists. A nonentity can answer no prayers. Now *I* feel secure in the belief that God exists, and I do not feel anywhere nearly as secure in the belief that my prayers are answered. Hence, by the pragmatic criterion that where there is a difference in practical consequences, there is a difference in meaning, the meaning of 'God answers my prayers' is different from the meaning of 'My prayers are answered'." In this retort there is a shift from the logical consequences of a proposition to the psychological consequences of believing it.

Are these psychological consequences *practical consequences* in the sense intended by Peirce? One Peirce scholar is certain that they are not. "But without question, [Peirce] did not wish to include private satisfactions and emotional responses within the scope of the 'practical.' For Peirce truth is public: the true is that on which a community of investigators will ultimately approach agreement. Hence there are, for Peirce, no private practical consequences of a belief apart from the consequences of holding that belief. A belief habit consists of an expectation of certain sensible effects, or of a habit of consciously reacting to objects in a certain way; and two apparently different habits that involve the same reactions and the same expectations are the same belief, according to Peirce, even though their emotional associations differ."[5]

Because James' theory of truth is very different from Peirce's, however, James has room to maneuver himself into holding a more "tender-minded" theory of meaning than that of Peirce. James' theory of truth, as we shall see, is individualist, relativist, utilitarian. This makes it possible for him to bring under "practi-

[5] Arthur W. Burks, *op. cit.*, p. 44.

cal consequences" psychological consequences. According to Burks and also Justus Buchler,[6] Peirce is a hard-nosed early verificationist, with one difference. Burks cites evidence from the *Collected Papers*, 1.624, 5.541, that Peirce was a little less "tough-minded" than the logical positivists. By 'verifiable' most logical positivists meant verifiable *in this world*, the tacit assumption being that there is no other world, and that hence the qualifier 'in this world' is a pleonasm. Peirce, in his later period, allows practical consequences to include experiences that one might have in an afterlife. For most positivists, the immortality of the soul is a cognitively meaningless hypothesis. For Peirce, it is not meaningless. However, even here Peirce restricts practical consequences to anticipated experience. Individualist psychological consequences are still excluded.

James' Adaptation of Peirce's Theory of Meaning

James, on the other hand, almost certainly means to include such factors under 'practical consequences'. Otherwise, some of the things we will find him saying in "The Will to Believe" will simply be false. He obviously assumes that "the religious hypothesis" is meaningful. Otherwise it could not be believed. Yet James assumes that it is possible to believe it. He says that at least the first half of "the religious hypothesis" is a proposition "which obviously cannot yet be verified scientifically at all." Its practical consequences cannot therefore be of the sort that are required by Peirce or logical positivism. But practical consequences it must have in order to satisfy the pragmatist in James. The only things that can be practical consequences here are the psychological consequences of believing "the religious hypothesis." In fact, our imagined interlocutor, the one who argued that his belief that God exists is pragmatically meaningful because it gives him a sense of security, speaks the language of James.

Toward the beginning of this section we posed a question. In declaring himself a follower of Peirce is James committing himself to a form of positivist verificationism, or do factors other than

[6] Justus Buchler, *Charles Peirce's Empiricism* (London: Routledge and Kegan Paul, 1939).

expected sensations and appropriate responses also come under his notion of 'practical consequences'? Assuming that Burks is right (that Peirce never counted the psychological consequences of believing among practical consequences), we must conclude that James radically modified Peirce's theory of meaning. For James includes both sense-verifiable consequences of a proposition and the psychological consequences of believing a proposition among his practical consequences.

Section 2

JAMES' THEORY
OF TRUTH

JAMES' THEORY of truth is one of his distinctive contributions. A theory very much like his was held by James' contemporary, F. C. S. Schiller, the English pragmatist. But James appears to have come by it independently, and it was certainly not shared by the other two best-known American pragmatists, Peirce and John Dewey. The theory was a novel and, to many people, a shocking perversion of the nature of truth. The critics found the theory to be shot through with fallacies, whereupon James accused them of misreading him. I agree with the critics in finding James' theory of truth to be philosophically scandalous. But it is instructive to examine the controversy around it. The reader will learn a good deal about the nature of truth by reflecting on what James said about it and what the critics found wrong with what James had to say. Some rather acute thinkers attacked James— for example, Bertrand Russell, G. E. Moore, J. E. McTaggart. Indeed, these three were among the very best philosophers of the time.

James' Reservations About Truth as
Correspondence with Fact

It is a commonplace that the truth of a proposition (statement, belief, hypothesis, theory, or whatever can plausibly be said to be true or false) consists in its correspondence with the facts. This James grants. But he observes that in saying this we have hardly said anything that can be useful. If I am faced with the problem of deciding which of two theories to choose, it will be of no help to me to be told that I ought to choose the one that corresponds to the facts. James is willing to allow that, in simple cases, such as when a cat is on the mat, we *can* say that the sentence 'A cat is on the mat' expresses a proposition that corresponds to the facts in some specifiable ways. The phrase 'a cat' refers to the cat, the phrase 'the mat' refers to the mat, both of which may be observed, and the phrase 'is on' expresses the relation that holds between the cat and the mat, which also may be observed. The fact cat-on-the-mat is a complex, just as the proposition expressed by the sentence 'The cat is on the mat' is a complex; every component of the fact corresponds to a component of the proposition, and the fact as a complex corresponds to the proposition as a complex.

When more complicated propositions are in question, however, say the proposition that gases are made up of elastic molecules in random motion, the cat-on-the-mat type of explanation is hard to apply. We are no longer talking about observable entities and their observable relations. We are now talking about theoretical entities and their theoretical interrelations. Suppose we want to know whether the kinetic molecular theory is true. It does no good to be told to see whether the facts correspond to the theory. The connection between the observable facts and the theory is indirect. From the assumptions of the kinetic molecular theory we deduce, by ordinary algebra and statistics, certain functional relations, viz., that the temperature of a volume of gas is proportional to the pressure times the volume. We can perform experiments to see whether the deduced functional correlations actually check. If they do, and if they agree with the rest of the body of accepted physical theory, and if they continue to be verified, then we accept the theory that implies them. The theory is then true insofar as it "works"; that is, it is true as long as its results are verified and cohere with the rest of what we take to be true. But all this can be put in less metaphorical language. A theory is meaningful if, and only if, it is possible to deduce from it, perhaps by way of other theories in addition, consequences that are experimentally verifiable (or falsifiable, let me add, in case the reader has forgotten that 'verifiable' has been used throughout the earlier discussions to mean 'capable of being found true or false'). If these consequences are experimentally found to be false, the theory that implies them is false. If these consequences are experimentally verified, then the theory is in all probability true; at any rate, we go on the assumption that it is true, until further notice.

But considerations of this sort suggest a theory of truth more like that of Peirce than that of James. Peirce said that the true is that upon which a community of investigators would in time come to agree. James, on the other hand, defines the true as that which it is expedient for us to believe. About truth, so defined, James says two things: one, that truth is not static, and two, that truth is manmade.

The Scope of James' Theory of Truth

BEFORE we continue, we ought to make it clear that James' theory of truth is not intended to apply to necessary truths or to propositions about one's own immediate sensory experiences. Thus, the theory is not to apply to "relations among purely mental ideas," e.g., that $1 + 1 = 2$ and that white differs less from grey than it does from black. Such propositions as these we are supposed to know with certainty before any questions can arise about truth *in the pragmatic sense.* James also distinguishes a certain class of contingent empirical propositions from another class of contingent empirical propositions and excludes the former class as well from the scope of his pragmatic theory of truth. He distinguishes reports of immediate sensory experience from contingent empirical propositions that go beyond what is immediately experienced. "The simplest case of new truth is of course the mere numerical addition of new kinds of facts, or of new single facts of old kinds, to our experience—an addition that involves no alteration in the old beliefs. Day follows day, and its contents are simply added. The new contents themselves are not true, they simply *come* and *are*. Truth is *what we say about* them, and when we say that they have come, truth is satisfied by the plain additive formula."[7] And in "The Function of Cognition" (*Pragmatism and the Meaning of Truth*, pp. 356–357), James writes:

> What can save us at all and prevent us from flying asunder into a chaos of mutually repellent solipsisms? Through what can our several minds commune? Through nothing but the mutual resemblance of those of our perceptual feelings which have this power of modifying one another, *which are mere dumb knowledges-of-acquaintance,* and which must also resemble their realities or not know them aright at all. In such pieces of knowledge-of-acquaintance all our knowledge-about must end, and carry a sense of this possible termination as part of its content. These percepts, these *termini,* these sensible things, these mere matters-of-acquaintance, are the only realities we ever directly know . . . these sensations are the mother-earth, the anchorage, the stable rock, the first and last limits, the *terminus a quo* and the *terminus ad quem* of the mind.

Facts-of-acquaintance, together with "relations among purely mental ideas," lie outside the scope of the pragmatic theory of truth. The theory is intended to apply to all kinds of propositions except these two kinds.

James' Definition of Truth

WITH THESE PRELIMINARIES out of the way, we are now in a position to examine James' definition of 'truth'. He derives that definition through the following deduction:

(i) The true is that which we ought to believe.

(ii) That which we ought to believe is that which it is expedient for us to believe.

∴ (iii) The true is that which it is expedient for us to believe.

[7] William James, *Pragmatism and the Meaning of Truth* (New York: Longmans, Green and Co., 1907), p. 62. In William James, *Essays in Pragmatism,* A. Castelli, ed. (New York: Hafner Publishing Co., 1948), p. 149.

James treats (i) and (ii) as incontrovertible, obvious, guaranteed to be true by the very meanings of the words involved in them. Presumably, they are instances of "relations among purely mental ideas." But far from being true by virtue of the very meanings of the terms involved, I think that (i) is in fact false. I take it that there are two things that (i) is saying. It is saying that (ia) whatever is true ought to be believed. It is also saying that (ib) whatever ought to be believed is true. Both these propositions, I think, are false.

The following example shows that (ia) is false, or, at least, that one could question it. Suppose that unknown to me (and under circumstances such that I will not find out unless I initiate elaborate inquiries), my wife has been unfaithful to me on one occasion. We have a happy marriage and happy children, whose continued happiness depends upon keeping the family together. Moreover, if I come to believe that my wife has been unfaithful to me on one occasion only, even so, I am so constituted that I will find it impossible to continue living with her, and, consequently, I will break up the marriage. On the other hand, if I do not find out the truth, we shall continue to live together in a perfectly satisfactory manner. Now would you, who know all the above facts, think that I ought to believe that my wife has been unfaithful to me on one occasion? You would have to be, I think, a heartless and unreasonable man to think that I ought. Yet it is true that my wife was unfaithful to me on one occasion. This shows that (ia) is false. *What* we believe or *that* we believe is seldom for us to choose. Once a fact is recognized by me, I cannot help but believe it. Therefore, there would be something extremely odd in my first finding out that my wife has been unfaithful to me and then trying to decide if I ought to believe it. But the oddness of that procedure does not tell against the point made. It is easily possible to imagine a situation in which you might believe of me that I ought not to believe a certain true proposition. Besides, even though it is odd to find out that something is so and then to try to decide whether one ought to believe it, it is not impossible. I may be the sort of person who decides that, everything considered, it would be better if I had never found out about my wife. I may say to myself: "I really oughtn't to believe that she has been unfaithful to me. And I know what to do about it. Dr. J. has developed a technique whereby he can erase all traces of the evidence from my memory as well as the memory that I once knew that my wife has been unfaithful. His fee is high, but it is a small price to pay to secure the continued happiness and well-being of my family."

I can imagine that some people would disagree with me about the wisdom of my believing that my wife has been unfaithful to me on exactly one occasion. They might be convinced that, inasmuch as it is true, I ought to believe it, and that is the end of the matter. I would agree that, inasmuch as it is true, I ought to believe it. But, inasmuch as my believing it would lead to tragedy in the lives of two adults and four children, while my not believing it (by being ignorant of it) would assure the continued well-being of the whole family, I ought not to believe it. And the judgment that I ought not, in this case, overrides the judgment that I ought. The reasons for not believing are much stronger here than the reasons for believing. At least, they seem so to me, and in saying this I do not think that I am in any way contradicting myself. Since there is at least the possibility that I may be right in judging that, all things considered, I ought not to believe the proposition about my wife, (ia) is not incontrovertibly true. Hence, (i) is not incontrovertibly true. Moreover, (ib) is not necessarily true either. Under the circumstances described, if I have any belief on the matter at all, I ought to believe that my wife has never been unfaithful to me. But that belief is false. Hence, not every proposition that I ought to believe is true. Thus, both parts of (i) are false, or, at least, it is possible that they are false. Hence, (i) is not necessarily true. I believe that it is in fact false.

Truth and Expediency

"But," James might say, "you have not gone far enough. You have not taken into account my second premise, namely, that that which we ought to believe is that which it is expedient for us to believe." Could we not reply, however, that in the case described it is inexpedient for me to believe that my wife has been unfaithful to me on one occasion? The consequences of my not believing it are that my wife, my children, and I continue in our present happy state. The consequences of my believing it are that all of us suffer horribly. Does this not make it obvious that the belief is inexpedient? And if it is inexpedient, by (ii) itself, I ought not to believe it. And yet the proposition that I ought not to believe is true. In fact, the propostion that it is expedient for me to believe is that my wife has never been unfaithful to me. Hence, it is false that all true beliefs are expedient, and it is also false that all expedient beliefs are true. This is so whatever we understand by 'expedient', whether 'expedient at least on an occasion of my having the belief', or 'expedient for a time', or 'expedient in the long run'. For in none of these senses of being expedient is it expedient for me to believe that my wife has once been unfaithful to me. Thus, James' second premise does not save his first premise. And since the first premise is false, the conclusion that the true is that which it is expedient for us to believe, is so far unsubstantiated.

Truth and Verification

BUT PERHAPS we have misunderstood James. Perhaps by 'expedient' he means some thing narrower than what the word means in everyday use. Now James again and again emphasizes that there is a logical connection between what is true and what can be *verified,* in the sense of "found to be true." "True ideas," says James, "are those that we can assimilate, validate, corroborate, and verify. False ideas are those that we cannot." The truth "works," in that it can be verified. We must try to see whether expediency can be tied to verification in a way that will save James' definition of the true as that which it is expedient for us to believe. Accordingly, the definition would be that the true is that which can be verified. From this it follows that necessarily all true propositions can be verified and necessarily all propositions that can be verified are true. Now by 'can be verified' James must have meant something stronger than the logical possibility of verifying. For, in the logical-possibility sense of 'can', any contingently false proposition would turn out to be true. It is false that Hitler is alive right now. But it is logically possible that right now there is a mass of evidence to make it practically certain that Hitler is alive. For one thing, it is logically possible that

Hitler is standing in front of me right now ranting about the Jews. We must suppose that by 'can' James means some sort of causal possibility. Perhaps he means to say that all true propositions would be verified, if put to the test, and all propositions that would be verified, if put to the test, are true.

The second half of this conjunction is a trivial truth, provided that by 'verified' we mean completely verified. But it is not at all clear that James' pragmatic conception of belief would allow him to talk about completely verifying beliefs about empirical matters of fact. According to pragmatism, the function of a belief is to lead us from experience to experience in a "satisfactory" manner, without shocks or surprises. If you believe that the yellow object in your hand is a lemon and that 'lemon' means, among other things, something whose juice is sour, then you would expect to experience a sour taste if you tasted the juice of the yellow object in your hand. Your expectation includes the expectation that you can squeeze juice out of the yellow object. Now try squeezing it. It doesn't squeeze at all. It is a clever imitation of a lemon. Your actual experience is different from what you confidently expected. You are surprised, perhaps annoyed. You will now adjust your beliefs in the light of this unexpected experience.

True beliefs, in James' view, do not lead us to unexpected experiences. But this "leading-function" theory of belief suggests that many of our beliefs are, so to speak, never completely "played out." Of course the longer a belief leads in a "satisfactory" manner, the more likely it is that our confidence that it is true will grow. But many of our beliefs have interminable practical consequences. Pragmatism generally assumes that the belief that this yellow object is a lemon is one that, in principle, some future experience might disconfirm. Hence, on the assumption that a belief about matters of empirical fact is necessarily something that points interminably to some as yet unrealized but causally realizable experience, there is no such thing as completely verifying many of our beliefs. For pragmatism all the evidence is never in for many of our beliefs. Besides to say that all the evidence is in is to imply that no future relevant experience is causally possible. But this is to imply that many of our beliefs are not beliefs. For, according to pragmatism, let us repeat, a belief about matters of empirical fact is necessarily something that points to some as yet unrealized but causally realizable experience. Thus, from the pragmatic point of view, it would seem that a belief that is completely verified is not an empirical belief at all, and that, therefore, a belief which is completely verified is not a true empirical belief, either. It would seem, therefore, that for a pragmatist the proposition "All propositions that can be verified are true," cannot be talking about complete verification.

That leaves the possibility that the version of James' theory of truth that we are now discussing, namely, that the true is that which can be verified, entails that all propositions that can be (incompletely) verified are *true to the extent that they are verified.* This seems to imply that there are degrees of truth. The notion of degrees of truth is a very strange notion, indeed. We do say such things as this: "His remark was closer to the truth than hers," and then go on to explain: "He said that the scarf was red. She said that it was orange. Actually it was crimson." But this perfectly straight-forward way of talking does not involve any strange notion of one proposition being more true than another. "The scarf is red" is not more true than "The scarf is yellow." The latter proposition is false; the former is true, but not as specific as "The scarf is crimson." If he had said that the scarf was orange and she had said that it was green, even though both propositions would be false, his statement would be closer to the truth in that orange resembles crimson more closely than green does. 'Closer to the truth' is a meaningful phrase in everyday discourse. The statement 'p is truer than the statement q' is not unless it means 'p is closer to the truth than q is'. Those who use, or are committed to using, the phrase 'p is truer than q' in an unfamiliar way must explain what they mean.

James could explain that 'true to the extent that it is verified' means that we are entitled to believe a proposition to be true, provided that the strength of our belief is (in some rough fashion) commensurate with the strength of the evidence. Inasmuch as this is a perfectly innocuous explanation, if this is what James did want to say, then his definition that the true is that which can be verified (in this life) would, so far, lead to no difficulty. Since this is a perfectly innocuous explanation of 'true to the extent that it is verified', we could without being unfair suppose that it is actually what James would have said. And so, James' implied claim that all propositions that would be verified, if put to the test, are true would be equivalent to the proposition that all propositions that, if they are put to the test, would be verified, albeit incompletely, are such that we are entitled to believe them to be true, provided that the strength of our belief is in a rough way commensurate with the strength of the evidence. And this last proposition seems to be perfectly sound. So far, then, James' definition of truth, namely, that the true is that which can be verified, would have no unacceptable consequences.

James may have been trying to suggest a theory along the following lines. "Facts-of-acquaintance," i.e. propositions that report or record one's own immediate sensory experiences, and "relations among purely mental ideas," e.g., that $1 + 1 = 2$, are true or false in an absolute sense. The pragmatic theory of truth is to be restricted to "theoretical" propositions only. These are propositions that cannot be known to be true or false in an absolute sense. They can only be confirmed or disconfirmed to some degree of probability, between 0 and 1, relative to a certain body of evidence. The evidence must include "facts-of-acquaintance" gathered by methods characteristic of the various empirical sciences. Theories whose probability is close to 1 are to be accepted as true "for all practical purposes." But they are not true in an absolute sense. Theories that have a probability near 0 are to be rejected as false "for all practical purposes." But they are not false in an absolute sense. Any theory will be susceptible of alteration in the light of future experience.

On this view, the truth of a theory is the same as its probability relative to a specified body of evidence. Hence, the truth of a theory is relative to the evidence. It admits of degrees; it changes with further evidence; it is expressed by some number between 0 and 1. Thus, if relative to the evidence the probability of a certain theory is 0.69, then relative to the evidence it is true to degree 0.69. Relative to the evidence we know it to degree 0.69.[8]

If this is what James meant to say, then his theory of truth would not be subject to certain criticisms. But to read him this way is to overlook the "tender-minded" side of his theory of truth. James proposes to explicate the meaning of 'true' as it is applied

[8] This may remind the reader of a suggestion made in Part II, Section 1 (pp. 112–113). There I said that Descartes would have fared better if he had admitted that some propositions cannot be known with absolute certainty. They can be known only to a certain degree of probability.

to all propositions other than "facts-of-acquaintance" and "relations among purely mental ideas."

In this general form, James' definition of truth entails that all true propositions would be verified, if put to the test. And the latter proposition seems to be plainly false. Suppose that I now have an impression that yesterday I had a mild headache at noon. Suppose, further, that yesterday at noon I did have a mild headache, but that no evidence exists of my having had it. Under the circumstances it is causally impossible for me to verify that I had a headache yesterday at noon, yet it is true that I did have one. Or, suppose that I did have a mild headache, but never paid attention to it. Suppose further that there is no evidence of my having had that headache, and suppose that I do not even have an impression of having had a headache yesterday at noon. I cannot verify that I had that headache, yet I did. Or, to give an even more obvious example, suppose that last night I was playing backgammon with my wife. No one else was present. At a certain moment during the game, there was a certain arrangement of the pieces on the board, which neither my wife nor I noticed. Now there is a true proposition about the configuration of those pieces, which it is causally impossible to verify. For one thing, we do not even know which proposition it is that we are to try to verify. It is causally impossible to test a proposition if we do not have the slightest idea what that proposition is.

Consider now the hypothesis of immortality. That I am immortal may be verified by me after my earthly life is over, if I am immortal. But if I am not immortal, the proposition that I am not immortal can never be verified by me. And if nobody is immortal, then the proposition about my not being immortal cannot be verified by anybody. But it is possible that nobody, including myself, is immortal. Hence, there are a great many propositions of the form: S is not immortal, which could be true, and if they were true, could not be verified by anybody. All propositions that would be verified could be verified: causal possibility entails logical possibility. But there are propositions that it would be logically impossible to verify, even if they were true; hence, these would not be verified ever.

The immortality example, as well as the others before it, should convince us that it is not the case that all true propositions would be verified, if put to the test. Some propositions that could be true could not be put to the test. Other propositions that are true cannot (causally) be put to the test, even though logically it is possible to verify them. Logically it is possible that God reveals to me that I had a mild headache yesterday noon. But there are no known causal laws according to which it is possible for anyone to test the hypothesis that I had a mild headache yesterday when I never noticed it, told no one about it, made no record of it, and do not now have even an impression that I had it. The false proposition that, if put to the test, all true propositions would be verified, is entailed by the definition that the true is that which can be verified. Therefore, that definition of truth is incorrect. A correct definition cannot imply falsehoods.

There is a way out of this difficulty. Restrict the class of "theoretical" propositions (the ones that can be said to be true or false in the pragmatic sense) to the class of propositions that we can actually check by the methods employed in the various experimental sciences.[9] This would get rid of such counterexamples as the ones about yesterday's headache, the backgammon board, and immortality. It follows from the very description of these cases that no one can confirm or disconfirm them by the methods that are employed in the various experimental sciences.

But of course this way out for James would involve a major alteration of his initial claim that his pragmatic theory of truth applied to all propositions other than propositions about "facts-of-acquaintance" and "relations of ideas." The initial claim is still demonstrably false.

The fact that "The true is that which we can verify" fails as a definition does not mean that there is no connection at all between truth and verifiability. Many true propositions can be verified, and we know that this is so because many of them are verified, at least to the extent that the evidence is overwhelmingly in their favor. In many cases, there is no evidence against them. But the fact is that not all true propositions can be verified.

[9] This is analogous to the restriction I suggested in Part III, Section 2 for the verifiability theory of meaning. There I said that the verifiability theory became much more plausible if it was proposed as an explicative definition of 'meaningful synthetic sentence normally used to make scientific statements'. (See p. 193.)

This fact prevents our taking its being causally possible to verify a proposition even as a *criterion* of truth. What a criterion is is very hard to say. The word 'criterion' has many different meanings, and it has no commonly recognized meaning in philosophy. In the present context, I am using it in such a way that "A is a criterion of B" entails that "Being A is a sure sign of being B." This is a strong sense of 'criterion', and in this sense "A is a criterion of B" entails "All B's are A's." For if there was a B which was not A, then being A would not be a sure sign of being B. In this strong sense of 'criterion', its being causally possible to verify a proposition is not even a *criterion* of truth. For we have seen that it is possible that there are true propositions that it is causally impossible to verify.

To sum up: James defines truth as that which it is expedient for us to believe. This definition is incorrect, if we understand the word 'expedient' in its normal sense. The definition is incorrect even when by 'expedient' we understand *would be verified, if put to the test*. Moreover, in either sense, being expedient cannot be even a criterion, let alone a *definiens*, of truth. There is a connection between truth and being found true upon examination. There is also an obligation to seek and to believe the truth. But the connection between truth and verifiability is not unexceptionable. And our obligation to seek and to believe the truth is not an absolute obligation. There are times when we ought not to believe certain propositions even though they are true. That a proposition is true is always a good reason for believing it. But it is not always a reason such that no other reasons could possibly lead to the conclusion that, everything considered, I ought not to believe that proposition. Even if I knew all the facts about my wife's infidelity, I might still judge that, everything considered, I ought not to believe the truth, and I might make this judgment even though I cannot otherwise help but believe what I judge I ought not to believe. And, if it sounds somewhat odd to speak of recognizing that I ought not to do something, when I cannot help doing it, then at least it must be granted that, even when I cannot help but believe the proposition about my wife's infidelity, I might still judge that, everything considered, it would be better (on the whole, more expedient) if I did not believe it.

We have so far talked about James' definition of truth. Let us now consider two claims that James makes about truth. He maintains that the truth is not static; that it changes. He also maintains that truths are manmade. Let us consider these claims in order.

James' Conception of Truth as Relative to Persons, Hence Changeable

THE CLAIM that the truth changes does not apply to the two classes of propositions we have already alluded to. One of these is the class of propositions that are about "relations among purely mental ideas." The other class is the class of contingent empirical propositions about facts with which we are acquainted by direct observation. About the former class of propositions, this is what James says:

> *Relations among purely mental ideas* form another sphere where true and false beliefs obtain, and here the beliefs are absolute or unconditional. When they are true they bear the name either of definitions or of principles. It is either a principle or a definition that 1 and 1 make 2, that 2 and 1 make 3, and so on; that white differs less from grey than it does from black; that when the cause begins to act the effect also commences. Such propositions hold of all possible 'ones', of all conceivable 'whites', 'greys' and 'causes'. The objects here are mental objects. Their relations are perceptually obvious at a glance, and no sense-verification is necessary. Moreover, once true, always true of those same mental objects. Truth here has an 'eternal' character. If you can find a concrete thing anywhere that is 'one' or 'white' or 'grey' or an 'effect', then your principles will everlastingly apply to it. (*Pragmatism and the Meaning of Truth*, p. 209.)

James' words are clear enough. Propositions about "relations among purely mental ideas" are not mutable. Propositions about immediately observed facts are also immutable. "Truth is *what we say about* them." What this means is that the truth of a contingent empirical proposition about immediately observed facts consists of its being a sincere description of whatever is immediately observed. Presumably such descriptions are not hypotheses subject to confirmation or disconfirmation by observations yet to come. Thus, the assertion that truth is mutable applies only to propositions that are true in the pragmatic sense.

Now is this assertion true? Before we can answer that question, we have to know what the claim is, as exactly as we can determine it. One clue to what James might mean by saying that truth is mutable is his saying that our beliefs are true so long as "they are profitable to our lives." This seems to commit him to two propositions. One, that for any period of time, if during that period a belief that p is "profitable" to S who holds it, then p is true for S. Two, that p is true for S only when it is profitable for S to believe that p. But it is possible that, during a certain period of time, it is profitable for S to believe that p, while during a different period of time it is not profitable for S to believe that p. Hence, it is possible that p, which is true for S at one time, is false for S at some other time. Also, it is possible that at the same time, it is profitable for S to believe that p, while it is profitable for S' to believe that not p. Hence, it is possible that, at one and the same time, p is true for S and false for S'.

So interpreted, the mutability of truth is a consequence of its relativity to people. James acknowledges that his theory of truth is relativistic. Here is an example of what he believes:

Mr. Russell[10] next joins the army of those who inform their readers that according to the pragmatist definition of the word 'truth' the belief that A exists may be 'true,' even when A does *not* exist. This is the usual slander, repeated to satiety by our critics. They forget that in any concrete account of what is denoted by 'truth' in human life, the word can only be used relatively to some particular trower. Thus, I may hold it true that Shakespere wrote the plays that bear his name, and may express my opinion to a critic. If the critic be both a pragmatist and a baconian, he will in his capacity of pragmatist see plainly that the workings of my opinion, I being what I am, make it perfectly true for me, while in his capacity of baconian he still believes that Shakespere never wrote the plays in question. But most anti-pragmatist critics take the word 'truth' as something absolute, and easily play on their reader's readiness to treat his own truths as the absolute ones. If the reader whom they

[10] See B. Russell, "Transatlantic Truth," *Albany Review* (January, 1908); reprinted under the title "William James' Conception of Truth," in B. Russell's *Philosophical Essays* (London: Longmans, Green and Co., 1910).

address believes that A does not exist, while we pragmatists show that those for whom the belief that it exists works satisfactorily will always call it true, he easily sneers at the naivete of our contention, for is not then the belief in question 'true,' tho what it declares as fact has, as the reader so well knows, no existence? Mr. Russell speaks of our statement as an 'attempt to get rid of fact' and naturally enough considers it 'a failure'. 'The old notion of truth reappears,' he adds—that notion being, of course, that when a belief is true, its object does exist.

It is, of course, *bound* to exist, on sound pragmatic principles. Concepts signify consequences. How is the world made different for me by my conceiving an opinion of mine under the concept 'true'? First, an object must be findable there (or sure signs of such an object must be found) which shall agree with the opinion. Second, such an opinion must not be contradicted by anything else I am aware of. But in spite of the obvious pragmatist requirement that when I have said truly that something exists, it *shall* exist, the slander which Mr. Russell repeats has gained the widest currency. (*The Meaning of Truth*, Longmans, Green and Company [1914], pp. 273–275.)

The passage just quoted is interesting for two reasons. One is that in it James clearly avows his relativistic conception of truth. The second is that in the last paragraph James thinks that he is answering Russell's (and Moore's) accusation that on James' view my belief that the Taj Mahal exists is true inasmuch as it profits me to believe it, even if the Taj Mahal did not exist. James would reply as follows: "How is the world made different for me by my believing it to be true that the Taj Mahal exists? First, the Taj Mahal must be findable (or sure signs of the Taj Mahal must be found) which shall agree with the opinion that the Taj Mahal exists. Second, such an opinion must not be contradicted by anything else I am aware of. It is an obvious requirement of pragmatism that when I have said truly that something exists, it shall exist." This answer would do only if James were a "toughminded" empiricist in his theory of meaning. For then the sentence 'The Taj Mahal exists' would include in its meaning the sentence 'If I went to a certain location in India, I would see the Taj Mahal'. And, then, of course, the proposition that the Taj Mahal exists would be true only if it was true that if I went to a certain location in India, I would see the Taj Mahal. But James is "tender-minded." He wants 'God exists' to be a meaningful sentence, and he also wants to say that, for some people, it is (pragmatically) true that God exists. But he cannot say about God the things that he can say about the Taj Mahal. God is not findable in sense experience, nor are there "sure [empirical] signs" that God exists. Moreover, the opinion that God exists is contradicted by many people who believe that God does not exist, and the believers are well aware of the fact that their opinion is contradicted many times over. It is absolutely clear that "when I have said truly that something exists, it *shall* exist . . . ," but it is by no means an "obvious pragmatic requirement." For, in the pragmatic sense of truth, a belief is true for S if, and only if, it is expedient for S to believe it. No argument exists in James to prove that my belief that such and such a thing exists is expedient for me *only if* that thing exists ("or sure signs of such an object are found"). As a matter of fact James can prove no such proposition, on pain of being inconsistent. We shall see in the next section that, according to James, the belief that God exists may be expedient for you, and "so far forth" true for you, even if God does not exist.

Here again we see that James' defense against Russell will not do. James' doctrine can be made plausible by the Taj Mahal example only if the doctrine is confined to propositions that can be confirmed or disconfirmed by methods employed in the various experimental sciences. Russell's criticism is perfectly sound against James' general doctrine that the pragmatic conception of truth applies to all propositions other than propositions about "facts-of-acquaintance" and "relations of ideas."

But let us return to the main point. James is a relativist with respect to truth, and his notion that truth is mutable follows from his relativism. Now let us take a closer look at the following proposition: (i) if during a period of time S believes that p, and S's believing that p is during that period profitable for S, then during that period p is true for S. This is one of the two relativistic consequences that we derived from James' dictum that our beliefs are true so long as they are profitable to our lives. What are we to understand by the proposition under consideration? One proposition it might be identical with is the following: (ii) if during a period of time S believes that p, and S's believing that p is during that period profitable for S, then during that period S will persist in believing that p. I say that this is one proposition that the original proposition *might* be identical with, because in its most usual sense, 'p is true for S' means simply that S believes that p is true. But, in the usual sense of 'true', it is possible that S believes that p is true, yet p is false. So that, if the original proposition (i) is to be identified with the second proposition, (ii), then it is evident that (i) is saying nothing about truth. Rather, it alleges that a certain circumstance has the causal influence of reinforcing belief in a proposition. This allegation may be true or false, but whichever it is, it is certainly not a proposition that tells us anything about truth.

By replacing James' *definiens* of 'true for S' with the *definiendum*, (ii) reads as follows: (iii) If during a period of time S believes that p, and during that period p is true for S, then during that period S will persist in believing that p. Again, if we mean by 'true for S' what we ordinarily mean, namely, that S believes that p is true, (iii) reduces to the tautology: (iv) If during a certain period of time S believes that p, then during that period of time S believes that p.

All this shows that James' theory of truth is not about truth at all. It is at best a stipulation to the effect that 'p is (pragmatically) true for S during time t' is to mean that S *believes that p during time t, and S's believing that p during time t is profitable for S during time t.* For '(pragmatically) true' we might as well substitute 'comforting for S' or 'good for S to believe'. Neither of these is synonymous with 'true' in any normally recognized sense of that word.

We said that James' notion that truth is mutable is a consequence of his notion that truth is relative to individuals. The mutability notion is no more accurate a description of truth than is the relativity notion. What James seems to have in mind where he talks of mutability is that one and the same proposition may be true for S at one time and false for S at another, and that at one and the same time the same proposition may be true for S and false for S'. Again, if we understand the phrase 'true for S' in its ordinary sense, the mutability thesis comes to this: S may change his mind about the truth of a given proposition, and different people may have incompatible beliefs. Both parts of this pronouncement are incontrovertible truths which a philosopher should have no special reason to declare. Who but an extremely naive person would even doubt them? And, if we understand by 'true for S' not what it means but the pragmatic sense that James stipulates for it, then the mutability thesis comes to this: At one time S may find it expedient (or comforting, or good) to believe that p, while at another time S finds it inexpedient (or uncomfortable or bad) to believe that p; and some people may find a proposition comforting to believe while others find that same proposition vexing to believe. Again, these are commonplace and banal propositions which a philosopher should have no special reason to declare. In neither case, neither when we interpret 'true for S' in its ordinary sense nor when we interpret it in its *pragmatic* sense, does the mutability thesis turn out to be a proposition about truth.

The fact is that a proposition cannot be true at one time and false at another. Moore makes a good point, I think, when he writes: ". . . that any idea [proposition] which is true once, would be true at any time, seems to me to be one of those truths of which Professor James has spoken as having an 'eternal,' 'absolute,' 'unconditional' character."[11] The sentence 'I am ill' may at one time be used to assert a true proposition and at another time to assert a false proposition. If I were to assert now that I am ill by uttering the sentence 'I am ill', the proposition I would assert would be false. Right now I am not ill. But if when I am in fact ill I assert that I am ill by uttering the sentence 'I am ill', then the proposition I am asserting is true. The same sort of thing is true of very many other sentences. Sentences such as 'I am ill', 'It is raining', 'This is white', 'That is a book' are instances of sentences whose assertive use obeys certain conventions, e.g., (i) that when I say I am ill, I am describing the state of my health *at the time of the utterance;* and (ii) that the personal pronoun 'I' refers to the one who is making the assertion. The proposition that at time t a certain person is ill is true if, and only if, the person in question is ill at t. And if the proposition is true—it is true. It makes no sense to say that it may be true at one time and false at some other time.

To say that propositions do not change their truth-values is, of

[11] G. E. Moore, *Philosophical Studies* (London: Routledge & Kegan Paul Ltd., 1922), p. 137.

course, not to say that the world does not change. Of course the world changes. What is a fact at one time is no longer a fact at some later time. Five thousand years ago there were no thermo-nuclear bombs anywhere on earth. Now there are many of them. Both of these propositions are true. From five thousand years ago to now what has changed is the world, not the truth-value of any proposition. In the years before Copernicus, many educated people believed that the sun goes around the earth. Now few, if any, educated people believe this. Well, the sun was not going around the earth before Copernicus, and it did not settle down to rest relative to the earth after him. The sun never moved around the earth. Educated people eventually found out the truth.

James' Conception of Truth as Manmade

THIS BRINGS us to the claim that truth is "manmade." What does that mean? The only argument for this in James is that what we believe to be true or what we believe to be false, and that we believe this rather than that, depends to a large extent on our personality and circumstances. All this is in all probability true. If that is all that James means by saying that "to an unascertain-able extent our truths are manmade products," then what he says is certainly true. But it is so commonplace an idea that one won-ders if that is all that James really had in mind. That it is not all that he has in mind is suggested by his saying such things as that "we make *our truths*." This suggests, as Moore pointed out, that "not merely the *existence* of our beliefs, but also their *truth*, depended upon human conditions."[12] We make our true beliefs *true*. Now there are beliefs of which this is true. We make them come true. What are called 'self-fulfilling prophesies' are of this nature. Suppose I believe that the bank where my savings are will fail. I broadcast my prediction, create a panic, and stampede the depositors into withdrawing all their savings. The bank fails. But beliefs that we make true are in a very small minority. Most of our beliefs are such that we can do nothing at all about making

[12] *Op. cit.*, p. 140.

them true or making them false. The belief that I will be dead tomorrow is one that I can make true—by committing suicide today. But nothing that I or anyone else can do will make it true that the earth is flat; nor that in June, 1965 men reached the moon. And, if there is no God, then nothing that anyone can do will make it true that there is one.

Section 3

"THE WILL TO BELIEVE"

THE PRINCIPAL theses of James' "The Will to Believe" are enunciated in the following quotation:

> Our passional nature not only lawfully may, but must, decide an option between propositions, whenever it is a genuine option that cannot by its nature be decided on intellectual grounds; for to say, under such circumstances, "Do not decide, but leave the question open", is itself a passional decision—just like deciding yes or no— and is attended with the same risk of losing the truth. (*Essays in Pragmatism*, p. 95.)

There are two propositions here. One is that, given a genuine option that cannot be decided on intellectual grounds, our "passional nature" must decide it. The other is that given a genuine option that cannot be decided on intellectual grounds, our "passional nature" may lawfully decide it.

Given that for James "passional nature" and "intellectual grounds" are exhaustive determinants of our beliefs, and given what James means by a 'genuine option', the first proposition is necessarily true. The key term is 'genuine option', by which

James means an option that is at once *living, momentous* and *forced*. By 'option' James means an opportunity to decide between doing one or the other of two mutually exclusive actions, or an opportunity to believe one or the other of two mutually exclusive hypotheses. By 'hypothesis' he means "anything that may be proposed to our belief." An option is *living for* S if, and only if, *both* hypotheses are *live for* S. A hypothesis is *live for* S if, and only if, it is not totally incredible to S. A *momentous* option is one in which it is important to make the right choice for two reasons. First, the right choice will yield important benefits, while the wrong choice will hurt us in significant ways. Secondly, the present opportunity to choose may be the only one we shall ever have. If we fail to choose wisely now, we may be forever passing up the chance of gaining an important benefit or avoiding a significant evil. Here is an example of a momentous option. I am offered a challenging job, which I will not be offered again if I refuse to take it now; the job frightens me considerably, because I am not confident that I am up to it; it is one that would make me very happy, if I took it and was able to measure up to it, but if I took it and did not measure up to it, my future would be bleak. Shall I accept the offer or refuse it? That is a momentous option. The opposite of a momentous option is a *trivial* option. Here the consequences of either choice are relatively unimportant to the person who is making the choice; or, if he should refuse to choose one of the alternatives, he will have other opportunities to choose it; or, if his present choice should prove inexpedient, he can undo what he has done. If, for example, my choice of a present for my wife should prove unsatisfactory, I can exchange it for something better.

A *forced* option is an option in the face of which refusing to choose is practically the same thing as having chosen one of the two possibilities, because the consequences of not choosing either possibility are the same as the consequences of having chosen that one of the two possibilities. Here is an example. I am on a sinking ship in shark infested waters. If I do not jump off, I will drown. If I jump off, I may be picked up, unless the sharks get me first. Now suppose that I am the sort of person who in those circumstances falls into a state of hysterical immobility. The consequences of this are identical with the consequences of my having intentionally chosen to stay with the ship. Of course, if a helicopter hovered over and by grabbing its life line I could be whisked off to safety, I would not be faced with a forced option. There would be a third choice, and in that case the option would be *avoidable*. But where there is no helicopter or some other way of escaping the ship, the option, "Stay with the ship or jump into the water," is forced.

From the fact that an option is forced it follows that commitment to one or the other of the two exclusive possibilities is unavoidable.* And, if the unavoidable commitment cannot be made on intellectual grounds, it follows that it must be made by our "passional nature." For, where a commitment one way or the other is unavoidable, if the intellect cannot decide, our passional nature is all that is left to settle the matter. Hence, James' first principal thesis is true by virtue of the meanings of the key terms in it; hence, it is true necessarily. The word 'must' in this context means: must *logically*. James' first thesis is thus a philosophical principle, not a psychological generalization. I believe that this principle is true. The assumption that intellectual considerations are not the only determinants of belief is certainly true. James divides the determinants of belief into "intellectual" and "passional" factors, and includes in the "passional" all extra-intellectual determinants of belief. It follows that, whenever believing one or the other side of an option is unavoidable, then if intellectual considerations cannot determine belief, the extra-intellectual determinants will, of necessity, settle the matter.

* There is an ambiguity in this as between commitment to one or the other of the two beliefs or to one or the other of the two consequences of the beliefs. Commitment to one or the other of the two beliefs is not unavoidable. What is unavoidable is one or the other of the two consequences. This can be illustrated in the following example. If I believe that the jar contains 1000 beans, I win a prize of ten cents. If I believe that the jar does not contain 1000 beans, I win nothing. This is a forced option because if I believe neither that the jar contains 1000 beans nor that it does not, I win nothing. The consequences of my suspending judgment are identical with the consequences of my believing one of the alternatives. Thus, one of the two consequences is unavoidable. But one of the two beliefs is not unavoidable. By having neither belief, I avoid both. If the option involves *actions* rather than *hypotheses*, however, both commitment to one or the other of the actions and to one or the other of the consequences are unavoidable, as in the example of the man on the sinking ship. The commitment, of course, need not be deliberate.

The second proposition is also true because it follows immediately from a proposition that James himself does not hold, but which I think is true. I think it is true that, given a living and momentous option that is not decidable on intellectual grounds, our "passional nature" may lawfully decide it.

This thesis seems to me to be true self-evidently. No elaborate machinery is needed to show its reasonableness. One or two simple examples may be more than enough to get the point across. Suppose, as I think is the case, that there is no sufficient evidence to prove that theism is true or more probable than atheism, and that there is no sufficient evidence to prove that it is false or less probable than atheism. Suppose, further, that although I can suspend judgment if I wish, i.e., the option is not forced, I am temperamentally so constituted that I find theism more congenial than atheism. I find, for instance, that the theistic view of the world makes more sense to me than the atheistic view of it; that in the theistic view I find a source of strength and comfort; that it gives me a greater capacity to face the disappointments, banalities and frustrations of day-to-day living, and to respond in a more balanced way to the rarer moments of personal success or even outstanding achievement. Suppose, in short, that living the life of a theist makes me on the whole a better man socially and a happier man personally. Why, under those circumstances, should I not firmly adopt the faith of a theist? Why should I not firmly believe that God is in his heaven and ultimately all's well? These seem to me to be purely rhetorical questions. It seems obvious that, under the circumstances, I should not only be doing no wrong by living by the faith of a theist. I ought, everything considered, to live by it. This, I think, is so even if theism is as a matter of fact false. The point is that I do not believe it to be true, while knowing at the same time that it is false. That is impossible. I do not believe it in spite of evidence to the contrary; I simply believe it in the absence of evidence.

And I would defend an even stronger principle than the principle that, under certain circumstances, believing something for which there is no evidence and which might well be false is justified. I have in fact already asserted the principle that there are times when I ought to believe what, as a matter of fact, is false. We have an obligation to believe what is true, but this is not an unqualified obligation. The example I have given against the principle that, if a proposition is true, we ought to believe it, involved the supposition that my wife had been unfaithful to me once. I believe that there are times when we ought to believe propositions against which there is conclusive evidence. It is best, everything considered, that I know nothing about my wife's unfaithfulness, that I remain forever ignorant of it or of any evidence for it. If I know that a proposition is true, I cannot help but believe it. "I know that p" entails "I believe that p." But there may be many propositions which are true; yet I do not know that they are true, and I ought to believe that they are false.

To sum up: There are three principles here. One is that, given a living and momentous option that cannot be decided on intellectual grounds, our "passional nature" may lawfully decide it. This entails James' second thesis, namely, that given a genuine option (an option that is living, momentous and forced) that cannot be decided on intellectual grounds, our "passional nature" may lawfully decide it. The third principle is even stronger than anything James proclaims or accepts by implication. Indeed, the principle is inconsistent with James' theory of truth. The principle is that there are times when I ought to believe a proposition against which there is available a mass of almost conclusive evidence. I believe both principles are true. To see that they are, it seems to me that we need only think about certain hypothetical cases.

The principle that entails James' second thesis and James' second thesis itself are not particularly exciting; they seem to be rather obvious truisms. But it should at the same time be said that emphasizing these obvious principles is not pointless because some philosophers have denied them explicitly or by implication. Descartes, for example, exhorts us to believe only those propositions that we can know to be true either incorrigibly or infallibly. Bertrand Russell believes that "We ought to give to every proposition which we consider as nearly as possible that degree of credence which is warranted by the probability it acquires from the evidence known to us."[13] These principles are less questionable when restricted to science than they are when taken more widely. To be sure, if I do become suspicious and

13 *Philosophical Essays*, p. 96.

investigate, I will get the evidence that shows, to a degree of probability amounting to practical certainty, that on one occasion my wife has been unfaithful to me. I will then firmly believe a true proposition in the spirit of the canons put forth by Russell. But what good is my not being duped about a matter of fact when that one piece of knowledge will destroy a happy family? Men would have an unqualified obligation to follow Descartes' and Russell's rules only if there was a necessary connection between believing only what the evidence warrants and acting as one ought, everything considered, or acting for the best, everything considered. But there is no such necessary connection. We can imagine all sorts of examples where no such connection exists.

James' Defense of His Ethics of Belief

JAMES' OWN DEFENSE of his second principal thesis, the one in which he affirms that our "passional nature" may lawfully decide an option of a certain carefully circumscribed sort, is radically different from the way I have defended it. I argued that it is true because it is entailed by a true principle, which does not require that the option be forced. The structure of James' own defense is not exactly clear, but it seems to conflate two propositions which should be distinguished from one another. One of these is James' second principal thesis. The other is an assumption that is presupposed by the tone of the whole essay. It is this: if we are "tender-minded," we stand a chance of knowing certain vital truths; and if we are "tough-minded," we stand no chance at all of knowing those vital truths.

It is not hard to see why James blends these two theses into one. Given his theory of truth, if believing a proposition is better than not believing it, then it is more expedient to believe it than not to believe it, and if it is more expedient to believe it than not to believe it, then it is true for us. The propositions that come under the heading of "the will to believe" are such as to be undecidable on any evidence available to us. Believing them cannot, therefore, be expedient or inexpedient, by way of our coming upon confirming or disconfirming evidence in this life. There remain only psychological grounds for judging the expediency-value of believing propositions of the sort in question. These, then, are the only grounds for assessing the expediency, hence the truth-for-us, of propositions of the sort specified. The link that thus connects the two theses is James' theory of truth. But that theory is false. The two theses should, therefore, be set apart from one another and examined separately. Possibly those critics who have found nothing of value in "The Will to Believe" have been prevented from seeing the truth in what James says just because James confused the issue, and the critics do not bother to straighten things out before they begin their critical assessment.[14] I have already defended James' second thesis. I shall devote the rest of this section to a critical assessment of the false doctrine that pervades the essay.

The provocative, unorthodox, and, in my opinion, false assumption of "The Will to Believe" is that, if we are "tender-minded," we stand a chance of knowing certain vital truths, but if we are "tough-minded," we stand no chance at all of knowing those vital truths. This is my own summary statement of the thesis pervading the essay, and I must explain what it means. Assume (as James does) that not all of what religion says is verifiable in the manner required by logical positivism. It follows that if we are "tough-minded," we shall dismiss religion for being devoid of cognitive content; that which is devoid of cognitive content cannot be either true or false. Hence, assuming that what religion says is unverifiable, if we are "tough-minded," we cannot consistently entertain the possibility that perhaps what religion says is true. If what religion says should be true, and vitally important, then the "tough-minded" stand no chance of ever believing or knowing that vitally important truth. But, if we are "tender-minded" pragmatists, we will not identify the whole of the meaningful with the verifiable.

Verifiability as required by positivism is fine for propositions

---

[14] An example of this type of criticism is B. Russell's in "Pragmatism," *Edinburgh Review* (April, 1909); reprinted in Russell's *Philosophical Essays*. In his much later work, *A History of Western Philosophy* (London: Allen & Unwin, 1945), pp. 814–816, Russell discusses "The Will to Believe" in a similar vein. A sympathetic reading is C. J. Ducasse's exposition of James. See Ducasse, *A Philosophical Scrutiny of Religion* (New York: The Ronald Press, 1953), pp. 160–167.

that have sense-verifiable logical consequences. But some propositions that have no sense-verifiable logical consequences are such that the psychological consequences of believing them are different from the psychological consequences of disbelieving them, or of suspending judgment about them. A man brought up in a certain way may be such that his believing firmly that religion is true causes him to be a much better man socially and a much happier man personally than he would otherwise be. A "tender-minded" pragmatist will include these psychological consequences under 'practical consequences'; where there is a difference in practical consequences, there is a difference in meaning. Where there is a difference in meaning, there is meaning, and where there is meaning there is the possibility of truth or falsehood. If what religion says should be true and vitally important, the "tender-minded" have a chance of believing what religion says. If they believe, they will enjoy the vital benefits of believing, and, in the process they will prove that religion is true. This is by way of a first approximation. Now let us explore in more detail James' application of these ideas to religion.

James' Contention that Religion Poses a Forced Option

According to James, "religion says essentially two things. First, she says that the best things are the more eternal things . . . an affirmation which obviously cannot yet be verified scientifically at all. The second affirmation of religion is that we are better off even now [in this life] if we believe her first affirmation to be true." The first affirmation of religion is vague. It amounts to saying that the passing things, the things that come and perish, are not the ultimately important things. Earthly joys and sorrows are trivial compared to the value of things eternal and imperishable. This is indeed an affirmation that cannot be scientifically verified. But why does James include the word 'yet'? Does he mean to imply that some day science may be able to confirm or disconfirm that affirmation? It seems obvious that science can never either confirm or disconfirm that statement, and I shall continue the discussion on that assumption.

The second affirmation of religion is surely scientifically veri-

fiable. It is a psychological hypothesis, one that, at least in principle, may be found to be true or false. It is not in principle
impossible to determine that a man firmly believes a certain
proposition, and also to determine whether or not his believing
that proposition causes him to be better off, with reference to
some set of agreed upon standards of being better off. Thus, "the
religious hypothesis" is scientifically unverifiable only in its first
half. The second half of the hypothesis is verifiable. When I
believe that the eternal things are the best, I may in fact find that
I am better off.

This far we may go along with James. But he would go farther.
He would say that the first affirmation would be true-for-you if
your believing it is expedient for you, as it would be if it made
you better off in this life. But we have already discussed equating
"true-for-S" with "true" (see Part IV, Section 2). The fact that
a man may persist in believing that the eternal things are the
best because it benefits him to do so is one thing. To say that,
therefore, his belief is true is quite another. Truth is not persistent belief.

James says that the religious hypothesis poses a genuine option
for many people. This is true. For many people the hypothesis is
living and momentous. It is also forced. If I am the sort of person
who will benefit vitally only from believing that religion is true,
then the option "Let me believe that religion is true or let me
believe that it is false" is a forced option for me because if I
suspend judgment, i.e., if I neither believe that religion is true
nor believe that it is false, then I lose the vital benefits just as
surely as if I had believed that religion is false.

James himself is somewhat unclear on this point. He sometimes
talks as if the option is forced because there is no third possibility
besides believing that religion is true and believing that it is
false. This is inaccurate. There is a third possibility—suspending
belief. What makes the option forced for the man in question is
that for him there is no third possibility besides gaining or losing
the vital benefits of believing that religion is true. Suspension of
belief carries the same penalties as his believing that religion is
false. This satisfies the definition of a forced option.

James' confusion on this point may be explained by the fact
that he holds a "tender-minded" variety of a pragmatic theory

of meaning together with a pragmatic theory of belief. For him, as for any pragmatist, two hypotheses that have the same practical consequences are not two hypotheses but one. Also, for him, as for any pragmatist, the intellectual content of a belief is exhausted by its practical consequences. But for a "tender-minded" pragmatist like James, among the practical consequences of a belief are the psychological consequences of believing it. It is therefore natural for him to conclude that there is no pragmatic difference between disbelief and suspension of belief in those cases in which the practical consequences of disbelief are identical with those of suspending judgment. This being the situation of the man for whom the religious hypothesis presents a forced option, James is led to believe that in that situation the man is forced to believe either that religion is true or that it is false.

This is a mistake on his part. The habits, actions, dispositions to behave and to have certain feelings, attitudes and moods, and the experiences of an atheist, an agnostic, and a theist may be as like or as unlike as you will. The essential difference among them in terms of what they believe is nevertheless clear. The atheist believes that theism is false. The theist believes that theism is true. The agnostic believes that he does not know. These are three distinct and mutually incompatible beliefs, and any one of them may be held by a man for whom the religious option is forced. It is simply an egregious error to identify belief with behavior, or with dispositions to behave in certain ways, or with dispositions to have certain feelings, moods, and experiences.

Having made clear why for certain people the religious hypothesis is forced, I would remind the reader that an option that cannot be decided on intellectual grounds does not have to be a forced option in order to be one that our "passional nature may lawfully decide." There are living and momentous options that are not forced and cannot be decided on intellectual grounds. For example, suppose that if I believe that I am immortal, I shall win $100,000, and if I believe that I am not immortal, I shall win $50,000, and that if I believe neither proposition, I shall win nothing. In this example, the consequences of suspending judgment by believing neither proposition are different from the consequences of believing either one of the two mutually exclusive hypotheses. Hence, the option is not forced, but it is living and momentous for me. By hypothesis, only my "passional nature" can decide what I shall believe. If I come to believe that I am immortal, the fact that the option is not forced does not make it any less fortunate that I have the more rewarding belief.

Thus, even if the religious hypothesis was not a forced option for someone, the fact that it is for that person living and momentous would be sufficient for saying that he has a right to believe it even if there were no intellectual grounds for the proposition that he believes. What comes under the right to believe has, therefore, no necessary connection with forced options. Thus, although James' principle that our passional nature may lawfully decide a genuine option that cannot be decided on intellectual grounds follows from the principle I affirm, James' principle is needlessly strong for justifying religious faith. The weaker principle I affirm is sufficient, provided that religious beliefs are not demonstrably meaningless.

The notion of a forced option is important in connection with James' assertion that, by being "tender-minded," we stand to gain vital truths that we would otherwise forfeit. Only to the "tender-minded" could the religious hypothesis present a *living option*. Only those who look upon it as meaningful can find that the religious hypothesis is not totally incredible. That much is clear. But once we have admitted that for a given individual, S, the religious hypothesis is both living and momentous, why should we also want to add that it confronts S with a forced option? The reason is that James wants to refute the dictum: "At all cost avoid error. It is better to risk losing the truth than to believe what might be false." His message is that, under carefully specified conditions, we not only may, and we not only must, of logical necessity, but we must also morally believe according to the dictates of "our passional nature." The crucial "must" here is normative. James says that we must (we ought to) seek the truth, and we must (we ought to) avoid error. But when we are faced with a genuine option between two hypotheses, H and not H, and we do not have enough evidence to show that one of them is true or more probable than the other, then suspension of judgment is tantamount to having chosen not to believe H. Now there is a fifty-fifty chance that H is true. If you choose to believe H, therefore, you stand a fifty-fifty chance of knowing a truth.

If you suspend judgment, you stand no chance of knowing a truth. Hence, in such cases, it is foolish to suspend judgment in obedience to the dictum: avoid error.

Three Difficulties in This Line of Reasoning

Now THERE are three things wrong with this line of reasoning. First, the form of argument in favor of believing H will also prove that one ought to believe not H. (Just read "not H" wherever there is "H.") What that argument "proves" is that, whenever we have an option of the above sort, we ought to believe both hypotheses. Then we are bound to add one more true proposition to our stock of beliefs. No matter that we would also be bound to add one more false belief to our stock of beliefs. But why be so squeamish? Why this "horror of being duped"? "Our errors," says James, "are surely not such awfully solemn things. In a world where we are so certain to incur them in spite of all our caution, a certain lightness of heart seems healthier than this excessive nervousness on their behalf."

The second thing wrong with this line of reasoning is that believing a true proposition to be true does not suffice for *knowing* it. For "S knows that p" entails that S has adequate evidence for p.[15] But one of the essential features of propositions that come under the will to believe is that S does not have adequate evidence for them. Hence, S cannot know them. Hence just those hypotheses that are supposed to be counter-examples to the dictum: avoid error at all cost, are the ones that are irrelevant to it. For it can never be a reason why that dictum is unwise that by heeding it we lose chance after chance of knowing vital truths. "Avoid error at all cost" is silly for the sorts of considerations I put forward in support of the principle that at times it is better to believe a falsehood, and that, therefore, there are times when we ought to believe what is false. It is silly to avoid the error of believing that my wife has never been unfaithful to me at the cost it entails. But I would never dream of arguing that

[15] I may believe that Japan has an emperor because I saw *The Mikado* recently. My belief is true, but I cannot be said to know it. I think that it is true for a silly reason.

"Avoid error at all cost" is silly, simply because slavish adherence to it might keep you from knowing certain truths.

What James should have said is that, whenever we are faced with a living and momentous option that cannot be decided on intellectual grounds, we are perfectly justified in believing that alternative that is more likely to make us happier individually and better socially. This is the principle I have been defending. The argument to justify believing hypothesis H would then proceed as follows. When we are faced with a living and momentous option between H and not H, and we do not have sufficient evidence to decide on intellectual grounds, and if believing H is more likely to make us happier individually and better socially, then refusing to believe H entails that we lose the probable benefits of believing H. To refuse to believe H under these circumstances, out of a dogged adherence to the principle "Never risk believing what might be false," would be perverse. Hence, we not only may rightfully, but we can go so far as to say that we ought to, believe H.

The third thing wrong with James' line of reasoning is that if the religious hypothesis is a forced option, and if, where there is no significant difference in behavior-habits and in dispositions to have certain feelings and experiences, there is no significant difference in belief, then with respect to the religious hypothesis there is no distinction between "Know the truth" and "Avoid error."[16] If "Religion is true or religion is not true" is such that refusing to believe that religion is true amounts to believing that religion is false, then there is no way of avoiding error by playing it safe. The point that is involved is this. We can ordinarily avoid error either by suspending judgment or by believing the truth. But, faced with a forced option, we cannot avoid error by suspending judgment. We can avoid error only by believing the truth. Hence, if "H or not H" is a forced option, then in that case "Believe the truth" is the same principle as "Avoid error." But James' purpose in pointing out that "Believe the truth" and "Avoid error" are two distinct principles is that in the case of propositions that come under the will to believe, we are wiser to obey the first and disregard the second. But it is just those cases in which the

[16] See George Mavrodes, "James and Clifford on 'The Will to Believe'," *The Personalist*, 44, 2 (1963), 191–198.

distinction is supposed to be so vital that are the cases in which the distinction disappears.

The assertion that by being "tender-minded" we stand a chance of knowing vital truths is false. It is the result of confusing (i) beliefs with behavior-habits, (ii) "knowing that p" with "believing truly that p" and (iii) truth with expediency. It is also the result of putting the logical consequences of a proposition on the same level with the psychological consequences of believing it. Finally, it involves the confusion that a distinction that exists between "Know the truth" and "Avoid error" persists in just those cases where it disappears. In sum, James' "tender-minded" theory of how one may achieve religious knowledge is a congeries of egregious errors. He is correct only in affirming the right of an individual to have religious faith, i.e., to believe religious propositions in the absence of evidence *pro* or *con*.

SELECTED BIBLIOGRAPHY

[1]   Alston, W. P. "Pragmatism and the Verifiability Theory of Meaning," *Philosophical Studies*, VI (1955), 65–71.

[2]   ———. "Pragmatism and the Theory of Signs in Peirce," *Philosophy and Phenomenological Research*, XVII (1956), 79–88.

[3]   Bradley, F. H. "On the Ambiguity of Pragmatism," *Mind*, XVII (1908), 226–231 on James; 231–237 on Dewey.

[4]   Buchler, J. *Charles Peirce's Empiricism*. London: Routledge and Kegan Paul, 1939.

[5]   Burks, A. W. Introduction to the Peirce Selections, pp. 41–53 in Max H. Fisch et al., eds. *Classic American Philosophers*. New York: Appleton-Century-Crofts, 1951.

[6]   ———. *Cause, Chance and Reason*. Unpublished manuscript. Chaps. 4, 5.

[7]   James, W. *Pragmatism: A New Name for Some Old Ways of Thinking*. New York: Longmans, Green and Co., 1907.

[8]   ———. *The Meaning of Truth*. London: Longmans, Green and Co., 1914.

[9]   ———. "The Pragmatic Account of Truth and its Misunderstanders," *Philosophical Review*, XVII (1908), 1–17.

[10]   Lovejoy, A. O. "The Thirteen Pragmatisms," *Journal of Philosophy*, V (1908), 5–12, 29–39; reprinted in A. O. Lovejoy, *The Thirteen Pragmatisms and other Essays*. Baltimore: Johns Hopkins University Press, 1963.

[11]   Matson, W. I. *The Existence of God*. Ithaca, N.Y.: Cornell University Press, 1965. Chap. IV.

[12]   Mavrodes, G. "James and Clifford on 'The Will to Believe'," *The Personalist*, 44 (1963), 191–198.

[13]   McTaggart, J. E. Review of *Pragmatism*, *Mind*, XVII (1908), 104–108.

[14] Moore, G. E. "Professor James' 'Pragmatism'," *Proceedings of the Aristotelian Society* (1907–1908); reprinted under the title "William James' 'Pragmatism'," in G. E. Moore, *Philosophical Studies*. London: Routledge & Kegan Paul, 1922.

[15] Russell, B. "Pragmatism," *Edinburgh Review* (April, 1909); reprinted in B. Russell, *Philosophical Essays*. London: Longmans, Green and Co., 1910.

[16] ———. "Transatlantic 'Truth'," *Albany Review* (January, 1908); reprinted under the title "William James' Conception of Truth," in B. Russell, *Philosophical Essays*. London: Longmans, Green and Co., 1910.

[17] Schiller, F. S. C. Review of *Pragmatism, Mind*, XVI (1907), 598–604.

[18] White, M. G. *Toward Reunion in Philosophy*. Cambridge, Mass.: Harvard University Press, 1956. Chap. XV.

THE FOLLOWING notational conventions, definitions, and rules are employed in the appendices.

Let '$\Diamond$' stand for *it is (logically) possible that.*
'$\sim$'stand for *it is not the case that.*

We define entailment as follows:

DE: $p \to q =$ Df. $\sim \Diamond$ (p and $\sim$q).

A convenient reading of this is: 'p entails q' means that it is not possible that p is true and q is false. We also define:

DI: p is incorrigible for S = Df.(i) (S believes attentively that p) $\to$ S knows that p, and (ii) $\Diamond$ (S believes attentively that p).

We assume the epistemological axiom:

EA: (S knows that p) $\to$ p,

and also the principle of inference:

PI: $[\Diamond$ (p and q) and (q $\to$ $\sim$r)] $\to$ $\Diamond$ (p and $\sim$r).

Because of DE, PI can be alternatively stated as follows:

$[\Diamond$ (p and q) and (q $\to$ $\sim$r)] $\to$ $\sim$(p $\to$ r).

THE FIRST PART OF THE DREAM ARGUMENT

(1) For any proposition, p, and for any person, S, {if p is a perceptual proposition, then (S is dreaming that he himself is attentively perceiving that p) $\to$ S attentively believes that p}.
(Assumption = Premise (1) on p. 82, above)
(2) For any proposition, p, and for any person, S, {if p is a perceptual proposition, then $\Diamond$ [(S is dreaming that he himself is attentively perceiving that p) and $\sim$p]}.
(Assumption = Premise (2) on p. 82, above)

∴ (3) If p is a perceptual proposition, then (S is dreaming that he himself is attentively perceiving that p) → S attentively believes that p.
(From (1))

∴ (4) If p is a perceptual proposition, then ◊ [(S is dreaming that he himself is attentively perceiving that p) and ~p].
(From (2))

(5) Let p be a perceptual proposition:
(Hypothesis)

∴ (6) (S is dreaming that he himself is attentively perceiving that p) → S attentively believes that p.
(From (3) and (5))

∴ (7) ◊ [(S is dreaming that he himself is attentively perceiving that p) and ~p].
(From (4) and (5))

∴ (8) ◊ [(S attentively believes that p) and ~p].
(From (6) and (7), by PI)

But

(9) ~p → ~(S knows that p)
(By EA)

∴ (10) ◊ [(S attentively believes that p) and ~(S knows that p.)].
(From (8) and (9), by PI)

∴ (11) ~[(S attentively believes that p) → S knows that p].
(From (10), by DE)

∴ (12) p is corrigible for S.
(From (11), by DI)

∴ (13) For any proposition, p, and for any person, S, if p is a perceptual proposition, then p is corrigible for S.
(From (12))

THE SECOND PART OF THE DREAM ARGUMENT

(1) For any contingent proposition, p, if (p → ~(S is dreaming)), then ◊ [(S attentively believes that p) and (S is dreaming)].
(Assumption = Premise (3) on p. 82, above)

Assume

(2) [p → ~(S is dreaming)] and (p is a contingent proposition).

∴ (3) S is dreaming → ~p.
(From (2))

∴ (4) ◊ [S attentively believes that p) and (S is dreaming)].
(From (1) and (2))

∴ (5) ◊ [(S attentively believes that p) and ~p].
  (From (3) and (4), by PI)

∴ (6) ◊ [(S attentively believes that p) and ~(S knows that p)].
  (From (5), by EA and PI)

∴ (7) ~[(S attentively believes that p) → (S knows that p)].
  (From (6) and DE)

∴ (8) p is corrigible for S.
  (From (7), by DI)

∴ (9) For any contingent proposition, p, if [p → ~(S is dreaming)], then p is corrigible for S.
  (From (2) and (8))

But

(10) The proposition that S is not dreaming is contingent and it entails itself.

∴ (11) The proposition that S is not dreaming is corrigible for S.
  (From (9) and (10))

∴ (12) S knows incorrigibly that he himself is not dreaming only if there is a proposition, q, which is incorrigible for S and entails that S is not dreaming.
  (From (11) and the criterion of incorrigible knowledge, i.e., (6) on p. 82, above)

∴ (13) ~(S knows incorrigibly that he himself is not dreaming).
  (From (9), (10), and (12))

∴ (14) No one knows incorrigibly that he himself is not dreaming.
  (From (13))

THE THIRD PART OF THE DREAM ARGUMENT

(1) For any proposition, p, and for any person, S, if p is a perceptual proposition, then p is corrigible for S.
  (Conclusion of the First Part of the Dream Argument)

(2) For any proposition, p, and for any person, S, {if p is corrigible for S, then S knows incorrigibly that p only if there is a proposition q such that (i) q is incorrigible for S, and (ii) q → p}.
  (The criterion of incorrigible knowledge = premise (6) on p. 82, above)

(3) For any proposition, p, for any person, S, and for any proposition, q, {if (p is a perceptual proposition and q is incorrigible for S) then ◊ [(in his dream, S has a clear and distinct intuition that q) and ~p]}.
  (Assumption = premise (4), on p. 82, above)

(4) For any person, S, and for any proposition, q, {if q is incorrigible for S, then [(in his dream S has a clear and distinct intuition that q) → (S attentively believes that q)]}.

(Assumption = premise (5) on p. 82, above)

(5) Let there be a person, S, and a perceptual proposition, p, such that S knows incorrigibly that p.

(Hypothesis)

∴ (6) p is a perceptual proposition and S knows incorrigibly that p.

(From (5))

∴ (7) p is corrigible for S.

(From (1) and (6))

∴ (8) There is a proposition, q, such that (i) q is incorrigible for S, and (ii) q → p.

(From (2), (6), and (7))

∴ (9) q is incorrigible for S, and q → p.

(From (8))

∴ (10) ◊[(In his dream, S has a clear and distinct intuition that q) and ∼p].

(From (3), (6), and (9))

∴ (11) (In his dream, S has a clear and distinct intuition that q) → (S attentively believes that q).

(From (4) and (9))

∴ (12) ◊ [(S attentively believes that q) and ∼p].

(From (10) and (11), by PI)

∴ (13) ∼[(S attentively believes that q) → p].

(From (12), by DE)

∴ (14) (S attentively believes that q) → (S knows that q).

(From (9), by DI)

∴ (15) (S attentively believes that q) → q.

(From (14), and EA)

∴ (16) (S attentively believes that q) → p.

(From (9) and (15))

∴ (17) If there is a person, S, and a perceptual proposition, p, such that S knows incorrigibly that p, then [{(S attentively believes that q) → p} and ∼{(S attentively believes that q) → p}].

(From (5), (13), and (16))

∴ (18) ∼(There is a person, S, and a perceptual proposition, p, such that S knows incorrigibly that p).

(From (17))

∴ (19) For any person, S, and for any proposition, p, if p is a perceptual proposition, then ∼(S knows incorrigibly that p).

(From (18))

APPENDIX II

FORMAL PROOFS OF THE EVIL DEMON ARGUMENTS

(a) Let 'Mp' (p is M) mean: p is a mathematical proposition such that ◊[([S believes attentively that p] and ~p) or ([S believes attentively that ~p] and p)].

(b) Let 'E(Z)' refer to the following entailment: x deceives y about p → either (i) x intentionally brings it about that y believes that p, and ~p, or (ii) x intentionally brings it about that y believes that ~p, and p, or (iii) x intentionally brings it about that y believes that p, and ~(y knows that p).

EVIL DEMON ARGUMENT I

(1) For any proposition, p, if Mp, then ◊ ([S believes attentively that p] and [the evil demon is deceiving S about p]). (Assumption)

(2) The evil demon is deceiving S about p → [either (i) S believes that p, while ~p, or (ii) S believes that ~p, while p, or (iii) S believes that p, while ~(S knows that p)]. (By E(Z))

∴ (3) For any proposition, p, if Mp, then ◊ ([S believes attentively that p] and [either (i) S believes that p, while ~p, or (ii) S believes that ~p, while p, or (iii) S believes that p, while~(S knows that p)]). (From (1) and (2), by PI))

But

(4) (S believes that p, while ~p) → ~p.

(5) ~p → ~S knows that p. (By EA)

∴ (6) (S believes that p, while ~p) → ~(S knows that p). (From (4) and (5))

Again

(7) (S believes that ~p, while p) → S believes that ~p.

But

    (8) (S believes that ~p) → ~(S believes that p), and ~(S believes that p) → ~(S knows that p).
        (Assumption)

∴ (9) (S believes that ~p, while p) → ~(S knows that p).
        (From (7) and (8))

Finally

   (10) (S believes that p, but ~[S knows that p]) → ~(S knows that p).

∴ (11) [Either (i) S believes that p, while ~p, or (ii) S believes that ~p, while p, or (iii) S believes that p, while ~(S knows that p)] → ~(S knows that p).
        (From (6), (9), and (10))

∴ (12) For any proposition, p, if Mp, then ◊ ([S believes attentively that p] and ~[S knows that p]).
        (From (3) and (11), by PI)

∴ (13) For any proposition, p, if Mp, then ~([S believes attentively that p] → [S knows that p]).
        (From (12), by DE)

∴ (14) For any proposition, p, if Mp, then p is corrigible for S.
        (From (13), by DI)

EVIL DEMON ARGUMENT II

    (1) For any proposition, p, and any contingent proposition, q, if (Mp and [q → S knows that p]), then ◊ [(S believes attentively that q) and (the evil demon is deceiving S about q)].
        (Assumption)
        (Note: q has to be a contingent proposition. "S knows that p" is contingent. A necessarily true proposition cannot entail a contingent proposition; and we do not want q to be self-contradictory.)

Assume

    (2) Mp and [q → (S knows that p)].

∴ (3) ◊ [(S believes attentively that q) and (the evil demon is deceiving S about q)].
        (From (1) and (2))

But

    (4) (The evil demon is deceiving S about q) → [Either (i) S believes that q, but ~q, or (ii) S believes that ~q, but q, or (iii) S believes that q, but ~(S knows that q)].
        (By E(Z))

∴ (5) ◊ [(S believes attentively that q) and [Either (i) S believes that q, but ~q, or (ii) S believes that ~q, but q, or (iii) S believes that q, but ~(S knows that q)].
(From (3) and (4), by PI)

But

(6) (S believes that q, but ~q) → ~(S knows that q)

and

(7) [S believes that ~q, but q] → ~(S knows that q)

and

(8) [S believes that q, but ~(S knows that q)] → ~(S knows that q).

∴ (9) [Either (i) S believes that q, but ~q, or (ii) S believes that ~q, but q, or (iii) S believes that q, but ~(S knows that q)] → ~(S knows that q).
(By (6), (7), and (8))

∴ (10) ◊ ([S believes attentively that q] and ~[S knows that q]).
(From (5) and (9), by PI)

∴ (11) q is corrigible for S.
(From (10), by DE and DI)

∴ (12) For any proposition, p, and any contingent proposition, q, if (Mp and [q → S knows that p]), then q is corrigible for S.

But

(13) the proposition "S knows that p" is (i) contingent and (ii) entails itself.

∴ (14) No necessarily true proposition entails that S knows that p.
(From (13) (i))

∴ (15) "S knows that p" is corrigible for S.
(From (12) and (13))

But

(16) For any proposition, p, if p is corrigible for S, then S knows incorrigibly that p only if there is a proposition q such that (i) q is incorrigible for S, and (ii) q → p.
(Assumption = the criterion of incorrigible knowledge)

∴ (17) Any proposition that entails "S knows that p" is either contingent and corrigible for S, or necessarily false.
(From (12) and (14))

But

(18) every necessarily false proposition is corrigible for S.
(By DI)

∴ (19) Any proposition that entails "S knows that p" is corrigible for S.
(From (17) and (18))

∴ (20) For any proposition, p, if Mp, then no one knows incorrigibly that he himself knows that p.
(From (15), (16), and (19))

THE ABORTIVE ARGUMENT

(1) For any proposition, p, if Mp, then ◊ ([S believes attentively that S knows that p] and [the evil demon is deceiving S about the proposition that S knows that p]).
(Assumption)

(2) (The evil demon is deceiving S about the proposition that S knows that p) → [either (i) S believes that S knows that p, but ~(S knows that p), or (ii) S believes that ~(S knows that p), and S knows that p, or (iii) S believes that S knows that p, but ~(S knows that S knows that p)].
(By E(Z))

∴ (3) For any proposition, p, if Mp, then ◊ ([S believes attentively that S knows that p] and [either (i) S believes that S knows that p, but ~(S knows that p), or (ii) S believes that ~(S knows that p), and S knows that p, or (iii) S believes that S knows that p, but ~(S knows that S knows that p)].
(From (1) and (2), by PI)

Now

(4) [S believes that S knows that p, but ~(S knows that p)] → ~(S knows that p).

But

(5) ~{[S believes that ~(S knows that p), and S knows that p] → ~(S knows that p)}

and

(6) [(S believes that S knows that p, but ~(S knows that S knows that p)] → ~(S knows that S knows that p).

But

(7) ~[~(S knows that S knows that p)→ ~(S knows that p)].
The argument aborts in Steps (5) and (7).

INDEX

Abortive argument, 128–33
    formal proof of, 296
    purpose of, 128
Agreement and disagreement
    ethical, 31–35
    See also Coherence test
Anselm, St., ontological arguments
    of, 208, 217, 225–34
Appetite, Platonic concept of, 54–55,
    57–60
Aristotle, 167
Arnauld, Antoine, 234–37
Assent, inability to withhold, 104–05
Assertion, pragmatic contradiction
    in, 141–42, 146
Attentive belief, 72–82, 240
    attentive perception and, 82,
    86–88, 92, 111–12
    in causal argument, 216
    in consciousness, 145–46
    defined, 73–75
    in evil demon argument, 119–20,
    124–27; abortive argument,
    129–31
    in existence, 139, 143; existence of
    matter, 154–55
    philosophical and exegetical im-
    portance of, 76–82
Ayer, A. J., 189–92; *Language,
    Truth and Logic,* 189–90

Being
    contingent, 152–53
    God as possible, 195–208
    See also Existence
Belief, 273–86
    assertion contrasted to, 141–42
    attentive, *see* Attentive belief
    dispositional, 73, 249
    inattentive, 73

incorrigible, *see* Incorrigibility
occurrent, 73–74, 77, 249–50
Platonic ethics determined by,
    32–33, 34–35
pragmatic theory of, 256–62,
    265–86; deduction, 256–57;
    ethics, 256–59, 265, 278–80,
    283; manmade truth, 272–73;
    mutable truth, 266–72; Peirce's
    theory, 249–51; verifiability,
    260–62, 279–81; "The Will to
    Believe," 273–86
    See also Faith
Berkeley, George, 160–61
Body, 135, 139, 154–55; mind with-
    out, 146–48
Broad, C. D., 200–1, 203–7; "Argu-
    ments for God's Existence," 200
Bourdin, Father, 89
Buchler, Justus, *Charles Peirce's
    Empiricism,* 252
Burks, Arthur W., 248n, 251–53

Cartesian Circle, 234–40
Castaneda, Hector-Neri, 72n, 83n,
    226n
Causal argument, 199; of Descartes,
    208–17
Cephalus, argument of, 36–38
Certainty (indubitability), 65, 67,
    102–03
    attention and, 76–77
    logical, 67–68, 103; primary, 151;
    see also Incorrigibility; Infalli-
    bility
    of mathematics, *see* Mathematics,
    certainty of
    "metaphysical," 238–39
    psychological, 67
Change in truth, 266–67

ABOUT THE AUTHOR

GEORGE NAKHNIKIAN is Chairman of the Department of Philosophy at Wayne State University, where he has taught since 1949. He received his B.A. and Ph.D. from Harvard University. For the academic year 1955–1956 he was Visiting Assistant Professor in Philosophy and Carnegie Intern in General Education at Brown University, and during 1965–1966 he was Fulbright Lecturer at St. Andrews University, Scotland. His published works include *Readings in Twentieth-Century Philosophy* (co-editor, with W. P. Alston), and *Morality and the Language of Conduct* (co-editor, with H. N. Castaneda). Professor Nakhnikian is an Advisory Editor of the *Natural Law Forum,* and a member of the editorial board of *The Encyclopedia of Philosophy.*

A NOTE ON THE TYPE

THE TEXT of this book is set in Caledonia, a typeface designed by W(illiam) A(ddison) Dwiggins for the Mergenthaler Linotype Company in 1939. This new typeface was inspired by the Scotch types cast about 1833 by Alexander Wilson & Son, Glasgow type founders, and Dwiggins chose the Roman name for Scotland—Caledonia. There is a calligraphic quality about this face that is totally lacking in the Wilson types. Dwiggins referred to an even earlier typeface for this "liveliness of action"—one cut around 1790 by William Martin for the printer William Bulmer. Caledonia has more weight than the Martin letters, and the bottom finishing strokes (serifs) of the letters are cut straight across, without brackets, to make sharp angles with the upright stems, thus giving a "modern face" appearance.

W. A. Dwiggins (1880–1956) was born in Martinsville, Ohio, and studied art in Chicago. In 1940 he moved to Hingham, Massachusetts, where he built a solid reputation as a designer of advertisements and as a calligrapher. He began an association with the Mergenthaler Linotype Company in 1929, and over the next twenty-seven years designed a number of book types for that firm, of especial interest are the Metro series, Electra, Caledonia, Eldorado, and Falcon. In 1930, Dwiggins first became interested in marionettes, and through the years made many important contributions to the art of puppetry and the design of marionettes.

This book was composed, printed, and bound by American Book–Stratford Press, Inc., New York City, N.Y.
Typography and binding design by Victoria Dudley.